Believing in the Church

lieving in the Church

The Corporate Nature of Faith

A REPORT BY
THE DOCTRINE COMMISSION OF
THE CHURCH OF ENGLAND

JMSturmer
1984.

LONDON
SPCK

First published 1981
SPCK
Holy Trinity Church
Marylebone Road
London NW1 4DU

ACKNOWLEDGEMENTS

Thanks are due to Faber and Faber for permission to quote from *The Collected Poems of Edwin Muir*.
The extract from *The Gospel and the Catholic Church* by Michael A. Ramsey is reproduced by kind permission of the Longman Group.
Thanks are also due to Mary Warnock for permission to quote from a sermon delivered in 1980.

Printed in Great Britain by
The Campfield Press
St Albans, Herts

ISBN 0 281 03839 2

Contents

Foreword by the Archbishop of Canterbury

I am glad to have a chance to express my thanks to the Bishop of Winchester and all who have served on the Doctrine Commission for the trouble and time they have given in writing this Report.

In recent years we have discovered again in our worship what it means 'to do things together'. The Commission set itself the task of examining the corporate nature of Faith. This is in itself a necessary corollary to the experience that has come to us in corporate worship.

Yet not everyone has found that experience. So much of what has been traditional is questioned, and often needs questioning. How is our common Faith expressed in the uncertainties of modern society? Is there a corporate belief that we can set against the excesses of individual notions? These are important questions and I warmly commend the Report for serious study in the Church.

ROBERT CANTUAR:

DR. John Taylor
Died :- 2001.

Members of the Commission

This report is submitted unanimously by the Doctrine Commission of the Church of England for the period 1977–81, consisting of the following:

The Rt Revd Dr John V. Taylor (Chairman)
Bishop of Winchester

The Revd John Austin Baker
Canon and Sub-Dean of Westminster, Rector of St Margaret's, Westminster and Chaplain to the Speaker of the House of Commons

The Revd Dr John Barton
University Lecturer in Theology (Old Testament), Fellow and Chaplain of St Cross College, Oxford

The Revd John W. Bowker
Professor of Religious Studies in the University of Lancaster

The Revd John H. Drury
Lecturer in Religious Studies in the University of Sussex

The Revd R. John Halliburton
Canon of Chichester and Principal of Chichester Theological College

The Revd Anthony E. Harvey
University Lecturer in Theology (New Testament), Fellow of Wolfson College and Chaplain of The Queen's College, Oxford

The Revd Dr John McManners
Regius Professor of Ecclesiastical History in the University of Oxford and Canon of Christ Church

Professor Basil Mitchell
Nolloth Professor of the Philosophy of the Christian Religion in the University of Oxford, Fellow of Oriel College

The Revd Dr Anthony C. Thiselton
Senior Lecturer in Biblical Studies in the University of Sheffield

The Revd W. H. Vanstone
Residentiary Canon of Chester Cathedral

The Revd Dr N. Thomas Wright
Fellow and Chaplain of Downing College, Cambridge

The Rt Revd David N. de L. Young
Bishop of Ripon

Among those originally appointed in December 1977 were:

Mr J. R. Lucas, who resigned before the preliminary meeting because he could not be present on any of the proposed dates, and was replaced in the summer of 1978 by Professor Mitchell;

The Revd Robin Nixon, who died before the second meeting, and was replaced in December 1978 by Dr Wright;

Canon David Jenkins, who resigned early in 1979 through pressure of other work.

CHAIRMAN'S NOTE

The Commission is greatly indebted to two people who, while not actually members, were appointed successively as Recorders of the meetings. The Revd John de Satgé served from the summer of 1978 until the autumn of 1979, when he was followed by the Revd Michael Perham, who has also edited and prepared the chapters for publication. Many thanks are due also to Miss Keri Lewis who, in the General Synod Office, has duplicated and distributed successive drafts of all the chapters with remarkable expedition, and to Mr Derek Cottrill, of The Queen's College, Birmingham, who has prepared the indexes. Were it not for these four, creative chaos would never have been given order.

After its preliminary planning meeting at Church House, Westminster in April 1978, the Commission met in eight residential sessions of two to three days each and wishes to record its gratitude to its various hosts: The Royal Foundation of St Katherine, Stepney (twice); the Regina Pacis Priory, Southgate; Crowther Hall, Birmingham; Westminster College and Westcott House, Cambridge; Pusey House, Oxford; and Ecton House, Northamptonshire.

✠ JOHN WINTON:
Ascension Day 1981

Introduction: The Voice of the City

In the festival play called *The Just Vengeance*, written in 1946, Dorothy L. Sayers imagined an airman, who had just died in battle, arriving at the city which for him was his native Lichfield and finding himself welcomed by townspeople from the past centuries and required to state his claim to citizenship.

RECORDER
    What matters here is not so much what you did
    As why you did it . . . Can you recite your creed?

AIRMAN
    I believe in God . . .

CHORUS
    (picking him up and carrying him along with it)
    . . . the Father Almighty, Maker of heaven and
    earth. And in Jesus Christ . . .

AIRMAN
    No! No! No! What made me start off like that?
    I reacted automatically to the word 'creed' –
    My personal creed is something totally different.

RECORDER
    What is speaking in you is the voice of the city,
    The Church and household of Christ, your people and
    country
    From whom you derive. Did you think you were un-
    begotten?
    Unfranchised? With no community and no past?
    Out of the darkness of your unconscious memory
    The stones of the city are crying out. Go on. [1]

In this book we attempt to take seriously the idea of 'the voice of the city'. We ask as honestly as possible whether this idea is tenable and, if tenable, whether it is not actually an indispensable factor in the human search for truth and meaning. That was how Aristotle saw it. 'The investigation of the truth', he wrote, 'is in one way hard, in another easy . . . no one is able to attain the truth adequately, while on the other hand we do not collectively fail, but everyone says something true about the nature of things, and while individually we contribute little or nothing to the truth, by the union of all a considerable amount is amassed.'[2] In this inquiry we understand tradition to be more than the deposit of past convictions and formulations. We see it as a still continuing process of *corporate believing,* a patrimony to be reinvested in each generation. We suggest that the corporate belief of a community provides the necessary matrix for the emergence of those personal creeds that are seemingly 'something totally different'.

Most of what is said about religious belief in these days seems to be marked by an exaggerated individualism. Believing has come to be regarded as such an interior and personal activity that it makes no more sense to say '*We* believe' than to say 'We are dreaming'. Since no two people can claim to believe exactly the same things, can we any longer speak of orthodoxy or heresy? This individualism has become entrenched equally among academics and in the discourse of ordinary people. Almost instinctively we of the western societies accord an authenticity to 'my personal creed' which we can no longer recognize in 'the voice of the city'. We are frankly suspicious of choruses that pick us up and carry us along with them. The roots of our scepticism run back through four centuries, and the hero-saints of our cult of independent thought are cast in the mould of Galileo. Michael Polanyi has trenchantly set down the fears we have inherited:

> We were warned that a host of unproven beliefs were instilled in us from earliest childhood. That religious dogma, the authority of the ancients, the teaching of the schools, the maxims of the nursery, all were united to a body of tradition which we tended to accept merely because these beliefs had been previously held by others, who wanted us to embrace them in our turn. We were urged to resist the pressure of this traditional indoctrination by pitting against it the principle of philosophic doubt.[3]

The extreme individualism in our understanding of religious belief today is also due to the historical pressures that have been brought to bear upon western man, urging him towards the privatization of many areas of experience. An economics of industrial growth in highly competitive national units has cast covetous eyes on the energies of our human capacity to act corporately and has reached out to possess and channel them mainly into the production of wealth, while encouraging us in all other spheres of activity to act individually and to enjoy our 'emancipation'. Religion, morality, recreation and the arts were collective experiences during the pre-industrial period; but one by one each of these has become a realm of private opinion and preference, unless it can be commercialized, that is, brought within the production process as, for example, television entertainment has been. Yet, ironically, this change of emphasis has not enhanced the value which our society sets upon this privatized individual thought, but rather diminished it. 'I believe' is taken to mean 'It is my view'. In a universe of private opinions all belief is relative, and the word itself has come to connote something essentially tentative or fallible. In earlier centuries belief was contrasted with unbelief; today it is contrasted with knowledge. When I ask the ticket collector, 'Is this the London train?', I am uneasy if he replies, 'I believe so.'

This is not universally the case. *Credo* and *Pisteuo* usually indicate a state of certainty. In the Bantu languages the verbs that mean 'to believe' have a root that conveys the idea of something firmly established, like the Hebrew *aman*. Indeed, there are many languages which have no separate word for believing as distinct from knowing. Rodney Needham recalls his perplexity at discovering that the Penan people of Borneo, who were sure of the existence of a supreme spiritual being, had no way in which their language could compose such a statement as 'I believe in God'. On finding the same situation among the Meru of Kenya, Needham comments: 'There might be no point in providing lexically for the assertion "I believe in God" when God's existence and presence are so taken for granted that no other possibility is either given in Meru collective ideation or occasioned in individual thought.'[4]

It would be wrong to suppose that corporate believing is limited to pre-critical cultures. The scientific community is a remarkable example of this. Its members live by, and for, a body of assumptions inherited and held in common. 'The creation and preservation of a free consensus is the overriding aim of Science,' says John Ziman.[5] The individual research

3

worker is bound to operate within the terms of that consensus and in a perpetual dialogue with it.

> The scientific enterprise is corporate. It is not merely, in Newton's incomparable phrase, that one stands on the shoulders of giants, and hence can see a little farther. Every scientist sees through his own eyes – and also through the eyes of his predecessors and colleagues. It is never one individual that goes through all the steps in the logico-inductive chain; it is a group of individuals, dividing their labour but continuously and jealously checking each other's contribution. The cliché of scientific prose betrays itself: 'Hence *we* arrive at the conclusion that . . .' The audience to which scientific publications are addressed is not passive; by its cheering or booing, its bouquets or brickbats, it actively controls the substance of the communications that it receives.[6]

The corporate believing of the community of science is, therefore, inherently self-critical. Individual members are relentlessly engaged in pushing out the frontiers of this public consensus but always in such a way as to be ultimately answerable to it, for their existence as scientists depends upon it.

Another kind of corporate believing can be found in the political parties where again we see toleration of a gradual development of doctrine but strong defensive measures against rebels and deviants. Lone independents may be respected, but their lack of answerability becomes a weakness as soon as their pursuit of private theory takes precedence over their service of a public policy.

It would seem, then, that believing is mainly belonging. It is, in fact, difficult to see how it could be otherwise since discursive thought is impossible without language, and language is a product of community. In the brains of humans and higher primates particular cells can respond to the impulse of a repeated image; the same cell reacts, for example, whenever a hand of any size or colour is seen, or even the drawing of a hand. In other words, each individual brain can identify and categorize. But it cannot in isolation give a name to its abstractions and so it cannot build them into a body of knowledge. For the meanings of words and gestures are an inherited tradition created through communal interchange. 'In learning to speak, every child accepts a culture constructed

4

on the premises of the traditional interpretation of the universe, rooted in the idiom of the group to which it was born, and every intellectual effort of the educated mind will be made within this frame of reference.'[7]

For an English-speaking person the real difficulty of learning a non-European language does not consist in memorizing the equivalent word for the same concept. It means feeling one's way into a different view of how the world is put together and what realities exist in it. There are some things that cannot be said, cannot even be *thought,* in such a different language. The mere device of introducing a foreign word as the vehicle for an alien idea cannot guarantee the incorporation of that idea into the thought of another people. For example, none of the indigenous languages of Uganda had a word for 'religion'. When an African of Uganda wants to speak about Islam or Christianity he uses the word *dini,* an Arabic-Swahili word which reached Uganda in the middle of the nineteenth century with the Arab traders from the coast. Even today nobody in northern Uganda would dream of describing his traditional clan ritual as *dini.* To do so would be a contradiction in terms, for *dini* is something which came into the country from outside, brought by foreigners, not as a replacement of the clan ritual but as something *sui generis,* entirely new in its reliance on the organization of ideas.[8] If you ask, 'Did they have no religion?', the answer is probably, 'Not as you understand it.' But if you ask one of them, 'What did your fathers believe?', his truest reply would have to be, 'I can tell you what they believed only if you talk the language in which they believed it.'

Language is only one of the factors in our human situation that ensures that believing is a much more corporate activity than we have tended to recognize. The sociology of knowledge has shown how cabined and confined, if not actually predetermined, the Independent Thinker actually is. The freely ranging mind can function only in relation to a social consensus which has already provided a system of assumptions, a vocabulary of thought and an apparatus of symbols, all of them taken for granted. The would-be rebel can do no more than respond to the expectations of his intellectual community. Just as personal identity is the product of relationships, so an individual's opinions, convictions and choice of action are formed out of, and in response to, the opinions, convictions and choices of his community.

5

This is not the repressive bondage it appears to be. On the contrary 'the voice of the city', shaping our individual thoughts and beliefs, is the source of our integrity and creativity. Those who do their thinking in isolation become strangely uniform and unoriginal: schizophrenics, who are the most isolated of all people, are frighteningly alike. On the other hand, genuinely new ideas seem to arrive very often as 'something in the air', occurring simultaneously to a lot of different people, apparently quite independently. This familiar fact, whether we account for it by sociology or metaphysics, points to the progressive and exploratory element in what this report calls 'corporate believing'.

When we examine it in this light we see that the tradition itself is an unceasing argument between conservation and development. To this dialogue the doubt and challenge of individual 'personal creeds' make their essential contribution. Each side, the orthodoxy and the disbelief, needs the other, and there is a difference between dissent and alienation. The alienated are those for whom the voice of the city has lost all plausibility, so that they have neither the interest nor the language to answer back. The dissenters remain with the dialogue, knowing that the roots which nourish their protest run into the soil of that communal belief.

Something of this interplay of individual minds with a corporate conviction is reflected in the manner in which the Doctrine Commission presents this report. The name or names of the authors of each chapter have been indicated, and they have been encouraged to disclose with integrity their personal emphasis. Yet each chapter was not only drafted in the light of long preliminary discussion, but was subsequently rewritten, twice over in most cases, to accommodate as far as possible the views that seemed to command general assent as the work was mulled over. So, while the separate chapters retain fairly the idiosyncrasies of their writers, the complete report is offered in the name of the whole Commission.

In the opening chapter Basil Mitchell suggests a way of reconciling the conflicts that have always existed in the Church with the conviction that there is an underlying unity of belief, and claims that this underlying unity is best safeguarded by a strong tradition whose stability nourishes the faith of individuals, while their freedom to question prevents it ossifying. Anthony Harvey then examines the meanings that can be given to the phrase, 'The Church believes', and after rejecting several plausible models, he finds that it is only by attending to the Bible as a 'story' whose significance has constantly to be reinterpreted that the Church maintains its definition and renews its life. The third chapter falls into two parts. The first calls attention to the corporate foundations of knowledge in everyday life, as a corrective to the view that makes both discovery and criticism depend on the individual. The second part applies this principle to Christian believing. Orthodoxy (for want of a better word) ideally is not the suppression of individual criticism nor should it encourage passive assent to second-hand doctrines. On the contrary, it relates to the transmission and preservation of the corporate memory which gives the Christian community its identity, and which also provides the framework for critical faith. Chapter 4 explores the idea of the Church as a story-telling community. It shows from various historical examples how liturgy is a recital of the story of such a kind that the participants are caught up into it and the story goes on in them. This is seen to be crucial to Anglicanism precisely because it accords less importance than many other communions to explicit definitions of its faith. Chapter 5 looks historically at the classical Anglican settlement and seeks to elucidate the characteristic balance between specific declarations of doctrine in a variety of forms and doctrine that is latent in and deducible from our worship, ceremonial and customs, and may survive residually but significantly in what is sometimes too dismissively called 'folk religion'.

Having thus reinstated the corporate foundation of all belief in a more sympathetic light than has been accorded to it in recent thought, the book turns to look again at the tension between the individual and the system. John Bowker uses the insights of systems analysis to show that a proper understanding of the necessity of institutions, with their corporate beliefs and boundaries to maintain continuity of information and decision-making, is the best safeguard against their abuse of this necessity. John Drury restates the tension between search and stability in more sharply personal terms, lest we appear to be turning bland about it. Taking George Eliot as his model, he reminds us that those who reject religious systems may be within Christian truth precisely in their anti-dogmatic stance. John McManners develops this thought to argue that the churches have been mistaken in identifying the Holy Spirit's guidance into truth with their

7

dogmatic propositions rather than with their worship and sacrificial living. His essay can be summed up in the words with which the Byzantine liturgy introduces the creed: 'Let us love one another that with one mind we may confess Father, Son and Holy Spirit.' In Chapter 8 W. H. Vanstone and David Young examine the charge that the Church pays an exclusive attention to its own story and fails to recognize that other faiths may contain the same truth. Their chapter submits that this criticism of any religious system presupposes an unreal disjunction between message and medium and ignores the 'performative' function of statements. In Chapter 10 John Austin Baker asks how development occurs in the specific field of doctrine, and how this technical question can be handled to make it a truer expression of our common living and believing. In the final chapter Anthony Harvey attempts to identify some of the areas in which our understanding of corporate believing may be particularly relevant, and suggests certain ways in which our approach may be of practical use to the life and mission of the Church today.

During its term of work just completed, the Doctrine Commission has succeeded in regaining recognition as an advisory body to which the House of Bishops may refer questions that have clearly theological implications. This may well be its most significant achievement. It coincides with the setting-up of a Doctrine Commission for the whole Anglican Communion by resolution of the Lambeth Conference in 1978. If this report provides some rationale for these developments in a day of openness and relativism, it will have been written to some purpose.

NOTES

1 Dorothy L. Sayers, *The Just Vengeance* (Gollancz 1946), p. 24.
2 *Metaphysics,* 93a; 30f.
3 M. Polanyi, *Personal Knowledge* (Routledge & Kegan Paul 1958), p. 269.
4 Rodney Needham, *Belief, Language and Experience* (Blackwell 1972), pp. 24-5.
5 John Ziman, *Public Knowledge: The Social Dimension of Science* (Cambridge University Press 1968), p. 135n.
6 idem, p. 9.
7 Polanyi, op.cit., p. 112.
8 See K. Russell, *Men without God?* (Highway Press 1966), p. 3.

1

I Believe: We Believe

When in that house M.P.s divide
If they've a brain and cerebellum too
They've got to leave that brain outside
And vote just as their leaders tell 'em to.

But then the prospect of a lot
Of dull M.P.s in close proximity
All thinking for themselves, is what
No man can face with equanimity.

(*Iolanthe,* Act 2, Scene 1)

It is a great pity that Gilbert never wrote an opera about the Church of England. If he had done, there would have been an obvious place for something like the sentry's song. For in religion, just as much as in politics, there is a problem of how to reconcile individual thought with corporate commitment. It is no empty metaphor when, in face of their doctrinal differences, members of the Labour Party insist that theirs is a 'broad church'.

To belong to a church is to believe what the Church believes. There is more to it, no doubt, than that, but there can scarcely be less. Yet there are many people who find it worrying. Some of them are worried by a demand that seems to them difficult or impossible to meet, and ask: 'How can I believe all that the Church requires me to believe?' Although they may be deeply Christian in character and cast of mind they either refrain from active church membership altogether or continue church members with an uneasy conscience. They feel condemned to remain as wistful unbelievers or equally wistful believers. Others, both 'inside' and 'outside' the Church, are untroubled by this particular problem themselves, but are bothered – even scandalized – by the presence within the Church of those who are troubled by it. Their worry is about belonging to an institution which seems so reluctant to define precisely what it stands for. So the Christian Church in

9

general, and more especially the Church of England, is thought by some to demand too much and by others too little in the way of belief.

It would be a mistake to represent it entirely as a conflict between intellectuals and the rest. Many of those who are irked by the demands the Church seems to make on them are ordinary people who refuse to 'swallow what the Church says hook, line and sinker'; and many of those who stress doctrinal commitment are highly sophisticated. In any case it is responsible for an enormous amount of anxiety and tension, made worse by a feeling on both sides that such a conflict ought not to exist.

In what follows I shall suggest a way of reconciling the great variety of emphasis and interpretation that has always existed within the Church with the conviction that there is an underlying unity of belief. The individual is never as independent or autonomous as is often supposed, but depends for most of his fundamental beliefs on a continuing tradition or traditions; and any tradition depends for its vitality upon the free criticism of reflective individuals. Hence there is a tension between the two which is inevitable and, when properly understood and accepted, fruitful.

By contrast the problem is often posed in terms which make it quite insoluble. On the one hand are the individual's beliefs – or, at any rate, his more fundamental ones – thought of as having been arrived at ideally, and to some extent actually, by a free and independent review of the relevant evidence; on the other the doctrines of Christianity as defined and accepted by the Church. To be a member of the Church is to bring the two entirely into line. The trouble is that it is hard to see how this can be done except by denying the individual's freedom to think for himself or calling in question the doctrinal authority of the Church. But is the reality at all like this?

The individual's belief

Most people, if asked in a television interview, 'What do you believe?' or invited to answer the question in a newspaper article, are not likely to be able to produce in their own words a clear, coherent and comprehensive answer straightaway. Still less are they likely to be able to provide a satisfactory justification of what they believe. Even if someone is given notice of the question and has had time to reflect on the answer, the result is still liable to be extremely inadequate. 'If this is the sum total of what I believe,' he may well think, 'my beliefs are very much more thin and jejune than I always supposed them to be.' In this respect intellectuals, who are used to putting things into words, are not much better off than the great majority of people. If we can properly be said to believe only what, given reasonable notice, we can clearly formulate and give reasons for, only intellectuals have much in the way of beliefs, and their beliefs are woefully meagre.

It is not surprising, therefore, that most people are reluctant to put their deepest convictions into words and feel that, when they do, what they succeed in expressing fails to do justice to what they really believe. If we ask why this should be so, there seem to be two reasons in particular. One is that beliefs are shown as much in a person's actions and habitual responses as in his reflective utterances. The other is that, even when beliefs are explicitly formulated and defended, it is done against a background of assumptions which are simply taken for granted. No doubt the person who is critical and reflective will endeavour to become aware of his attitudes and assumptions and try to make them consistent and coherent, but even in the most highly intellectual people, the process is, in the nature of things, never complete.

How, then, does the individual come by the beliefs which he has not got round to formulating and defending? Some are the product of the sort of intuitive discernment which enables one, without conscious attention, to recognize and interpret what is going on around one. But most are taken over, without his knowing it, from the innumerable influences upon him: parents, friends, the general cultural assumptions of the age, above all, perhaps, the language in which his thoughts and attitudes have to be expressed, whose implications and resonances are only to a limited extent under his command. Thus most people depend for most of their beliefs upon others. Whatever modifications they themselves introduce, or however selective they are, the greater part of their scheme of thought, like the language in which it is expressed, comes to them from an existing tradition or traditions. The 'way they see things', both literally and metaphorically, is affected deeply by influences beyond their control. 'No man is an island' is as true of beliefs as of everything else. The existence of shared beliefs is something that is necessary if individuals are ever to be in a position to develop beliefs that are peculiarly their own.

What difference does it make if the individual actually places himself in a tradition and declares his adherence to it – if, for example, in answer to the question about what he believes, he is content to reply 'I am a socialist' or 'I am a humanist' or 'I am a Christian'? Is he faced by any problems which the uncommitted man does not have? He clearly is. No doubt the 'free thinker' is less free than he thinks he is – his individualism is less complete than it appears – but, since he is not associating himself with any particular tradition, he can admit his general indebtedness without needing to define or defend the relationship between his personal convictions and those of any one tradition and without having to vindicate the coherence of any such tradition. By contrast the committed socialist or Christian faces two problems: one of definition – how can he be satisfied that what he believes is genuinely socialist or Christian?; and a moral one – how can he reconcile the demands which the tradition makes upon him with his duty to pursue the truth?

The problem of definition can be stated simply. To be a socialist or a Christian he must share with other socialists and Christians, past and present, the beliefs which make them socialists or Christians – or at least a good many of those beliefs. But not only, as we have seen, are his own beliefs for the most part inadequate and incomplete, the 'shared beliefs' of socialists and Christians are open to divergent interpretations and admit of considerable controversy. (Consider the proceedings of the Labour Party Conference or the General Synod.) It is not simply a matter of taking one list of entirely clear and unambiguous statements and comparing them with another list of clear and unambiguous statements to see how well they fit.

Corporate belief

When we look at traditions, whether political or religious, which have a continuous history, what we find is a range of beliefs and a variety of interpretations. Not all individuals or groups within the tradition accept, or have in the past accepted, all of these, but all have accepted some of them. In the face of this variety it is tempting to say that we are dealing with people who really believe different things. They are regarded, and regard themselves, as belonging to the same tradition as a result of a combination of historical, sociological and other causes which do not require any fundamental agreement in belief. What believers see as development is really just change, and what they see as differences in interpretation and emphasis are really plain disagreements. What, after all, is there in common between a strict evangelical fundamentalist and a radical theologian, let alone between either of these and an Irish monk of the early Celtic Church, except that they trace their history to the same crucial events whose character and significance they nevertheless understand very differently?

But no sooner have we persuaded ourselves, along these lines, that there is no genuine community of belief between members of such political and religious traditions than other considerations come to mind which compel us to think again. When, for example, we encounter an entirely non-Christian culture, such as that of contemporary Hinduism or of Athens in classical times, we become aware at once of fundamental differences, in comparison with which the differences between Christians appear insignificant. There is then apparent a recognizable family resemblance between Christians of whatever period which does not hold between Christians and these others, however difficult it may be, as it always is with family resemblances, to characterize it precisely. (One relevant point of resemblance lies in the importance attached to belief in relation to other marks of religious affiliation.) There are, of course, certain respects in which some Christians are more like some Hindus than they are like some other Christians – in their degree of puritanism, for example, or their attachment to ritual, or their ascetic mode of life, but even in these cases the reasons given generally turn out to be different, and so does the extent to which reasons are thought to be necessary.

Furthermore, when we review the course of Christian history and the development of Christian thought, we feel bound to stigmatize some of the movements that have occurred as grave errors, departures from or distortions of the true teaching of the gospel. Divine forgiveness was trivialized in the sale of indulgences, divine righteousness distorted in the persecution of heretics, divine sovereignty misapplied in the divine right of kings. The Church's evaluation of erotic love suffered for centuries from the dualistic ideas which had coloured the earlier asceticism of the Church. More generally the attempts of theologians, justified though they were, to express the Christian doctrine of God through the concepts of Greek philosophy can be seen in retrospect to have favoured

13

too abstract and impersonal a notion of God's attributes and thus to have encouraged, by way of reaction, a damaging association between reformation and irrationalism. Such judgements are, of course, themselves controversial and to that extent illustrate the lack of unanimity which generates the sceptical problem. The point is, however, that we are unwilling to regard such judgements as altogether inappropriate or irrelevant. The constant impetus to reform which is so striking a feature of historic Christianity witnesses to an insistence upon the need to identify the true gospel and to rescue it from error and corruption.

These considerations should persuade us to consider the matter more carefully. When we were tempted to deny to Christians, or to socialists, any genuine community of belief, what was our standard of comparison? We may suspect that we were making our criteria of identity unduly simple or unduly strict. The concept of identity is notoriously problematic and scepticism about identity is the natural response to any attempt to impose requirements that are excessively severe. When Hume concluded that there was no continuing self, it was because he insisted on looking for a single continuous 'impression' of the self which was present to him whenever he was conscious. The problem of personal identity still perplexes philosophers and it is apparent that the solution must be a good deal more complex than Hume supposed. The continuing identity of a system of belief has received very much less attention from philosophers but is likely to prove equally complex.

Total unanimity not only in what was believed, but in how it was expressed, and in the reasons given and how they were expressed, no matter how the believers or their situation changed, would be appropriate more to robots than to human beings; and yet this is the standard that we were covertly employing. Its absurdity becomes apparent if we consider the simplest possible case, where two people only are concerned. If we say that they are of one mind, we are not ascribing to them this lifeless replication. What happens is that they achieve a sort of stereoscopic effect by viewing the matter from different standpoints, making use of varying metaphors, and yet saying recognizably the same things. The idea as it grows between them draws its life from the observation and imagination of them both, and the excitement of discovering that it is the *same* idea that they are each entertaining demands a process of

14

recognition which is not simply automatic. The legend of the *doppelgänger* owes much of its horror to the fear of encountering someone whose thoughts, desires and feelings, being indistinguishable from one's own, can never, even for a moment, puzzle or surprise one. When two different people discover that they share the same convictions, the excitement comes from the unlikeliness of such a complete congruence of minds, in which each, in his or her own unique way, recognizes and expresses the same truth.

An equally simple model of *development* can be constructed using two people only. When Augustine returned to the faith in which Monica had nurtured him, must we deny that he remained in the *same* faith, if he went on to explore its implications in directions that Monica had never thought of? In general, does any parent or teacher, who has tried to pass on a particular view of life, regard it as a failure if the child later gives expression to it in new and unsuspected ways? Of course many outcomes are possible. The child may abandon the parent's or teacher's faith, or radically alter it in such a way that a sense of having failed to hand on the faith is rightly felt. The point is simply that there are more ways of succeeding than to have the child remain for ever content with the very formulations it grew up with. Indeed that would scarcely count as success at all, because with genuine belief fresh challenges should properly evoke fresh responses.

Corporate belief and individual judgement

By indefinitely extending these examples we can form some conception of the communion of saints in which all 'agree in the truth of thy holy word', and in which that truth, being inexhaustible, is constantly being reflected and refracted by innumerable individual minds, each moulded by its own personal history and coloured by its unique blend of intellect and imagination. No one will want, upon reflection, to say to another 'You are wrong', but all will be surprised by encountering unsuspected aspects of the truth in which they agree.

This ideal state of affairs plainly does not exist in our earthly life, but once the inappropriate criterion of corporate belief, which tempted us to scepticism, has been firmly put aside, we can trace family resemblances which, while they fall short of the ideal congruence of minds we have been envisaging, are nevertheless enough to represent genuine continuity and

15

convergence. One important reason for this is that, among the entire range of beliefs that are found in the tradition, some occupy a more central place than others. Not only are they more often believed than others, but they are commonly relied upon to explain and justify others, so that adherents of the tradition feel especially bound to accept some version of them or, if they cannot do that, at least to defend their not accepting them by showing how the gap thus created can be filled by other conceptions which are no less central to the tradition. Theological debates about the doctrines of the incarnation or the resurrection provide examples of this, (as do disputes about Clause 4 in the constitution of the Labour Party). Theologians who are unable to accept the doctrine of the incarnation in its traditional form and emphasize its 'mythical' character, continue to see in the life and death of Christ the crucial instance of God's involvement in the suffering of the world, and those who seek to 'demythologize' the resurrection continue to stress the radically new life which inspired the early Church. It is entirely consistent with this pattern that, both in religious and in political traditions, distinct denominations or groups develop which emphasize certain strands in the total tradition as affording the clue to the rest. Indeed, given the inherent complexity of the issues, their existential importance and the inability of the individual fully to comprehend them on his own, such divisions can scarcely be avoided.

It would, of course, make things a good deal easier if it were possible in all cases to reconcile the conflicting beliefs and interpretations, or failing that, to provide some simple and definitive test which would determine once and for all what is the correct formulation of the tradition, but neither is possible in practice. This state of affairs creates less concern in politics than it does in religion, because political parties, even when based upon a definite ideology, are ready as a rule to accept pragmatic compromises and to regard doctrine as of secondary importance. It is more difficult for religious believers to agree to differ when what is at stake is the character of saving truth. Even if they see no present prospect of resolving them, they are unwilling to regard their disagreements as ultimate.

There are two strategies for circumventing this problem which are commonly adopted both in political and in religious movements, but which inevitably fail. The first is sectarian and operates by circumscribing rather narrowly what is allowed to be truly socialist or truly Christian; what a restricted group believes and only what it believes has any title to the name. The second is latitudinarian; it seeks some simple and capacious formula which is vague enough to be acceptable to all who wish to identify themselves with the tradition. The first fails because the original problem breaks out again within the narrow perimeter of what is regarded as 'true socialism' or 'true Christianity'. The history of sectarian protestantism and of extreme left-wing socialism vividly illustrates this fissiparous tendency. Whatever the definitions accepted initially, there are changes and developments as time goes on which lead to competing interpretations, and these in due course demand to be similarly isolated and protected from corruption. The second fails because it leaves out too much that is felt by many to be of central significance; though intended to be all-inclusive, it cannot include those who hold to be essential what it is content to regard as dispensable.

Ultimate truth and provisional understanding
Let us, now, look back again at the individual's situation and compare it with that of the religious tradition with which he seeks to identify himself. When we do this, we find that they have one important feature in common. Just as the individual is aware that his attempts to give expression in words to his deepest convictions are always inadequate and incomplete and often marked by inconsistency and incoherence, so the Church's own attempts to articulate its corporate beliefs are recognized to be inadequate to convey their full significance, which transcends all efforts, whether individual or corporate, to capture it. We are bound to ask whether there is any way in which, without denying this incompleteness, we can do justice to the conviction that this transcendent truth not only exists, but is also to some extent grasped by these inadequate statements.

There are certain experiences which point in the required direction. Sometimes one has the good fortune to encounter an inspired teacher who has the almost uncanny gift of divining what a pupil is trying to convey, no matter how muddled and confused his or her attempts to express it. 'Yes,' he will remark, 'I wonder whether something like this could express what you have in mind?' and there will follow a lucid and beautifully constructed statement which the pupil recognizes at once as expressing, far better than he could ever have done himself, just what he had all along been getting at. Something

17

similar occurs when a scientist has a hunch that the explanation of an apparently unrelated set of facts lies in a certain direction and has a certain shape which, at this preliminary stage, he can only sketch in largely metaphorical terms. The early stages of the atomic theory or the wave theory of light must have been like this. When, after prolonged efforts to get the theory into clear focus and test it by experiment, he finally works it up into a full and scientifically acceptable form, he may find himself exclaiming, 'This is what I meant all along.' There may be room for disagreement as to how far along the path to 'full' understanding the student or the scientist has to have been for this retrospective claim to be justified, but he can reasonably be given credit for having meant what he subsequently came to understand fully at a comparatively early stage in the proceedings. If this is true of the individual, could not something similar be true of an entire tradition? If the sympathetic teacher can discern what one member of his class is trying to say and present him with an acceptable statement of it, he can presumably do the same for others too. And he may then find that a number of them are trying to say substantially the same thing, even though it may seem to them and to an outside observer that they are at odds with one another. In such a case he may be able to do what a skilled chairman sometimes can, namely, achieve a recon-ciliation between apparently opposing statements, which is not just a compromise between them. He *may* be able to do this but, of course, not invariably. There are positions that are not reconcilable, and the teacher will find some of the suggestions put to him either individually incoherent or straightforwardly false. It would, as we have seen, be wildly implausible to suggest that all the views put forward as Christian by contem-porary Christians, let alone all those put forward in the past, could in principle be rendered fully intelligible and shown to be consistent with one another by some celestial interpreter. We know enough already to be able to tell that some of them are false, and some plainly incompatible with others. We can often recognize distortions and trace the cultural influences which led to them. But for the illustration to be serviceable there is no need to postulate so unlikely a convergence of views. It would be enough if the more important disagreements were such that the contending parties could in the end be brought to see that they were endeavouring to express substantially the same truth.

If this were so, could we not say that what the Church (corporately) believes bears to that truth the same relationship as the undergraduate's suggestions in his essay or the scientist's hunch to the fully developed theory that would adequately express their meaning? And, if we could say this, we could also say that the individual believer adheres to the credal affirmations of the Church in the faith that it will turn out to be so. He does not (or, at least, should not) suppose that what the Church is now saying, or what is being said in its name or on its behalf, represents the final and complete truth of the matter, but rather regard it as an incomplete and unsatisfactory, but not wholly misleading, way of getting at the fuller truth which alone could adequately complement and complete these anticipatory stutterings. The individual is in effect saying something like 'What I am getting at is what the Church is getting at' or, more fully, 'I believe that there is a set of truths which would adequately express what the Church is trying to say (but which is never articulated fully, adequately, etc.) and I profess my adherence to that set of truths.'

Analogies from science and literature

One feature of the scientific analogy which makes it attractive in itself and readily transferable to the religious case is that scientific theories frequently develop through the exploitation of metaphors, which are more than merely aids to discovery. Waves and particles are obvious examples. More and more is learnt, as research progresses, as to how these are to be interpreted and applied, and as to what inferences are to be drawn from them; yet they cannot be finally dispensed with. The scientist who, at a comparatively early stage, has a hunch that one such model provides the clue to his inquiries does not entirely discard it when, at a much later stage, he has solved many of his problems with the aid of it. It is this that makes it not unreasonable to claim that, at that earlier stage, he had a genuine, although incomplete, grasp of the theory he was later to develop. Since the use of metaphors, analogies, images, is an even more striking feature of religious thinking than of scientific, there is at least as good reason for crediting the religious believer with a genuine, although limited understanding of the truth which these figures point to.

In some ways there is an even closer analogy with the interpretation of literature. The plays of Shakespeare, for example, like all great literature, are in a sense inexhaustible; they are

19

open to indefinite reinterpretation. Critics often maintain that it does not make sense to claim that one interpretation is truer than another. Whatever can be seen there *is* there to be seen. Nevertheless some interpretations are manifestly dotty or distorted, as a visit to Stratford will often show, whereas the interpretations of Johnson and Coleridge have lasting validity. It is arguable that it is not Shakespeare's primary aim to convey a message and there are critics who warn us against looking for any answer, let alone a definitive one, to the question, what is Shakespeare trying to say? Hence a less ambiguous parallel is provided by a philosopher, like Plato, who resembles the poet in his use of imagery and parable, and shares his inexhaustibility, yet is quite manifestly endeavouring to convey truth. If it is plausible to call western philosophy a 'series of footnotes upon Plato', this is because his work never ceases to generate questions and suggest answers. It continues to admit of innumerable interpretations, but the interpreter cannot feel free, as perhaps he can with Shakespeare, to ascribe to Plato himself whatever exciting or stimulating thoughts he gets from studying Plato. Platonism is no longer a recognizable philosophical school with a continuous history, but, when it was, a man could properly call himself a Platonist only if he could reasonably maintain that Plato himself would not have disowned him.

One might test the position we have been trying to develop by starting at the other end. Suppose one wanted to convey a difficult and important message in such a way that it could continue to be received and transmitted into the indefinite future. How should one proceed? It would need to be memorable, and must, therefore, seize the imagination. It must, so far as possible, be protected from ossification, because it is a message that is to be lived as well as intellectually acknowledged by those who receive it; and this demands the resonant language of metaphor and analogy. To understand it must involve the active co-operation of the recipients and this will be assisted if it largely takes the form of a story to be re-enacted. Such a message would inevitably be subject to different and even divergent interpretations in at least two ways. Different elements in the message would be emphasized and developed by different persons and at different periods; and the message as a whole would be interpreted in terms of varying philosophical concepts. It would thus be impossible to arrive at an entirely definitive formulation of the message acceptable to all believers at all times, but this would not mean that some interpretations could not be seen to be seriously distorted or considerably diluted. In practice one would expect there to develop a number of rival schools of interpretation, differing from one another in style and emphasis.

This is in fact what we find. It is a situation that creates problems, but the problems are inseparable from a tradition that is alive and not ossified. There is, as we have seen, no satisfactory way of avoiding them either by the sectarian or by the latitudinarian route. But if entirely definitive formulae are not to be had, it does not follow that the task of interpreting the tradition is a hopeless one. Those who see through a glass darkly do not fail to use all their resources to understand what they see. If the Christian message is to be related, as it must be, to contemporary knowledge and if this requires, as it does, the use of some philosophical framework, there must be those whose task it is, on behalf of the Church, to enter into the contemporary philosophical debate and look for the most suitable concepts in terms of which to express the Church's teaching about the nature and purpose of human existence. To leave this undone will be to leave 'a room swept and garnished' for occupation by purely secular ideologies or by superstitions. If some social and political arrangements are more compatible than others with a Christian understanding of human life, it is important to discover them and work for them. If, as is inevitably the case, these questions are controversial, then controversy must be engaged in with as much clarity and charity as possible. The individual believer's commitment to the tradition and the Church's commitment to it both involve a certain acceptance of the provisional nature of what is believed, together with an underlying faith in the truth it is believed to point to.

The demands of truth

At this stage in the discussion the first question considered: how the individual can be satisfied that what he believes is genuinely Christian, leads on to the second: how he can reconcile the demands which the tradition makes on him with his duty to pursue the truth. An individual identifies himself with a tradition in the belief that truth is to be found there and that in working through it and in helping to develop it he is moving towards a fuller understanding of truth. No doubt for most believers this conviction is implicit, for people do not as a rule become believers as the result of a reflective intellectual process nor is it to be expected that they should. Nevertheless they would not wish to remain believers if they were persuaded that the tradition to which they subscribed was fundamentally in error. Not only does the believer expect to find truth within the tradition he has identified himself with, but, if our earlier argument is correct, he cannot expect to find it on his own without the help, whether acknowledged or not, of any tradition at all. The earnest seeker after truth cannot be a free thinker, or, to the extent that he can, it is only by availing himself of the fruits of others' labours, who are content to work within existing traditions.

But, if it is to be a means to the discovery of truth, the tradition needs, as we have seen, to be a critical and a reflective one, and this requirement introduces certain tensions whose character has already become apparent. The problems for any system of belief arise when fresh facts or well-supported theories run counter to the tenets of the tradition as currently formulated. To ignore these problems altogether is to display indifference to truth. To adhere unreasonably to the accepted formulation is to risk ossifying the tradition. To abandon it too readily may well be to forfeit the benefits to theory of a more tenacious policy, as well as making for practical ineffectiveness. In this sort of situation a tradition needs both strength and flexibility and it is natural for these virtues to become exemplified in different persons. If Christian teaching is to be brought into relation with the best thought of the day, it must be someone's task to do this, and the task is bound to be to some extent experimental and exploratory. Some, at least, of those who undertake it will be by temperament and training innovators; and all of them need considerable freedom if the job is to be properly done. Tension between them and the more steady and conservative thinkers (as between radicals and conservatives in the Church at large, for these divisions are not confined to intellectuals) is to be regarded as a symptom not of weakness, but of vigour. The strength of a tradition can be largely measured by its success in containing this tension and enabling it to be creative.

In religious, as in political and other traditions, these divisions sometimes take on an organized and institutional form. Rival schools in interpretation arise, each fastening upon some important element in the total tradition, which is felt to have been neglected or distorted, and making it a major clue to the understanding of the whole. It is conceivable that, given the limitations of human life, a fuller and richer approximation to the truth may sometimes be achieved by such rival attempts to develop the resources of the tradition than by trying to reconcile their claims by means of some compromise formula. This does not, of course, mean that *genuine* reconciliations are never possible, and should not be sought so far as possible; only that the continued coexistence of separate streams of the tradition may have positive value, so long as there remains a common determination to respect the whole tradition and to recognize that each interpretation represents only an approximation to the truth.

The notion that the individual who identifies himself with a traditional system of belief must be less concerned with truth and is less likely to achieve it than the entirely independent thinker, arises from a wholly unrealistic idea of the way in which truth is to be discovered. Both the conservation and the discovery of truth must be primarily corporate endeavours. The twin dangers of excessive dogmatism and rootless individualism are to be guarded against not by rejecting all traditional restraints but by developing traditions which are able to stimulate and control individual exploration. Once this is understood, some at least of the stresses and strains which affect every living tradition can be seen to be inseparable from its continued growth.

This emphasis upon growth and discovery may seem at first sight to be out of place when dealing with a specifically religious tradition. The great religions have traditionally been understood as more than the products of a merely human search for truth. They offer answers to man's insistent questions about the meaning of his life, which are believed to have a transcendent origin and authority. The gospel could not otherwise be the vehicle of saving truth, nor could it be a constant challenge to the standards which individuals and societies are content to live by. In a fundamental sense, therefore, the Christian revelation is not something that has yet to be discovered, but a treasure that needs to be safeguarded. However, our earlier discussion of what it means to hand on from one generation to another 'the same' message shows that growth and discovery are essential to it. Here is a situation in which 'it takes all the running we can do to stay in the same place'. If the message is from God it cannot be a process of *merely* human growth and discovery, but it must be

23

at least that if the message is to be genuinely understood and appropriated by succeeding generations. The history of the Christian Church as a human institution has been marked both by serious failures of charity and by intellectual errors, that is to say, by inappropriate responses to the challenges presented to it, but fresh responses were constantly demanded and failure to respond at all was as much apostasy as wrong responses. The safeguarding of the message has to be an active task, in which the guidance of the Holy Spirit evokes creative as well as sustaining energies.

2

Attending to Scripture

I believe: the Church believes

These two phrases, and the relationship between them, lie at the heart of the problem to which the previous chapter addressed itself, the problem of 'how to reconcile individual thought with corporate commitment'. For there can be no doubt that there *is* a significant difference between saying what it is that I personally believe as an individual and what I assent to as a member of the Church. Unless I have renounced all spirit of inquiry and responsible decision, I shall be bound to say that there are many religious questions on which I have my own view, and many religious convictions which I have my own way of expressing. But I shall also feel bound to say, as a faithful member of the church to which I belong, that my faith is not simply my own version of Christianity, but is the faith of the Church. What I believe is, in essentials, what others believe. Indeed, on a number of points, what I and others believe is so much of a piece, and so distinctive, that we sense ourselves to be a part, not merely of Christendom, but of a particular denomination within the worldwide Church.

So much may be agreed. But difficulties arise as soon as we try to find a form of words which will express this difference. On the one side we have a simple phrase to express the individual's belief. The individual can say, without more ado, 'I believe in such and such', or 'I believe that such and such is the case'. But on the other side it is not quite so easy to find a phrase which has the same naturalness. 'The Church believes . . .' seems to raise questions. How are we to fill in the rest of the sentence? What does it mean for an institution – even so untypical an institution as the Church – to 'believe'?

An immediate response to this difficulty might be to object that this is in any case the wrong phrase. 'The Church believes' has an unfamiliar ring; what we should put in its place is 'the Church teaches'. *Ecclesia docens* is a well-tried concept. Why not work with the pair, 'The Church teaches – I believe'?

But a moment's reflection will show that this will not do. It is true that one of the functions of the Church must always be to teach. Children, young people, converts, all need to be 'taught' what the Christian faith is about, and the Church has traditionally responded to this need by providing a 'catechism' as a basis for instruction. But it is also clear that the teacher–pupil model, even if it is appropriate in the early stages of Christian discipleship, does not by any means fit the reality of adult membership of the Church. Christians are not persons who are for ever going to school in their Church. The exploration and deepening of their faith is a far more complex and subtle process, involving a constant dialogue between the individual and the institution. The individual's personal struggle to live out his faith in his own personal circumstances becomes part of the corporate experience of the Church which is then mediated to, and is in turn tested by, the next generation. The language in which the essentials of the faith are conveyed must be such as to find a response in the individual Christian, and that response will itself affect the language which is customary at any particular time within the Church. There are, of course, methods of teaching in which this kind of dialogue has a place. But the traditional, didactic model of a 'teaching' Church set over against a 'learning' believer is incapable of expressing the dynamics of vigorous and healthy church life.

But (it may further be said) the model of the classroom was the wrong one in the first place. Christians may not be for ever at school in the Church; but they are nevertheless members of an institution which has rules, standards, policies and attitudes. Situations will constantly arise in their lives in which it is necessary to decide on a course of action, a word to be spoken or a position to be held or repudiated, such that it can be said that they have acted as Christians and as faithful members of the Church. In such situations they will naturally appeal to the Church for guidance, and the Church will respond by giving its 'teaching'. The model, that is to say, is not the classroom but the tribunal. The belief of the Church is expressed in its *magisterium*.

But again, this is not how it works out in practice. Even in the Roman Catholic Church (where the notion of *magisterium* is most at home) it is impossible to make a neat distinction between the 'Church' which gives directives and its members who assent to them. When new issues arise for decision, the experience and Christian insight of church members themselves must be attended to before judgement can be given; moreover, it is far from being the case that the Church presumes to make all the individual Christian's decisions for him. It may offer advice, and propound general principles. It may authorize bishops to make pastoral decisions in the interests of the Christian community which may deeply affect the life of the individual. But the ultimate decision still lies with the conscience of the believer. Even in its strictest application, the concept of *magisterium* does not validate the model of a 'teaching' Church set over against a submissive and acquiescent individual.

If, then, we cannot work with the idea of a 'teaching' Church which imparts its belief to its members, it seems that we must beware of models which set the Church *over against* the individual, and explore instead the model of a single corporation of belief. What the Church believes is not something which judges and controls what its members believe: it *is* what its members believe. But again this model needs to be handled carefully. At first sight, it might suggest that the belief of the Church is simply the consensus of its members: what they all believe is what the Church believes. But not only would it then be impossible in practice to establish what, at any particular time, the Church does believe (the range of beliefs among its members being so bafflingly wide); but (more importantly) this model also fails to fit the actual experience of the individual Christian. In claiming that he holds the belief of the Church, he does not intend to say that he believes his religious views to be identical with those held at this particular moment by the majority of his fellow Christians. Indeed, he is not primarily concerned with consensus at all. His appeal is not to the supposed unanimity of church members (which may not even exist, and is certainly not easily ascertainable). Nor is it (usually) to statements issued by authoritative ecclesiastical figures. It is rather, as we shall see, to a certain tradition of faith which is still, one way or another, controlling the conduct and belief of church members and which has come to control his own. He shares with others, not a series of identical beliefs, but a respect for, and loyalty to, the form in which the Christian religion has come down to him, a form which controls his own life and thinking, and tends to make his beliefs come out broadly the same (though often different in detail and formulation) as those held by other Christians.

It is now becoming clearer why the phrase, 'The Church believes . . .' caused us initially a certain unease. The phrase suggests that we ought to be able to spell out in a series of statements what it is that the Church does believe. If we could adopt the model of the *ecclesia docens*, then this might be a possible programme. But, as we have seen, this model does not fit our actual Christian living. Equally inappropriate is the consensus-model: it would be impossible to ascertain what, at any given time, the consensus amounted to; and in any case it is clear that this is not what a Christian *means* when he talks of the faith of the Church. In other words, 'The Church believes . . .' is a phrase which makes us uneasy because we sense that it is difficult to fill in the object. On certain specific matters (as later chapters will show) there may be authoritative (though not ultimate or permanent) decisions to refer to. But there is no series of propositions which constitutes, at any given moment, the total belief of the Church. The Church, like the individual, discovers what it believes only by interpreting the faith which it has received in the light of its present experience.

Points of reference: the creeds

We need to direct our search, therefore, in a different direction: not towards a formulation of the Church's belief, but towards the points of reference and orientation which provide the framework for, and control over, the Church's believing. And since we naturally tend to expect this 'believing' to be expressed in the form of doctrinal propositions, we shall look particularly for points of reference and control which seem themselves best suited to offer a basis for such propositions. Indeed, we shall not hesitate: what we are looking for is most obviously exemplified by the creeds. These have remained fixed, stable and (in the main) unifying for a millennium and a half. They are willingly repeated by worshipping Christians all over the world. Surely these constitute, if not what the Church actually 'believes', then at least the framework in which she does her believing?

Some of the problems raised by the creeds in the Church of today, and the differing (and sometimes mutually incompatible) attitudes which individual members of the Church of England may have towards them, have already been discussed in *Christian Believing*[1] and there is no need to go over the same ground again. But that discussion was primarily concerned with the *truth* of the propositions contained in the

creeds, and the personal difficulties caused to the believer if he
feels unable to assent to one or more of them. Our present task
is rather to understand the function and authority of the creeds
as points of reference and control for the corporate believing of
the Church. And for this purpose it is important to assess them
not so much on their truth as on their content. We may agree
with the statement in *Christian Believing*[2] that 'the creeds still
commend themselves as the most intrinsically authoritative
and creative extant summaries of the essentials of the Christian
faith to a large proportion of Christian people the world over';
but we must now ask whether the 'essentials' of the faith are in
fact those areas of Christian doctrine in which the Church's
contemporary believing most needs guidance. To put the
question somewhat crudely: quite apart from the question of
their truth, do the creeds have the right Christian priorities?

The point may perhaps be made clearer by an example.
Suppose a man becomes a Christian because he has
experienced the reconciling power of Christ; or has found, in
Jesus, a new dimension in human suffering; or has come to
acknowledge Jesus as his personal saviour; or finds that only
Christianity 'makes sense' of our relationship with the physical
universe. Each of these converts, if asked what was the most
important part of his Christian belief, would answer somewhat
differently; but we would agree that his answer was a
legitimate understanding of some of the central truths of the
faith. But if so, we have to recognize that these truths are not
prominent among the 'essentials' of the faith contained in the
creeds. The most important part of the 'believing' of these
individuals can hardly be said to be represented by (still less
controlled by) the historic tradition of the Church as expressed
in the creeds.

The same is true, not only of individuals, but of whole
churches. For the Lutheran tradition, for example, one of the
most important (and at times the most important of all)
Christian doctrines has been that of justification by faith. But
this is not present, even by implication, in the creeds, and
therefore certain confessional formulae have been needed in
order to provide a framework for the believing of the Lutheran
Church. Moreover, the doctrinal questions which agitate the
churches today are not necessarily – indeed are not often –
ones which fall within the range of topics covered by the
creeds. There is, for example, earnest debate at the present
time over the extent to which Christian belief and practice

allows or demands political action. But this debate cannot be settled by reference to any creed: the historic tradition of the Church as formulated in the creeds simply does not make any reference to the question. Proponents of 'personal Christianity' or 'the social gospel' may accuse each other of having neglected an essential part of the faith. But in saying this, they are not referring to any doctrinal formulation where these 'essentials' might be set out, for no such formulations exist. At the time when the creeds were perfected, the questions at issue were those which are the subjects of the various clauses. The priorities expressed in the creeds were determined by the questions which were being debated at the time. The questions being debated today are often quite different. The frame of reference for discussion, and for evaluating the beliefs of those who take part in it, has to be looked for elsewhere.

This last point helps us to see that, however important the place which has been occupied (and perhaps is still occupied) by the creeds in the life of the Church, we cannot regard them as an ultimate arbiter of Christian believing, for they were themselves compiled with explicit reference to a higher authority from which they received their own, namely, Scripture. As Geoffrey Lampe showed so clearly,[3] a church which accepts the authority of the creeds does so only because it is believed that they correctly express what is contained in Scripture. It follows that in our search for points of reference and orientation in relation to which the Church's believing takes place, we cannot rest with the creeds; we must go behind them to the Scriptures themselves, which are the source of the authority which the creeds possess.

Points of reference: Scripture

We are led by this route to locate the ultimate authority for doctrine in Scripture itself. We now have to ask how it is that Scripture possesses this overriding authority in the Church and how it is exercised. But first we must notice a fact about Scripture which fundamentally affects its suitability to perform the controlling function over Christian belief which we wish to ascribe to it. The form of Scripture is not such that we can easily deduce from it general statements of what it is that we believe. Its most characteristic mode of writing is that of narrative; it contains also poetry, exhortation, controversy and many other modes; but it contains relatively little of the kind of doctrinal statement from which a reasoned presentation of the Christian faith could be logically deduced. It is true that St Paul, when engaged in theological argument, makes statements which lend themselves more readily to doctrinal elaboration: and it is no accident that some parts of his writings have formed the primary basis of some of the greatest attempts in modern times to found a systematic presentation of the Christian faith on Scripture. But this does not alter the fact that the characteristic mode in which Scripture conveys to us the things concerning God, Jesus and man is not (in this sense) 'doctrinal' at all. It is mainly (though not exclusively) *narrative*.

It could be said that, from very early times, the task which has seemed to present itself with greatest insistence to the theologian has been that of overcoming this basic inappropriateness of Scripture. The Christian wants general truths about God and man; Scripture tends to tell him only of specific events that happened. It has been for the theologian to grapple with this intractable amalgam of narrative, poetical description, exhortation and vision, and to distil from it the kind of doctrinal propositions which the believer seems to require. In the past he has done this with the aid of other sources of knowledge – in particular, philosophy – which seem to offer material more serviceable for his construction. More recently, a determined but short-lived attempt has been made to recover from the Bible itself the kind of theological material which can be used for the construction of a doctrinal system: we have seen the search for a 'biblical theology', or even a 'biblical metaphysic'. Underlying this immense effort has been the conviction that the ultimate theological task is to identify doctrines which may be held to be true on the basis of their foundation in Scripture, despite the apparent unsuitability of Scripture to provide the foundation for anything of the kind.

But, once again, we must ask whether we are using the correct model. Is it really the case that our 'believing' depends on the success of this arduous theological enterprise? Do we really have to wait for definitive theological formulations securely based upon Scripture before we can say that we 'believe'? The facts of our Christian experience hardly bear out such an assumption. At least three of our characteristic Christian activities suggest a quite different model.

First, *worship*. It is true that liturgy implies doctrine; but it could not possibly be maintained that liturgy *is* doctrine. In our worship we hear again and again that 'story' which is the main burden of Scripture. We attend to it, we respond to it, we participate in it, we re-enact it. To put somewhat crudely a point which will be developed in a later chapter: in worship we seek to bring the story of our own lives into conformity with the story of our salvation. This activity is certainly a part of what we mean by our 'corporate believing'.

But not only in worship. The same happens, secondly, in our *daily living*. An element of deliberate imitation is present in the 'believing' of virtually every Christian. Sometimes this is a conscious discipleship of the person of Jesus as he is known from the gospels; sometimes it is no more than a dim realization that a certain kind of self-sacrificial service is of the essence of Christianity and is to be taken upon oneself as best one may. But again, this effort to live in such a way that the story of one's own life conforms with the Christian story is an integral part of our 'corporate believing'.

Thirdly, *evangelism*. The activity of conveying the Christian faith to others rarely resembles bringing a package of doctrinal statements to the tribunal of another's judgement. Our believing has to be expressed through our zeal to bring our beliefs to others; but this takes place through a complex combination of dialogue, example and persuasion. Sometimes, it is true, we shall be challenged to say precisely what it is that we believe; but we cannot expect that our Christian formulations will necessarily be meaningful to our listeners, and we shall need to search for many ways of making our meaning clear, ways that take us a long way from the propositions with which we began. More often, perhaps, we shall be telling the Christian story, and the response we shall be looking for is the recognition in another that this story speaks to his condition as well as to ours.

This analysis of some of the constituents of our corporate believing allows us to make room for a point which we have had made very forcibly to us, namely, that the great majority of Christian believers are, and have always been, people for whom the niceties of theological definition have relatively little interest. If we survey the actual membership of the Christian churches, it cannot be the case that the criterion of membership consists primarily in the ability to formulate and assent to doctrinal propositions. Even among intellectual Christians, other expressions of 'believing' will be equally important. Christian believing is a manifold activity, with manifestations that appeal to the heart and the imagination as much as to the mind; and for such a response, it is entirely appropriate and understandable that the primary authority should consist at least as much of 'story' as of 'statement'.

But is it true?

But this cannot be the end of the matter. We may accept that our believing is, to a great extent, a response to a story, expressed in worship, service and evangelism; but we shall still want to ask whether all this is *true* – that is to say, whether the story itself and the Church's response to the story are worthy of belief, even to the exclusion of beliefs held with equal conviction by members of other religions or of none. In the Christian context, a definition of belief may give pride of place to such things as 'faith', 'trust', 'commitment', and so forth; but it must still be fundamentally related to 'truth'. It must be possible to say that we believe certain things because they are true.

But suppose that, instead of trying to identify certain propositions which are implicit in the Christian story and declaring them true, we ask whether the story itself is true. This opens up a number of senses of the word 'true'.

We shall want to say, first, that the Christian story is historically true. In particular, we shall claim that the story of Jesus, as related in the gospels, is a true story in the sense that the principal events comprised in it really happened. We shall be ready, of course, to admit certain qualifications to this claim. We shall not expect the story of Jesus to be immune to the kind of distortions and uncertainty which would attend the records concerning any notable person of antiquity; and we shall be prepared to concede that there are legendary features and ecclesiastical interpretations so deeply entwined in the text that it is no longer possible to separate them out with any certainty. But, given these necessary qualifications, we shall claim that Jesus lived and died much as the gospels say he did. In this sense, the Christian story is 'true'.

But stories are true in other senses too. If we are moved to say that *War and Peace* is a 'true' novel, we do not mean that its account of the battle of Borodino is historically true. We mean that the novel as a whole is true to experience, true to human nature. Any story which has the power to move and inspire and become memorable is likely to have the kind of realism which is itself a form of 'truth'. If the story of Jesus showed him to be some kind of freak, acting irrationally and unpredictably, and

33

without any notably admirable personal qualities, it would not be true in any but the limited sense of accurately reporting what was alleged to have happened. We would certainly wish to claim for our story that it is true in a wider sense than this.

And there are still other ways in which a story may be judged to be true. The narrative may contain teaching given by its hero, and the truth of this teaching will contribute to the general truth of the story. It may also contain reports of past events and predictions of future ones – and these too, if they are not true, may affect our judgement whether the whole story is true, whereas if they are true they will again contribute to the general truth of the story.

In all these ways – and possibly more – we shall wish to say that the story of Jesus is true. We can therefore fill out the object of our believing: we can say what it is that we believe to be the case by reference to a story which not merely demands a response in our lives and imaginations, but challenges our intellect to pronounce that it is true. But this alone does not fully answer our question about the nature of 'corporate believing'. We have seen that to share the faith of the Church is to join in a complex activity of believing which is ultimately controlled by the Christian story. But we still have to ask, why this, and why only this, story? Or (to put the question in more traditional terms), what gives the story (or rather the whole complex of stories) contained in Scripture an authority over our believing greater than that of any other story? What (in brief) do we mean by 'the authority of Scripture'?

The inspiration of Scripture

It is tempting to reply that Scripture is necessarily authoritative for us because it is 'inspired', or because it is the product of divine revelation. No doubt the great majority of Christians would wish to make a claim along these lines. They sense that the Bible is (at least in certain respects) unlike any other book; and the words 'inspiration' and 'revelation' seem best suited to account for this unlikeness. In practice, however, great difficulties have always attended the attempt to formulate such a doctrine.

In the past, difficulties have clustered around the problem of the relationship between the ultimate divine author of the inspired books and the human writers whose personalities, gifts and limitations seem not to have been eliminated by the process of revelation. A number of models were tried: most popular was that of a musical instrument in the hands of a musician. But it cannot be said that the problem was ever resolved to general satisfaction.

Further difficulties have been caused by the increasingly widespread realization that the Bible, however unlike other books in certain respects, is nevertheless *like* other books in many important ways. Its text (like that of other writings from antiquity) has been subject to corruption, so that we cannot always be sure exactly what the writer wrote; its literary conventions were not the product of the period and culture of the authors, and are not always immediately intelligible to us today; and the writers themselves were undoubtedly subject to constraints and influences which need to be allowed for if their work is to be adequately understood. All these factors greatly complicate the task of formulating the sense in which the words written on the pages of a modern Bible are 'inspired'.

Another factor which may have to be taken into account is the relationship between the words themselves and the events and circumstances which they describe. Clearly there is a large number of words in the Bible which could not have been written had not certain events taken place; and if the words are 'inspired', then the process of inspiration must involve some influence upon events and circumstances such that the necessary conditions were present for those particular words to be written. A long historical process was necessary to produce the precise circumstances in which any book of the Bible was written; and further historical conditions were needed to ensure that the book was preserved, studied and received. A doctrine of the inspiration of Scripture, therefore, may have to allow for the 'inspiration' of those events which enabled Scripture to be written (and in fact a number of Roman Catholic scholars have recently been thinking along these lines). But it then becomes difficult to set any boundary to this phenomenon of inspiration. Almost any event in ancient history may be distantly connected with the events which were the immediate conditions for the Bible being written. And if there is virtually nothing which is *not* part of the process of inspiration, the concept of inspiration ceases to have any meaning.

Difficulties such as these are not necessarily insuperable. Indeed, to many they will seem serious only if they are treated in isolation rather than as a part of the necessary conditions and limitations which attended the incarnation of God in man.

35

However much it may be true that the story of Jesus Christ is the story of a unique intervention by God in the history of mankind, this intervention was not such as to suspend the constraints which shape the life of every human being: it was not a dazzling manifestation of God in barely human form, but a willing obedience to the limitations of a true humanity. And so it must be with all those other interventions by which God prepared the way for this definitive self-manifestation and opened up paths for its subsequent influence. If Scripture is 'inspired', it is inspired by the same God who accepted the constraints of the incarnation. It is not invested with an other-worldly, totally self-authenticating power; as with the incarnation itself, its uniqueness and authority can be glimpsed only through the limitations imposed upon it, as upon any other book, by the circumstances of composition, editing, copying and circulation. A doctrine of inspiration cannot, any more than a doctrine of the incarnation, expect to achieve perfect consistency. For inspiration, too, is mysterious; it is part of the mystery of the incarnation itself.

These difficulties, therefore, however baffling, need not be such as to call into question the whole enterprise of formulating a doctrine of inspiration, nor to suggest that it is meaningless to speak of the Scriptures as 'inspired'. The Christian will certainly continue to feel that there is some inherent quality or power in the Bible (or at least in parts of it) which give it unique authority for him, and he will encourage theologians in their efforts to achieve an adequate and intelligible formulation of it. But at the same time, it is possible to answer the question why Scripture is authoritative in a simpler and more pragmatic way. To take a simple analogy: if it is asked why the American Constitution is regarded as the ultimate authority in the United States, an answer could be looked for in the particular qualities, comprehensiveness and finality which would be likely to have won the assent of the American people. But it would also be correct, and in some ways more illuminating, to offer the answer that the Constitution is authoritative because at a certain moment the nation accepted its authority and has never yet repudiated it (though in fact it has amended it). Similarly we can say that Scripture is authoritative because the Church came to accept and still accepts its authority. That is to say, we can answer our question, not (or not only) by seeking some quality in Scripture which accounts for the authority it possesses, but by studying the role which it actually

36

plays in the Church. In the process, we may also gain some insight into its function as a control over corporate believing.

Attending to Scripture?

At an earlier stage in the argument we reached the conclusion that corporate believing, though it cannot be expressed in a series of doctrinal propositions, nevertheless requires some authoritative framework or point of reference; and that since this could not be provided by the historic creeds, we would have to go further back still to the Scriptures themselves. If this is the case, then the answer to our present question has already been given: Scripture is authoritative because all other sources of authority in the Church are ultimately dependent upon it, and if one were to deny authority to Scripture one would end up by denying the possibility of any authority in the Church whatever; indeed, it is hard to see how the Church could continue to exist as an identifiable community. But before we accept this conclusion it is necessary to look again at the function which doctrinal formulations may still perform in the Church, and ask whether, given the archaic character, the obscurity and the endless difficulties of interpretation of the Bible, corporate believing may not in fact be related more securely to certain propositions which are (or ought to be) widely accepted by Christians today than to the scriptural authority which allegedly lies behind them.

These who feel instinctively (as many do) that there must be statements of Christian truth upon which all Christians can agree and which are fundamental to our profession of the Christian faith, may turn first to certain propositions contained in the New Testament which have held such an important place in theology down the centuries that they can surely be regarded as basic and normative statements of Christian belief. Among such propositions will doubtless be those which appear to have a credal or confessional character even in New Testament times, such as 'Jesus is Lord', or 'God raised him from the dead'. Anyone who denies the truth of these statements, it will be felt, can hardly be regarded as a Christian. Conversely, the ability to affirm these truths is surely a guarantee that Christians do share, at least in fundamentals, the same faith. This instinctive feeling is certainly well grounded, in so far as familiar and basic propositions of this kind are generally assented to by the great majority of Christians. But the ability of such formulations to serve as authoritative points of reference for Christian believing depends upon the meaning they convey to different people. For many centuries there could be assumed to exist a common language in religious matters, such that propositions of this kind could be used as a test and standard of belief. Those who assented to them could be assumed to agree on what they meant and to understand also what opinions they excluded. But today our situation appears to be different. Before we assent to any doctrinal statement we need to ask, not so much, 'Is it true?' as, 'What does it mean?' In what sense can we say today that Jesus is 'Lord'? What meaning can we attach to the proposition that someone was 'raised from the dead'? We shall find that opinions will differ widely, even with regard to propositions which in the past have seemed fundamental, on whether they are 'meaningful', or 'relevant', or even 'mythological'. Nor can the difficulty be solved simply by attempting to reformulate these truths in contemporary language. This task, which is constantly being entrusted to denominational and ecumenical commissions, can result only in formulations which will commend themselves (if at all) as 'one way of putting it'. A commission composed of a different group of individuals would undoubtedly have chosen a different form of words; and no church member will feel committed to employing only *that* way of putting it to the exclusion of all others. In short, it seems that basic doctrinal propositions of this kind, though they may still be used by Christians to indicate a common area of belief, can no longer be relied on to convey the same meaning to even the majority of Christians today, and cannot therefore be used as an authoritative standard for Christian believing or as a criterion of membership of the Church.

A somewhat similar desire for authoritative statements of Christian doctrine is felt by those who are concerned with some of the questions which are being most keenly debated at the present time. In discussions about the ethics of homosexual behaviour, for example, or about the alleged 'politicizing' of the gospel, there must surely be some standard of what is and is not 'Christian' by reference to which different opinions can be assessed. It is also natural to assume that this standard is, or at least could be, expressed in terms of a doctrinal statement. But again, any such statement will prove elusive. Committees will labour to produce reports on these subjects, and their conclusions, even if unanimous (which is by no means always the case), will be widely debated in the Church. It may seem reasonable enough at the outset to ask what is 'the position of the Church' on a particular issue; when it comes to the point, it will be found again and again that the most that can be offered is a balance of opinion one way or the other. The reason for this is not that doctrinal propositions are in conflict with one another; it is rather (as we shall see) that the different parties to the discussion, though they all recognize the authority of Scripture and (often to a lesser extent) the tradition of the Church, nevertheless each regard a different passage of Scripture or aspect of the tradition as carrying decisive weight with regard to the question at issue. Discussions of this kind throw us back, once again, on to discussions about the authority and relevance of Scripture.

This conclusion need not be regarded as a negative one. All believing and practising Christians (and not only theologians) are committed to the task of working out their Christian position on the many moral and religious issues which they encounter, and what will count will be the earnestness and integrity with which they seek the truth rather than their ability to agree on a series of doctrinal propositions. As we have seen, the existence and reality of 'corporate believing' does not depend upon the production of agreed statements and dogmatic definitions. Indeed, many would feel that the health of the Church depends upon there being as few formal statements of doctrine as possible, since their effect can be only to exclude some honest and adventurous inquirers from the Church, and to cause pains of conscience to loyal Christians who find they cannot assent to them. As Simone Weil tellingly observed, you cannot *command* someone to believe. The essential thing is rather that the Church should be seen to be remaining faithful to the authority of Scripture, as mediated to it by its historic tradition, and to express this faithfulness by a constant wrestling with the problems involved in discovering the force and relevance of the biblical story to the circumstances of Christian living today. It remains to elucidate in somewhat more detail the way in which Scripture continues to exercise this authority over the corporate believing of the Church.

We must first reiterate a point that was the subject of one of the chapters of *Christian Believing*,[4] namely, that Christianity is essentially a 'historic' faith. Whatever direct experience of God people may have, or claim to have, in our own day, this needs (for a Christian) to be integrated into the revelation of God in Christ which took place at a particular time in history and of which we can have knowledge only as we have knowledge of other events which belong to the past. It is true (as *Christian Believing* pointed out) that this 'pastness' of the definitive Christian story will strike different people in different ways. Some will welcome it as adding to the solidity and mystery of their religion, others will find it an obstacle in the way of a truly contemporary discipleship. But all will have to recognize that without these past events, and without the means by which we have knowledge of them, there could be neither Christianity nor Church.

Can Scripture be relied on?

If then we are (in this sense) bound to the past, we must ask how reliable are the records of that past which is so important to us. We cannot expect that the records by which these decisive events have been transmitted to us should have been immune from both the accidents and the distortions to which all historical documents are subject; indeed we have already commented on some of these. On the other hand, it is arguable that the sources of our knowledge about Jesus are as plentiful, and the chain by which we have received it is as secure, as in most other cases of historical knowledge of the ancient world. It is not on these grounds that doubts may arise about the reliability of our tradition. It is rather that (particularly since the rise of modern biblical criticism) we have become aware that our sources are not, and can hardly be expected to be, dispassionate and objective records of what took place. They contain not just facts, but an interpretation of those facts, and one of the main achievements of contemporary New Testament scholarship might be said to have been to identify the various interpretations which the first Christian writers laid upon the events they sought to describe.

This contemporary approach to the writings of the New Testament – particularly the gospels – has certainly had the effect of greatly reducing the amount of knowledge that we may confidently say that we possess about Jesus. Some reports of his sayings or activities are now widely believed to be due to the creative imagination of the evangelists or their sources; others describe miraculous events which the modern reader may find frankly incredible and may prefer to attribute to the alleged credulity of a distant age rather than to any

40

supernatural powers in the historical Jesus. But the fact that we believe these writings to be 'inspired' does not mean (as we have seen) that they ought to be immune from the circumstances and accidents which affect the transmission of all historical information about the remote past, and there are at least three reasons why we should continue to regard them as essentially reliable.

Historical documents preserving 'bare facts' – that is, facts without any interpretative comments or additions – scarcely exist. The fact that Scripture offers us a record of events already interpreted does not make it different from – or necessarily less reliable than – other historical writings.

In the second place, while we may admit that the differences between the gospels in their treatment of various aspects of the life and work of Jesus may sometimes be substantial, and may confront not only scholars but believers in general with serious difficulties, yet there is sufficient coherence and consistency in the broad outlines for it to be reasonable to believe that the different writings represent varying but not incompatible responses to the same basic sequence of events. If the differences between the gospels had been really substantial, we might have expected that different churches would have selected and made use of some to the exclusion of others. But, although there were some inevitable uncertainties in the early centuries when the canon was being formed, and although these uncertainties occasionally gave rise to heretical movements (such as those of the Marcionites and the Alogi), it remains true that the Church as a whole came to acknowledge the authority of all the main writings of the Old and New Testaments, evidently finding in them sufficient self-consistency to outweigh their acknowledged differences in theological and historical content.

Third, the greater part of Scripture stands closer to the events it records than any other writings available to us. However much these records may be found already to contain an interpretation of the original events, they do not thereby lose their primacy in the chain of tradition. It would be unreasonable to ask for the bare facts at a stage before any interpretation had been placed upon them. Such facts are barely recoverable even in theory, and even if they were they would have little significance as a basis for religious faith. We must of course be ready to identify these elements of inter-pretation, and to recognize that they place us at a certain

41

distance from the original facts; but no documents exist which will bring us closer, and to deny authority to the Bible for this reason would be to deny ourselves any reliable access to the facts whatever.

In short, by virtue of their privileged place in the long chain of transmission and interpretation by which the vital facts of the Christian past reach us today; in virtue of a basic consistency which holds together the diversity of the various interpretations; and in virtue, finally, of their sheer irreplaceability at the fountainhead of the Church's access to its own past, the biblical writings must necessarily continue to be authoritative so long as there continues to be a Church which professes to proclaim Christianity as a 'historic' religion.

Scripture and tradition

But the significance of these original facts, and of the interpretations to which they gave rise, has constantly to be grasped and expressed anew. In this enterprise, Christians learn from the experience of previous generations. In some cases, the interpretative contribution of one man or one period is so influential that it comes to determine the interpretation accepted by a whole church – as with Luther, Calvin, or perhaps the Caroline divines. Elsewhere, the weight of interpretative tradition may be more widely spread in time and geographical extent, but still have a strong consistency which defines a particular church – as in the case of Orthodoxy. But in all the historic churches a Christian is never bound only to the original history-with-interpretation offered by Scripture; he has also to acknowledge his debt to the subsequent tradition of interpretation inherited by the denomination in which he finds himself. In this sense he recognizes the 'authority' of tradition.

It could not be expected that any interpretation would be valid and meaningful indefinitely. Being a Christian involves searching for, finding and living out an interpretation which is appropriate to oneself and one's contemporaries. The way this is done in practice varies in different traditions. An evangelical group may feel that they are attending directly to the Bible in order to find appropriate ways of living out their faith, whereas a Christian of Catholic or Orthodox background will instinctively seek the guidance of authoritative expositors. But members of the first group will also recognize the need to act in concert with other church members, and will in fact have a certain 'tradition' of biblical interpretation (such as a particular series of commentaries); and equally, catholics will recognize that their appeal to the 'teaching of the Church' does not exempt them from the responsibility of personal attention to Scripture in order to work out their own response, and thereby ultimately to contribute to the tradition itself.

This activity of constantly working out an interpretation of, and response to, Scripture may not of course be undertaken by all members of a church: some, if not many, will be happy to follow the guidance of those who are engaged in it. But it remains an essential, if not a constitutive, activity of any church which claims the name of Christian. An example will make this clear. Suppose a group of Christians begins to read the poems of T. S. Eliot instead of passages of Scripture. They may claim that they find Eliot more edifying, and speaking more directly to their situation; and this could well be true. But if, as a result, they cease to attend to Scripture, and so cut themselves loose from the historical foundations of the faith, we shall be bound to ask whether they can be said still to be within the Church and still to be involved in the corporate believing of their fellow Christians. Again, if Christians accept a subsequent writing as more authoritative than, or equally authoritative with, Scripture (as in the case of Mormons or Christian Scientists) they cease to be members of the historic Church. Harder to define, though still empirically identifiable, is a degree of selectivity or bias in attention to Scripture such that faith and practice become significantly deviant (as with Jehovah's Witnesses or British Israelites). In all these cases the relationship of the believer and his church to Scripture, and the authority ascribed to it and to tradition, appear to offer a criterion by which we may pronounce whether he and his denomination are members of the Church. Conversely, it would seem that the 'corporate believing' of the Church, if it is to remain faithful to those origins in the past which, as we have seen, constitute its irreplaceable foundation, involves a constant reference to the ultimate source of authority which is the Bible. Nor need this 'attending' be thought of as an academic exercise or routine obligation. There have always been and still are countless Christians who would testify that God speaks to them through the Bible in a way that he does not through any other book. By attending to the Bible, the Church not only maintains its existence and definition, but receives constantly renewed life.

The answer, then, to our question why *this* story, rather than any other, should have such a controlling influence over our believing and acting as Christians is that it is only the recognition of this story as its ultimate point of reference (that is, as 'authoritative') which enables the Church to continue as an identifiable society. As an individual I am of course free to believe what I like. I may find greater 'inspiration' in other 'stories' or writings, I may express the truths which I find in them in ways quite different from those customary among other Christians. But in so far as I am a member of the Church, I associate myself with a 'corporate believing' which consists in a recognition of, and a constantly changing response to, 'the authority of Scripture'. There may be no point at which this ever-moving response to the historic givenness of Christianity can be caught, immobilized and presented as a still shot, a systematic statement of belief (though an important part of the response itself will consist of personal attempts by theologians to do precisely this). But this does not prevent any individual who consciously associates himself with the Church from recognizing that, by so doing, he is making his own personal understanding of the faith to a certain extent subservient to that collective activity of attention to, and interpretation of, Scripture which is an essential part of 'corporate believing'.

NOTES

1   pp. 32–42.
2   p. 41.
3   *Christian Believing*, pp. 55 ff.
4   'The Pastness of the Past', pp. 6–13.

Knowledge, Myth and Corporate Memory

The problem and the task

The problem

The modern western intellectual tradition is largely founded on our capacity to distinguish *knowledge* from mere belief or opinion. From Socrates and Plato onwards, it has become customary to regard knowledge as that which can be apprehended and tested by the individual for himself, while opinion or belief is thought of as that which the individual has merely 'taken over' from the community, or has learned from others at second hand.

Plato illustrated this principle by means of some everyday examples. If someone asks for, and receives from others, travel directions for the way to Larissa, we may say that he acquires *beliefs* (correct or incorrect) about the way to Larissa. But only the individual who has actually made the journey for himself may be said to have *knowledge* of the way to Larissa. Similarly, Plato urged, in understanding the principles of geometry or even the principles of moral conduct, what is learned passively from others, or taken over from the community, may be said to constitute correct or incorrect belief. But the individual who actively engages with the problems of geometry or moral conduct, and works out the issues for himself, may be said to have genuine knowledge of them.

The encouragement and growth of this kind of approach, with its emphasis on individual critical thought, has been the legacy not only of greek philosophy, but also of the Renaissance and more especially of the Enlightenment of the seventeenth and eighteenth centuries. Critical thought begins when the individual no longer takes for granted as true what he has merely taken over from parents, teachers or the general assumptions of the community into which he is born. To doubt the opinions of others and to question the traditions of society is the starting-point on the road to knowledge.

So deeply, however, is this outlook embedded in the

foundations of our thought that we may fail to notice a problem to which it all too readily gives rise. The respective parts played by the individual and by the community in the growth and criticism of knowledge tend to become opposed to each other and polarized. Worse, the part played by the community comes increasingly under suspicion and relegated to a secondary category, while the role of the individual is accorded a privileged position and comes to occupy the centre of the stage. From this angle, the very idea of 'corporate knowledge', or a knowledge grasped, transmitted and tested by the community, seems to be almost self-contradictory. Communities are thought to hand down opinions, beliefs, myths or codes of conduct, but only the individual, it seems, can grasp and test knowledge.

The problem receives sharp focus in the history of philosophy both in the rationalism of Descartes and in the empiricism of Hume. The well-known dictum of Descartes, 'I think, therefore I am', expresses the principle that true knowledge begins only when the isolated ego shuts itself off from all other resources of knowledge except its own thoughts, and subjects everything else to doubt. It was not without reason that Archbishop William Temple described the moment when Descartes shut himself away with his own thoughts as perhaps 'the most disastrous moment in the history of Europe'.[1] The empiricist tradition, however, is no less individualistic in its approach to the problem of knowledge. Receiving knowledge is still a matter of the individual's receiving ideas or impressions from the outside world, as if his mind were a sheet of blank paper. Indeed, so firmly is this approach rooted in individualism that Hume saw grounds for scepticism about evidence for the very existence of the external world. Berkeley was saved from the doctrine that all I can know is my own states of mind only by invoking, theologically, the idea of God as guarantor of some further reality.

It is this dominant tradition in the history of western thought that poses the 'problem' to which we refer in this essay. For this account of the nature of knowledge has far-reaching implications for our attitude towards parallel issues in Christian faith and practice. Once again, the shape of the problem emerges all too clearly in the attitude of the thinkers of the Enlightenment. In the legitimate and proper quest for critical thought and tested knowledge, the value of religious tradition, or the 'deposit' of faith handed down by the community, tended to be underrated. Individual critical reflection took the centre of the stage at the expense of the wisdom cumulatively gathered over the centuries by successive generations in interpersonal experience. Little or no attention was given to the public or intersubjective world which pre-existed individual reflection, and was of special significance for Christian faith and practice.

The task

The thinkers of the Enlightenment saw only one side of the picture, and it is still the side which receives most attention today. We are not making some kind of special appeal to theology or religion when we assert that the individual does not in fact begin his quest for knowledge *de novo,* as if he were an isolated individual abstracted from history and society. A shared public world pre-exists both him and his own thinking. This public world shapes his thought in such a way that it not only provides and transmits shared resources of knowledge, but also shapes the terms on which he examines and tests that knowledge. It conditions what he regards as appropriate criteria for evaluating it. If an individual were cut off from birth from the shared resources of language and knowledge of human society, he could scarcely achieve much beyond a semi-instinctual quasi-animal awareness of a tiny world of private individual experience. In particular, without the resources of language he would lack the conceptual tools necessary for critical evaluation and even access to the resources of a community's corporate memory.

The task of this essay is first to redress the imbalance which leads all too often to a devaluing of the corporate foundations of knowledge, and then to apply what we have said about corporate knowledge to questions about Christian believing. Our argument, in practice, is set out in three overall stages. In the first half of the chapter we introduce some of the more theoretical and philosophical considerations which lead us towards an appreciation of the corporate foundations of human knowledge. Every effort is made to avoid unduly technical discussion, but it would weaken our argument if we failed to allude to the work of one or two important thinkers in the history of ideas, including those who have worked in the area of the sociology of knowledge. One of our aims is not only to elucidate the part played by public or interpersonal knowledge, but also to show that appeals to the knowledge transmitted through tradition on the basis of the corporate memory of the Christian community in no way rests on a kind of special pleading for religion which would have no place in a more general account of human knowledge.

In the second main stage of the argument we then apply these arguments and concepts to issues of Christian belief and practice. Philosophical and sociological concepts of knowledge, training, custom and habituation come to a fresh focus in Christian theology when we reassess the significance of tradition, authority, orthodoxy, creeds, the reading of the Bible and the use of the sacraments. Some aspects of the discussion look back to what Anthony Harvey has said about the need to understand the authority of the Bible in terms of its function or role rather than in terms of some quality which it is said to possess. But our arguments in this section find their closest affinity and parallel in the claims made by John Bowker in his chapter on Religions as Systems about what he calls 'mechanisms of transmission and control'. Creeds, sacraments, the use of the Bible, and other 'mechanisms', ensure the preservation and transmission of corporate memory, with the result that the community (cf. Bowker's 'system') remains *this* community, with its ongoing resources of corporate knowledge and identity. The importance of continuity of 'identity' for corporate believing has already been touched on briefly by Basil Mitchell in the first chapter.

In the third main stage of discussion we look more closely at the actual interrelation of roles performed by the community and by the individual in the growth and criticism of knowledge within the context of Christian faith. First we ask whether any light is shed on this part of the discussion by invoking the term 'myth'. Myths embody stories which have (or at least had in the past) the status of believed truth within a given community. Yet they lend themselves to reinterpretation by the individual in accordance with revised and more critical knowledge. Does the idea of myth, then, serve to carry the discussion forward constructively? Or might we perhaps find a more fruitful and less distracting model elsewhere?

Our major purpose in this final section, however, is to expand the following argument: to understand most clearly the corporate or interpersonal dimension of Christian belief, and to see why it *necessarily* rests on corporate knowledge, we must appreciate that the grammar of faith involves not only an inner or 'vertical' dimension of response to God, but also a social or 'horizontal' dimension of public behaviour. The Christian lives out his faith, or shows what it amounts to, in a public interpersonal world. He cannot, as it were, 'believe privately', in the sense that faith towards God necessarily involves attitudes towards other people.

These practical or 'self-involving' aspects of faith have been noted by Basil Mitchell, and are later developed in more detail by John McManners. He urges that love for the brethren demands a measure of freedom and tolerance for the individual. And so it does. But the complementary point is also true: love for the brethren places a constraint on the individual to heed the corporate memory and testimony of the community, and invites some degree of modesty in his assessment of the scope and basis of his own private judgement. The repression of individual conscience ignores one side of the dialectic; the notion of Christian belief as a merely 'individual' or 'private' affair ignores the other. Any theology that simply *opposes* the individual and the community, as if to invite us to choose one or the other, is inadequate. Our task is to try to elucidate the positive roles of both sides of the dialectic, but more especially to call attention to the corporate foundations of knowledge and to the necessary role played by corporate memory in making faith possible for the individual. Some readers may wish to omit the three most technical philosophical sections (pp. 54–9). A few may even prefer to hurry on at this point to the main theological argument (pp. 60–76).

The corporate foundations of knowledge

'Common sense' and human language

Knowing, believing and especially understanding depends on some kind of sharing and on some kind of experience of continuity. We have already noted that the traditional 'theories of knowledge' in rationalism and empiricism failed to take adequate account of this. The individual who from birth was totally isolated from society would not be the 'knowing subject' of Kantian philosophy. The recognition of this very important fact may be said to represent the fundamental starting-point of a movement in the history of ideas which has come to be known as the sociology of knowledge. Thus, from this viewpoint, one writer observes: 'There is no such thing as an isolated man . . . Kant was operating with a construct rather than a reality . . . What he [man in the concrete world] becomes conscious of must, or at any rate may, depend on the shape which his mind has acquired in the process of social living'.[2]

We are not obliged, however, to appeal to the sociology of knowledge for this basic insight. Behind his or her appeal to 'common sense' lies the ordinary person's tacit and perhaps barely conscious recognition of the importance of the experience and judgements of the community in the growth and transmission of knowledge. 'Common sense' represents what 'everyone' already knows. It draws on the community's cumulative wisdom and shared experience. As *sensus communis*, it stands in contrast to some merely individual or idiosyncratic interpretation of the world, offering the corporate judgement of the wider community in the course of whose experience something has become accepted as self-evident. On the basis of what is common sense, an individual does not have to begin reflecting on a problem *de novo*.

From this point of view, it is no accident that Vico, as an opponent of Descartes and the whole Cartesian method, appeals to the *sensus communis* as something always present in the tradition of the humanities going back to the classical concept of practical wisdom. Wisdom represents the accumulated body of experience and skills which the community (or a special sub-community) may bring to bear on a question. As such it is usually practical rather than purely theoretical. Vico contrasts this 'wisdom' with the mere 'reason' of the Stoics, urging that the sense of what is right and true is acquired not simply by theoretical reflection, but by *living out one's life within the community*; what is fundamental in the historical context of its ongoing life and experience.

Over the last fifty or so years, several writers have shown that the positive role of 'common sense' (in the broadest meaning of the term) as an aspect of knowledge was never really lost sight of in the history of ideas. It was merely temporarily swamped out by Enlightenment rationalism, with its obsessive suspicion of tradition. This is most noteworthy in the tradition of German philosophy which approaches problems of knowledge under the heading of 'understanding' or 'hermeneutics', and in sociological work which stresses the importance of typification and social interaction as points of departure for exploring questions about relevance and meaning.[3] Even in accordance with the narrower meaning of the term 'common sense' as 'knowledge of everyday life', from a sociological viewpoint, communities encourage common-sense knowledge. The younger generations are often reminded of 'common sense' by their elders, even though amidst the conditions of rapid change prevalent in modern industrial societies, each generation also works out its own corporate common-sense knowledge in the light of its own corporate experience.[4]

The corporate foundations of knowledge are exposed more clearly when we consider, next, the relation between knowledge and language. Because of the heritage of oral or written language, a human being is never dependent merely on his own experience for information or knowledge. If he were left entirely to the limitations of his own individual experience, he would be relatively helpless and ignorant, even in a very primitive society. Language makes it possible to pool, to store and to transmit the common stock of knowledge shared by the community not only geographically but, more important, from generation to generation. False trails may be set aside and the repetition of errors avoided. The method of trying to begin *de novo,* either for the growth or the criticism of knowledge, may seem attractive as a theory amidst the security of one's own bookshelves or library; but it strikes out the life-line through which the individual gains access to the intellectual resources and cumulative experience of past generations, and which is stored in language. Seen in these terms, the belittlement of tradition as an object of suspicion and doubt, seems to stem not from 'criticism' but from arrogance.

Once this basic point about language has been accepted, we are free to consider more complex issues which arise on the basis of the relation between language and thought. It is unfortunate that this relation has sometimes been formulated in mistaken ways which claim too much, or from another viewpoint, too little. Sometimes a crude account is suggested according to which language is said to determine the scope and limits of thought on the basis of vocabulary-stock or even surface-grammar. Such a view has been shown to rest on a mistaken view of language, including the mistaken assumption of a one-to-one correlation between words and concepts. However, even if the influence of language on thought (and thought on language) does not operate significantly at the level of mere linguistic morphology, language-habits become important at the level of language-*use*, or the 'grammar' of concepts. I have explored these issues in some detail elsewhere, concluding that language 'hands on an inherited tradition which then makes it easier or more difficult for a later generation to raise certain questions, or to notice certain aspects of life'.[5] Language shapes the frame of reference through which knowledge is *grasped*, and within which it is *criticized*. It does not exclude certain questions or concepts as impossible, but it does encourage certain ways of seeing the world, and of deciding what counts as a test or as a solution in the examination of the problems which have been posed. In the kind of terminology used in the sociology of knowledge, language is the storehouse of the day-to-day typifications of experience which we share with others, and on the basis of which the growth and criticism of knowledge proceeds. 'Language', it may be added, may also be understood (in the context of the present discussion) to include a very wide range of potentially symbolic material, such as non-verbal artifacts which may nevertheless 'speak' in such a way as to transmit attitudes, values and knowledge, from the past.

The transmission of corporate memory

Our considerations about language suggest that the corporate foundations of knowledge may be viewed not only in terms of a society spreading outwards from the individual in space, but also spreading backwards and forwards in time. From this angle, the individual biography of a single thinking individual represents only a single passing episode in the cumulative development and testing of human knowledge. Although we should be on our guard against the kind of relativism which comes from views of historical or sociological necessity sometimes implied by certain thinkers in the sociology of knowledge, there is much truth in Karl Mannheim's dictum that all human thought represents a 'thinking further' of what others have thought before us. Even the way that people raise questions and the terms in which they examine and *test* knowledge, builds on the thought and experience of others. Corporate memory is preserved and transmitted in the form of what we could happily call 'tradition', were it not for the widespread disparagement of the word 'tradition' and the failure to appreciate its positive role. Tradition transcends the scope of immediate individual knowledge and experience, and provides the framework within which one's own thought develops and becomes critically sharpened.

If the corporate memory of a community constitutes an important source of its knowledge, and if the biography of the individual thinker represents no more than an episode in its transmission and critical control, it follows that the community which wishes to preserve its knowledge, experience and cultural identity will employ *instruments for the transmission and institutionalization* of its corporate knowledge. What is recollected in corporate memory will be transmitted in proverb, story, sermon, myth or, equally, in (for the scientific sub-community) the pages of a modern technical journal. What is believed to be of value for the community, or on which its cultural identity is thought to depend, will be *reiterated in formulae* such as laws, ethical maxims, creeds, rites, songs and so on. In the context of religious or specifically Christian belief, the *reiteration of shared knowledge* on the basis of corporate memory finds expression in creeds, sacraments, sermons and the reading of narratives of the foundation-events out of which the community was born. That this is something which is *essential* to, but not *distinctive* to, the Christian community is confirmed in a later chapter by John Bowker's discussion of mechanisms employed for the maintenance of 'systems' in such a way as to preserve their continuity and identity.

We shall examine these last claims further in the next section when we consider the significance of all this for questions about Christian belief. Meanwhile, however, we note that corporate memory represents much more (for almost any community, including that of scientists) than a mere access-point to knowledge of the past. As John Ziman forcefully argues in his book on the corporate foundations of knowledge in science, even the scientist does not simply consult his journals and books for knowledge of the past. In science (and we may note in passing, in matters of Christian faith) corporate memory provides a frame of reference in the light of which the scientist (and the Christian) assesses or interprets knowledge and determines procedure in the *present*. [6]

To see the force of these points, it is not necessary to appeal to those who are acknowledged authorities in the academic world. However, it would be a mistake to imagine that these arguments could not be underpinned, if necessary, with reference to recent and more rigorous argument on the part of those who have undertaken lengthy and thorough research into the issues involved. A host of writers have shown in some detail how, from a sociological point of view, the corporate memory of the community hands down ways of seeing the world, ways of asking questions, and ways of classifying people, places, things and events, which determine, or at least condition, the terms on which knowledge grows and undergoes criticism by a present generation and its individual thinkers.[7] This does not of course mean that this frame of reference may not itself undergo conscious criticism and a measure of revision. If this were not possible, we should be imprisoned in historical relativism, and the very notion of human rationality would be evaporated of content in the inevitability of being determined solely by contingency. It does mean, however, that, as we have already claimed, the growth and criticism of knowledge takes place as part of a process of *dialectic* between corporate and individual knowledge.

Inherited knowledge as the indispensable context for individual understanding: a philosophical example

Those who may still have reservations about the present arguments may find themselves wondering how much depends on considerations now fashionable in the sociology of knowledge rather than arguments which are grounded more broadly in philosophy. After all, there are schools of thought in sociology which seem to lay such heavy emphasis on the role of class-interest, educational expectation, and so on, in determining our view of what counts as 'reality or objectivity' that some may hesitate to accept an account of human knowledge which seems to owe much to the insights of sociology.

Such misgivings would be understandable, but they are misplaced. For in relatively recent years a recovery of the realization of the importance of corporate knowledge has emerged in certain areas of philosophy, as well as in the sociology of knowledge. We select for attention the contribution to the debate by two very different philosophers, namely, Gadamer and Wittgenstein.

The tradition of philosophy which is represented by Gadamer approaches questions about 'reality' or Being from the standpoint of the problem of *understanding*. For this reason, this tradition of philosophy is sometimes given the name 'hermeneutical philosophy', or (in Gadamer's phrase) 'philosophical hermeneutics'. Understanding, it is argued, can *never* be the product of the individual's autobiographical reflection alone. Inherited knowledge constitutes the framework or context into which, so to speak, the individual slots his own perceptions and experiences in such a way that they acquire *significance* or meaning, to be understood *as* what they *are*. Gadamer calls this inherited knowledge and the way in which it operates 'effective history', or (in a specialized and entirely positive sense of the term) 'tradition'.

This ongoing process of effective history is *prior* to actual self-conscious critical reflection on the part of the individual because it is mediated through family, society, the national culture and so on, constituting the basis on which individual awareness and critical judgement become *possible*. It provides the background against which it makes sense for the individual even to think about what is in his mind. Hence Gadamer observes, 'The self-awareness of the individual is only a flickering in the closed circuits of historical life . . . The prejudgements of the individual, far more than his judgements, constitute the historical reality of his being'.[8]

Gadamer rejects the antithesis between *authority* and reason, or between corporately based knowledge and individual reflection, which he associates with Enlightenment rationalism. Rationalism and individualism, he urges, give rise to 'a mutually exclusive antithesis between authority and reason'. However, in actual practice the notion of authority gives recognition to the fact that knowledge is grounded in the experience of others in the community: 'It rests on recognition and hence on an act of reason itself which, *aware of its own limitations, accepts that others have better understanding*. . . There is no such unconditional antithesis between tradition and reason.'[9]

All education, in fact, depends on this principle. Schools give the pupil access to resources of knowledge which are wider than those of individual experience or even that of the family. Through transmission of specialist knowledge which has been acquired even beyond the local or national community, universities draw still more widely on resources of corporate knowledge. The use of these corporate resources and of the cumulative understanding of successive generations in no way contradicts the use of individual 'reason' or the student's thinking for himself. The student who attempted to ignore the lessons embodied in the understanding and tradition of the academic community would be regarded, with either pity or contempt, as falling victim to his private intellectual arrogance. He could hardly plead that he had to choose *between* 'reason' and 'tradition'. Indeed, only on the basis of exercising his rational judgement *within* the context of effective history could he claim to achieve a proper *understanding* of the subject-matter before him. I have discussed Gadamer's approach to these issues more fully elsewhere.[10]

The contribution of Ludwig Wittgenstein

It may be hoped that each stage of the present discussion will spell out more clearly the nature and importance of the corporate foundations of knowledge and the inadequacy of any account of knowledge which is centred only on the individual. However, the English-speaking reader who hesitates to place any confidence on the sociology of knowledge may be only marginally reassured by the work of Gadamer. In the later writings of the philosopher Ludwig Wittgenstein we encounter a thinker whose stature and influence is beyond question, and whom no one could ever accuse of yielding to mere fashion or intellectual gamesmanship. Wittgenstein's earlier writings show beyond all doubt his total commitment to wrestling with the problems of logic, and indeed much of his earlier work concerned the nature of logical necessity.

Yet Wittgenstein himself saw that abstract reflection in isolation from the context of human life related only to part of the whole picture. In his later writings he consistently called attention to the corporate or social foundations of language, and its grounding in the institutions or practices of human life. In his last notes, entitled *On Certainty*, he turned his attention to the corporate foundations of knowledge. Because (it is generally agreed) Wittgenstein cannot easily be summarized without reduction and loss of what he wished to say, we shall include one or two direct quotations in our brief account of his work in these last notes.

Wittgenstein argues that propositions which appear to represent truths of 'common sense' (cf. our discussion on pages 49-51) do so because they presuppose a certain inherited frame of reference. This frame of reference constitutes a 'foundation' on the basis of which normal day-to-day research and action can take place. This foundation of inherited thought belongs to, or has emerged from what was once, 'the *scaffolding* of our thoughts', for, Wittgenstein adds, 'Every human being has parents.'[11] He writes: 'The *truth* of certain empirical propositions belongs to our frame of reference . . . All testing, all confirmation and disconfirmation of a hypothesis takes place already within a system.' What actually '*counts* as its [a proposition's] test' depends on the system to which it belongs.[12] Contrary to the individualism of the rationalist tradition, Wittgenstein observes: 'The child learns by believing the adult. Doubt comes *after* belief"; and even then, 'my doubts form a system . . . From a child up, I learned to judge like this.' 'If you tried to doubt everything, you would not get as far as doubting anything. The game of doubting itself presupposes certainty.'[13]

It would be a mistake to regard Wittgenstein's approach in *On Certainty* as somehow radically different from his observations on language in the main writings of the later period. These last notes represent a logical development of the central place occupied in the *Philosophical Investigations* by 'training', 'custom', 'rules' and especially 'forms of life'. What gives point to Wittgenstein's masterly explorations of concepts, or 'logical grammar', is precisely his recognition of the crucial importance of what he calls 'the surroundings' of words and language in the ongoing stream of life. But 'life', or 'practice', is grounded in the shared conduct and attitudes of the language-using communities. Only in the ongoing stream of life and thought do words have meaning. Wittgenstein's whole discussion of 'private' language forms the background to his claims about corporate knowledge. An individual trying to manipulate concepts in total isolation from how others have used them is like someone saying: '"But I know how tall I am!" and laying his hand on top of his head to prove it.'[14] It is 'as if someone were to buy several copies of the morning paper to assure himself that what it said was true'.[15] Even checking and testing is a more-than-individual affair. 'Only in the stream of thought and life do words have meaning.'[16]

Examples from the history of science
Because of the pressures of space, we must limit this part of the discussion to only one more type of example of work on the corporate foundations of knowledge, even though many different writers and approaches might have been mentioned. One of the best known, although he is also widely criticized, is Thomas A. Kuhn. Although, as far as I know, he does not seem to make more than a relatively minor acknowledgement

to Wittgenstein, Kuhn is remarkably close to some of the themes which we have noted in *On Certainty*, except that Kuhn's special interest is in the foundations of knowledge in science. Like Wittgenstein and Gadamer, Kuhn urges that the advancement and criticism of knowledge takes place within the context of the growing framework of experience and knowledge handed down by the community. This frame of reference takes the form of a system, 'paradigm', or a way of seeing the world, which conditions the terms in which certain questions are posed, or problems solved. Indeed Kuhn argues that the paradigm influences what problems are put on the agenda, and what may be said to count as their solution.

Kuhn defines paradigms as 'models from which spring coherent traditions of scientific research'. He comments: 'Men whose research is based on shared paradigms are committed to the same rules and standards for scientific practice.'[17] Each generation of scientists operates with a kind of 'network of theory through which it deals with the world'.[18] This network is the legacy of the scientific community. From time to time in the history of science, paradigms are found to be inadequate, and at such moments a 'revolution' occurs in the models and methods adopted by the scientific community. However, this in turn gives rise to a new era of 'normal' procedure, during which current paradigms are once again taken for granted as a basis for research and inquiry.

Scientists, Kuhn urges, view the world 'through their own research training and practice', and use 'conceptual categories prepared by prior experience' on the part of the scientific community.[19] Thus, 'What a man sees depends both upon what he looks at and also upon what his previous visual-conceptual experience has taught him to see.'[20] What he has been 'taught' to see owes as much, if not more, to the community or even 'tradition', as to his own individual inquiries. For these individual inquiries have normally been carried out within a framework received from the community.

A number of writers have put forward criticisms of Kuhn's arguments, and those which are most widely known come from Karl Popper. Popper gives special emphasis to two points. First, he insists that there has never been any *one* particular paradigm which has dominated scientific inquiry in such a way as to set its entire agenda. Second, even if scientists do accept and use some corporate framework of knowledge, such a framework certainly does not *dictate* what knowledge is possible. He concludes: 'A critical discussion and a comparison of the various frameworks is always possible.'[21]

If we had argued in this essay that the growth and criticism of knowledge was wholly and entirely a corporate process, Popper's comments would cause pause for thought. However, as they stand, his criticisms serve only to underline what we have already said about the dialectic between the corporate and individual aspects. Indeed, the debate which has followed the statement of Kuhn's claims serves to show that even when a new paradigm in the history of science seems to suggest a divergent conclusion about 'what is the case', individual exponents of the new paradigm nevertheless may be seen often to *rely* on what was taken to be 'the case' under the old paradigm, or at least in the work of predecessors. Kepler continued to rely on the astronomical observations of Tycho Brahe; Einstein made use of observations undertaken by Leverrier in accordance with a mechanistic pre-Einsteinian paradigm. In the transition from Newton to Einstein it is simply not the case that all work carried out within the framework of the earlier paradigm was dismissed as 'wrong'.

The lesson to be learned from all this is that Kuhn's approach cannot be understood in a simplistic way, and that to accept its implications for our argument about corporate knowledge reinforces the claim that neither side of the dialectic can be ignored. The inescapable conclusion which emerges from the whole discussion up to this point is that arguments about corporate knowledge require no special pleading on behalf of religion or the Christian community. The same fundamental considerations appear whether we look at the history of science, at Wittgenstein, at 'hermeneutical' philosophy, or at basic facts about language and even the role of common sense. It is also clear that corporate knowledge in no way stands in contrast to critical thought, but, rather, constitutes a precondition for it. We may now turn, in the second half of our essay, to examine the bearing of all this discussion on questions about corporate believing, with special reference to criteria for 'authentic' Christian faith and the theological problem of tradition and 'orthodoxy'.

The transmission of
corporate knowledge and corporate memory in the community of Christian faith

The roles of the individual and the community
in the quest for authentic faith

Just as both sides of our dialectic are fundamental for the growth and criticism of knowledge in general, so also in questions about Christian faith neither the role of the community nor that of the individual should be under-estimated. There is what we may term (for want of a better shorthand word) a 'vertical' dimension to faith, in the light of which faith can never be reduced to a mere acceptance of 'orthodoxy', or of the tradition passed on by the community.

In his letter to the Galatians, for example, Paul insists that there is nothing second-hand about his call or his gospel: 'For I did not receive it from man . . . it came through a revelation of Jesus Christ' (Gal. 1.12). Nearer to our own times, the prophetic protest against any merely second-hand faith has been voiced with special force by Søren Kierkegaard. Kierkegaard writes: 'The most ruinous evasion of all is to be hidden in the crowd . . . to get away from hearing God's voice as an individual.'[22] Christianity, he comments in his *Attack upon 'Christendom'*, 'has been abolished by expansion, by these millions of name-Christians the number of which is surely meant to conceal the fact that there is not one Christian'.[23] The very notion of a 'Christian state' or of a 'Christian world', he continues, is 'shrewdly calculated to make God so confused in His head by all these millions that He cannot discover that He has been hoaxed; that there is not one single Christian'.[24]

Becoming a Christian, Kierkegaard urged, is not merely a matter of taking over the orthodox Christian beliefs of the day. It involves inner transformation and personal commitment. Hence: 'It would help very little if one persuaded millions of men to accept the truth, if precisely by this acceptance they were transferred into error . . . Truth becomes untruth in this or that person's mouth.'[25] A faith that merely takes up the routines prescribed by a tradition is for Kierkegaard (and for Paul and for Jesus) not 'true' faith. Nevertheless, it would be a mistake to assume that this contradicts the notion of a *corporate framework* of knowledge *within* which the individual may reach authentic faith. Jesus, Paul, Luther and Kierkegaard were all conscious of the limitations and seductions of tradition; but all lay down their calls to faith within a framework of knowledge and experience which transcended individual autobiography. When they spoke of God, Jesus and Paul spoke of the God of Abraham, of Isaac, and of Jacob. When Luther spoke of God, this was the God of Israel, the God of Jesus, and even, for Luther, the God of the Church Fathers. When Kierkegaard insisted that the 'jovial mediocrity' of Danish-state Christianity did not represent authentic, obedient faith, his standard of comparison was not simply his own experience or reflection; his complaint was that 'being a Christian becomes something different from what it is in the New Testament'. 'Official Christianity . . . is in no sense the Christianity of the New Testament.'[26]

The example of Paul is parallel in this respect to that of Kierkegaard. Paul does not abstract his first-hand knowledge of the risen Christ from the frame of reference of what was believed about Jesus Christ in the primitive Church, or from beliefs about God embodied in the Old Testament. These elements contribute to the overall framework within which he was able to reflect on, interpret and understand his encounter with Jesus Christ. Indeed, the examples of Paul and Kierkegaard help us to see more clearly the interplay of each side of the dialectic. For both are concerned about the authenticity of Christian faith; that it should be, in this sense, a critical faith. But what is at issue in any prophetic summons to authenticity is a relation to the referent of faith in which both the *identity of the referent* and the *basis of the relationship* is not merely a product of the individual's own religious aspirations. We have already seen, however, from our examination of corporate knowledge in the previous section that *questions about identity and continuity can be answered only within the larger framework of shared experience and public knowledge. Conceptual or linguistic reference, we saw, depends on a pre-existing framework of conceptual or linguistic regularity,* which may be described in terms of *rule, custom, training or a succession of interrelated forms of life flowing on through history.*

Once again, it is a matter of holding together the two poles of a dialectic, rather than opposing the parts played by the individual and the community. Sometimes the life and thought of the community drifts into implausibility and even, at times, into glaring self-contradiction. At such times the prophetic summons of a Luther or a Kierkegaard is vital to the rediscovery of the community's true identity and of the authenticity of Christian faith. There is force and truth in the well-known dictum of Calvinist theology that the Church that has been reformed always stands in the need of reformation: *ecclesia reformata semper reformanda.* Sometimes it is the prophetic insight of an individual thinker and man of faith that spearheads the necessary corrective. The classic example is Luther's ringing declaration at the Diet of Worms: 'Here I stand. I can do no other.' Nevertheless, Luther saw that challenge not as a summons to innovative departure from the corporate memory and knowledge of the community, but as a call to return to it and to heed its testimony more seriously. He could boldly assert the importance of reason and the integrity of conscience not because he saw himself in the way that Descartes conceived of the isolated 'I' of individual reflection, but because, in his own words, his conscience was 'captive to the word of God'; because it gave expression to a more authentic focus, as he saw it, of the corporate knowledge of the community. Contrary to widespread popular misunder-standing, Luther not only appealed to the faith and testimony of the biblical writers, but also quite consciously invoked the corporate witness of the Church Fathers. Augustine, Ambrose, Cyprian and Chrysostom all feature in his thought. In this sense, Luther's great affirmation of 'Here I stand' is entirely compatible with the equally famous patristic dictum that 'there is no salvation outside the Church'. Certainly any 'theory of knowledge' which Luther's faith might be said to presuppose would have more in common with Irenaeus and Augustine than with the kind of individualism represented by Enlightenment rationalism or by Descartes.

The conclusion which we draw from these allusions to Luther and Kierkegaard is that the kind of 'individualism' which is usually ascribed to them (and to many other examples of prophetic or reforming figures) is not the kind of individualism which it is often imagined to be, at least from the standpoint of questions about corporate knowledge. The appearance of an *opposition* or *polarization* of individual and corporate knowledge is merely an *appearance* which necessarily dictated by the historical situations which lay behind their criticisms or protest. They did not see themselves as innovators, not least because their understanding, testing and criticism of 'tradition' depended, in turn, on appeals to the corporate memory of the community, and presupposed the continuity of its 'effective history'. What is true from a philosophical point of view applies also in Christian theology: 'I must not saw off the branch on which I am sitting.'[27] The point requires no special theological pleading. Individual criticism rests on corporate foundations of knowledge.

The transmission of corporate memory in inherited patterns of belief and practice

Over the centuries the Christian community has had its own ways of maintaining and preserving the stable background against which the faith could spread, and also could undergo critical examination and testing. *Creeds, liturgy, pastoral oversight* and perhaps most notably *the use of the Bible and of the sacraments* represent such instruments. They effectively anchor the community's present both in the founding events of its past and within the overall framework of its ongoing life in a way which transcends individual experience and provides a control against undue novelty or individual innovation.

It is significant, therefore, that our earliest accounts of the Eucharist and of baptism place these observances within a tradition which even by the time of Paul is already described explicitly as a 'tradition' (*paradosis*).[28] Paul recalls: 'For I received . . . what I also delivered to you' (1 Cor. 11.23). Participation in the Lord's Supper is seen as a 'proclamation' of the founding events of the death and resurrection of Christ which give the community its life, its existence and its identity (11.26). It constitutes a 'remembrance' (*anamnesis*) in which the present community, through its corporate memory, both reflects on the founding events and pledges itself anew to their present significance and practical effectiveness. All this is far more, but certainly not less, than what sociologists describe as the *legitimating formulae* whereby the shape of a society's institutional order and values are passed on from generation to generation. Baptism, in the same way, from the earliest pre-Pauline theology, grounds the experience of the individual believer in the once-for-all saving events which found the community: 'Do you not know that all of us who have been baptized into Christ Jesus were baptized into his death? . . . The death he died he died to sin, once for all' (Rom. 6.3 and 10; cf. 4-11).

Every Christian who rightly and duly participates in the sacraments sees himself as, in a sense, 'there' at the founding events of the community ('You proclaim the Lord's death';

'Do this in "remembrance" of me'). At this level individual biography is transcended, and corporate memory *makes possible* a common biography. The creeds, sacraments, Bible readings and liturgy all amount to a *reiteration of shared experience*. Whether this should be described as a mythological way of grasping reality will be discussed shortly. Our primary concern at this point is to assert the significance of all this for continuity and identity, and hence for knowledge. Corporate memory provides access to an understanding and knowledge of realities which transcend individual experience.

These considerations shed a new light on the concern for *orthodoxy* which has been a persistent feature of much Christian thought from the era of the New Testament onwards. As long as this concern is seen merely as an attempt to impose on a minority the view of some controlling party or dominant interest, a concern for orthodoxy necessarily appears in a negative and restrictive light. Thus it is often said, for example, that the Pastoral Epistles and other 'secondary' literature of the New Testament reflect a self-preserving defensive posture which is at odds with the self-denying faith and creative fervour of the great Pauline writings or the teaching of Jesus. But even the earlier writings speak of the need to hold fast to a tradition, and it is clear that the concern expressed in these writings is not a matter of mere authoritarianism or a defensive judgementalism. What is at stake is whether the Christian way is turned into 'another gospel' (Gal. 1.8). The concern which is expressed appears quite other than negative and restrictive when it is seen that what is at issue is the maintenance of that degree of continuity which is necessary for Christian *identity* and more especially for participation in the *patterns of behaviour which have been instituted and prescribed* by those events on which the community itself has been founded.

At this point it would have been helpful to draw on what has been said about 'roles' in sociology and in the sociology of knowledge. The difficulty is that in everyday speech the word 'role' tends to have a negative meaning as that which is somehow artificial or insincere. Existentialist philosophers have rightly criticized and attacked the whole notion of an individual having to assume 'roles' imposed by the social conventions and expectations of society. Such expectations put pressures on the individual to live in a way which is second-hand, superficial or 'inauthentic' for him. This mood of suspicion has (also rightly) found its way into the area of

Christian faith, where (following Kierkegaard whose approach we have just discussed) many are on their guard against the danger of reducing authentic Christian faith to the mere 'taking over' of second-hand attitudes and routines. To assume the *role* of one who merely 'goes to church' is not necessarily the same thing as having authentic Christian faith.

Nevertheless, when all this has been said and accepted, it remains the case that Christian believing involves taking up certain *patterns* of attitudes and behaviour, which can be said to be recognizably 'Christian' precisely because they are patterns. They can be identified because they embody an element of regularity and repetition. Certain attitudes and behaviour may rightly be 'expected' of the Christian if he is genuinely a Christian. In this *sociological* sense, Christian belief does entail adopting a 'role', although some may still prefer to think of them simply as 'patterns of response'.

The central point which now emerges is that, in accordance with sociological inquiry, roles presuppose a process of repetition or habituation, and usually also carry with them some explicit or implicit status. This status, in turn, often (although not always) depends on some authoritative act or event such as that of appointing, employing, directing, allowing and so on. A person assumes the role of waiter, managing director, husband or secretary, because he or she has been given, and has accepted, that 'understood' status and role. Usually a given status carries with it certain rights and privileges on one side, and certain obligations on the other. A secretary is obliged to type letters, but has the right to a salary, and so on. 'Belonging' to the firm with its pensions, its holidays and its rules also provides rights and obligations.

Christian believing also is founded on an event or events which make possible the offer and acceptance of a given status and the ascription of appropriate roles. Because of God's saving acts in Christ, the status of 'son', or 'one of the redeemed' (and so on) may now be offered and accepted, and the role of worshipper, obedient servant (and so on) 'taken over' or appropriated. For all this to be meaningful, however, there *must* be a relatively stable background of repetition, habituation or 'expected' belief and conduct. Language which identifies appropriate roles (forgiven sinner, obedient son) now functions as a firm semantic marker for identifying what we mean when we talk about being a Christian or having

Christian faith. From a sociological viewpoint these are 'institutional' responses.

The early Church gave expression to its sense of the need to preserve such a framework by the place which it accorded to creeds, catechism and what was then (in an entirely positive way) called 'tradition'. The early Christian confession of Christ as Lord brought into focus the Christian's expected pattern of behaviour as servant and worshipper. The creeds, confessions and 'traditions' thus mediated to later generations the corporate knowledge and memory on which the authenticity of faith depended. Habitualized action depends on shared experience and corporate knowledge. The individual, cut off from the community, could never discover and test (entirely on his own) what is 'expected', 'appropriate' or 'relevant'. But it is 'built into' Christian faith, through its very grammar, that Christians adopt the role of servant to their Lord, of obedient subject to their King, of adopted sons to their Father. Moreover, these roles constitute stable elements in the Christian understanding of *God*. On the basis of corporate knowledge and experience *God is* Lord, King, Redeemer and Father, because in these roles (habituated patterns of action) he has been experienced in Israel and in the Christian Church.

It now becomes clear why *corporate memory* (especially as this is articulated and preserved in the biblical writings) represents much more than a mere 'source' for knowledge of the past. Corporate memory is the frame of reference which gives meaning to the present, and even guides present action. There is nothing necessarily 'pious' about using ancient writings in this way; still less does this represent antiquarianism. In modern society, for example, ancient legal documents may sometimes be used as 'sources' from which to study the past, but more often laws, even from earlier times, serve to guide present judgements and procedures, especially when the community wishes to retain what it regards as a cultural *identity* reaching back into the past. The possession and 'effective history' of corporate memory is what makes a society (or a nation, or a church) *this* society, and not some other.

We must return, however, to the relation between corporate memory and *roles*. At this point the sociological descriptions of Peter Berger and Thomas Luckmann prove to be especially helpful. They argue that roles can be adopted and made operative only on the basis of 'an objectified stock of knowledge common to a collectivity of actors'. They then comment: 'In the common stock of knowledge there are *standards of role-performance* that are accessible to all members of a society, or at least to those who are potential performers of the roles in question.'[29] In these terms, a Christian concern about the place of the Bible, or about tradition or orthodoxy, has little or nothing to do with intellectual conformity as such. What is at stake is the maintenance of conditions under which it still makes sense to speak of 'standards of role-performance'.

When we apply these considerations to what have traditionally been described as the problems of heresy and orthodoxy, it is important to make one point clear. In order to be able to speak of standard role-performance, it is certainly not necessary that *every individual* who claims to be part of the Christian community should *actually perform* every role prescribed as standard to Christian belief. What matters, from this standpoint, is whether, when deviation or eccentricities occur, they are identified as permitted *deviations or eccentricities.* If the community itself were to revise what it has hitherto regarded as standard role-performance *across the board,* then in the case of the Christian community, the two consequences would follow what we have already described: first, what it would now mean to stand in *this* tradition or to use *these* concepts would become problematic; second, language about *God* (as, for example, redeemer of the redeemed, and so on) would also lose its grounding and its stability. If these concepts were cut loose from what the community had regarded as paradigm cases of their use, we should be left with the kind of individualism which Lewis Carroll gently mocked through the lips of Humpty-Dumpty: 'When *I* use a word, it means just what I choose it to mean – neither more nor less' (*Through the Looking Glass,* chapter 6).

The problem of 'myth' and the relation between belief and behaviour

The use and abuse of 'myth' to describe the transmission of corporate memory

Theology and other related disciplines often employ one particular concept or category in order to bring together many of the considerations which we have set out above. The

67

category in question is that of *myth*. Myth hands down corporate memory not in the form of abstract theory or systematic ideas, but in the form of story (although not strictly of factual report). In particular, myths have the status of *believed truth within a given community*.

The popular notion of myth as that which is false emerged precisely because the truth of myth is relative to the beliefs of a community. When myths are viewed from a standpoint which is different from that of the myth-making community, their content may be regarded as false. Thus, in popular thought, myth is generally associated with falsehood because the standard paradigm of the myth in modern western culture is the stories of the gods and goddesses of ancient Greece.

As well as being grounded in the thought and experience of a community, myths also lay claim to truth which is believed to be significant for *present* thought and conduct. In accordance with our earlier observations, they function characteristically as 'legitimating formulae' for attitudes handed down through corporate memory, which the community wishes to preserve and validate for the present generation. Myths thereby draw the individual into the frame of reference bequeathed by corporate experience. Yet an individual, or even a whole generation in later times, may wish to reformulate or revise the beliefs and practices which are being legitimated, in accordance with truth perceived outside the community or in the light of recent experience and knowledge. Hence myths may undergo *reinterpretation* in the course of the dialectic between corporate memory and critical reflection.

It may seem, in the light of these basic characteristics, that myth represents the category best fitted to express and describe the nature of the dialectic which is at present under discussion. Have we not already given an account of how corporate memory and critical faith interact and condition each other within the Christian tradition?

We shall be forced to conclude, a little later in our argument, that the term 'myth' in fact raises more problems than it solves. However, it would be cavalier not to examine more closely some of the advantages which might be claimed for its use, especially since such an examination carries our discussion of corporate memory further. We shall focus on each, in turn, of the three major characteristics of myth to which we have already drawn attention.

First, myths, we observed, take the form of stories or

narratives, not that of abstract systematic doctrine. Thereby they have the power to draw the hearer into the 'world' of the story. The individual and the present generation are enabled to be *'there'* at the great founding events of the community, as these have been held and transmitted by corporate memory. They operate, therefore, at a far deeper level than mere concepts or intellectual 'information'. Stories also do justice to the uniqueness of persons as persons. They are not concerned with mere generalities, but with what *this* person did on *that* occasion. A person comes alive as a person not when we describe his general characteristics or attributes, but when we tell stories about what he did on particular occasions. We see his unique personhood through personal traits of behaviour. In myth, this applies especially to stories about gods or about God. Indeed, many have argued that this anthropomorphic way of describing God brings us to the very heart of what may be said to constitute myth. At all events the highly personal God of the story or narrative belongs no less equally to myth and to the biblical and Christian tradition.

A second characteristic shared by myth and the biblical material is that truth about God is presented from a number of different angles in which language utilizes analogy, model, metaphor or symbol. The reality to which the material itself stands witness somehow (at least in the judgement of a community) transcends the language which is used. Christians often speak of the truth of the Bible as 'inexhaustible', seeing attempts to speak of God as like the attempt to cup hands around the ocean. This gives rise to attempts in biblical inter-pretation to move beyond the conscious horizons of the author of the text. There is often, it is urged, 'something more' than that of which the author himself was aware. Similarly, the re-interpretation of myth depends on the belief of a later generation or individual that it is possible to reach 'behind' the myth to understand it 'better' than the original community, at least in relation to later problems and questions.

Third, and perhaps most important of all, both myth and the biblical writings embody language which may appear to be merely descriptive, but which in fact serves also to summon the reader to appropriate attitudes and conduct. It invites the latest generation to share in the attitudes and conduct which were demanded by the founding events of the community. There is thus a *reiteration of shared memory, shared reality and shared experience, but also a reiteration and reappropriation of shared attitudes,*

shared imperatives and shared practices. What may appear to be
only a statement (Christ was raised; Christ is Lord) is seen *also*
to function as a self-involving commitment (We are raised; we
are Christ's servants).

If this were all that need be said (or more significantly *had*
been said) about myth, we might have been free to draw what
positive insights we could from the use of this category to
describe corporate memory in the Christian tradition. But the
history of modern research into the nature of myth reveals
pitfalls and difficulties which far outweigh any advantages in
such use. Moreover, even the three characteristics so far
discussed all too often in modern discussion carry with them
unwanted implications which prove to be seriously misleading
when applied to the Christian story.

First, we spoke of myth as story. But partly because it takes
this relatively unreflective, unselfconscious and unsophisti-
cated form and avoids more precise abstract reflection, many
modern writers have associated it with a world-view which is
necessarily uncritical, primitive and pre-scientific. This view of
myth owes much, once again, to the period of the Enlightenment, and betrays the influence of Fontenelle, Eichorn and
Strauss. But although recent research has shown the
inadequacy of such an account of myth, it persists in many
quarters and has been popularized in the theological world
through Bultmann (even if other understandings of myth also
coexist uneasily in Bultmann's writings). It is argued, for
example, that precisely because of its pre-scientific nature,
myth ascribes the occurrence of certain events in the world to
supernatural causes. Hence the advent of a more sophisticated
world-view is said to demand the reinterpretation of all such
references to supernatural causality, which is assumed to
represent a viewpoint owing more to cultural factors than to
religious convictions. The complex mass of literature which
has emerged on this subject, however, shows that these issues
cannot be foreclosed in this oversimplistic fashion.[30]

Second, while it is true that neither myth nor the Christian
story articulates the reality to which it points in such a way that
there is nothing more to be said, we must guard against the
mistaken view that language is simply some kind of opaque
wrapping which can be detached from the pure thought which
it expresses but also obscures. How do we gain access to the
reality said to lie 'behind' the myth or story, other than
through the myth or story itself? It is very easy to speak

disparagingly (or more often, patronizingly) of what the community in earlier generations was 'trying' to say, as if to imply that its original formulations may now be set aside. But there are two quite different senses in which something may be said to need 'reinterpretation'.[31] There is, on the one hand, the analogy of the code which needs to be translated. Once we have the key to the code, we may translate the code into our own everyday languages, and then dispense with the original, which is now obsolete. The Enlightenment view of myth encourages this approach to the New Testament. But we may also take up a very different analogy. A masterpiece may need to be interpreted to a later generation. The modern 'commentary' may shed a flood of light on it, and be necessary for full understanding in the changed culture of a later time. But in this case, the original will not be thrown away. The whole purpose of the interpretation is to help the hearer to return to the original masterpiece, this time with eyes to see. The second analogy describes the task of biblical interpretation; the first does not. But the term 'myth', with all its slipperiness and accumulation of mistaken theories, allows the second kind of interpretation to be confused with the first. The Christian story indeed needs fresh *interpretation* from generation to generation; but in terms of the theory of knowledge presented above, it also contains irreducible paradigms which cannot be dispensed with without 'sawing off the branch on which I am sitting'. It embodies the corporate memory of the Christian community.

Third, in stressing the practical or self-involving function of myth, many writers adopt an unduly negative attitude towards the descriptive function of story or narrative. Bultmann, for example, believes that this 'objectifying' or descriptive aspect simply impedes the practical impact of its language, even to the point of misleading the modern reader about the content of its message. But self-involving language cannot be effective if it is *wholly* instrumental or 'practical', without being anchored in some understanding of reality. The self-involving or practical aspect becomes operative precisely because it is grounded in an understanding of 'what is the case', or in the founding events of the community. This is one of several reasons why a number of modern writers insist that 'myth', as a category, cannot do justice to the particularity, uniqueness, or once-for-allness (however this is expressed) which marks the Christian story. We are not obliged to depend for this point on waning remnants of the once fashionable 'biblical theology' movement. No sane account of the faith of the New Testament communities can brush over this aspect, and it is noteworthy that correctives have emerged in New Testament studies to the older idea that early Christian preaching was wholly 'confessional', as if descriptions of events were of no interest at all to the primitive communities.[32]

It seems, then, that the category 'myth', in spite of the promise which it seems initially to hold out, does not in the end take us very far along the path of trying to clarify the nature of the relation between corporate knowledge and individual criticism. At very least it leaves too many loose ends which lend themselves easily to misunderstanding.

Two further perspectives: the problem of interpretation and the self-involving nature of Christian belief

If the idea of 'myth' fails, in the end, to carry the discussion forward constructively, we may perhaps suggest two other alternative perspectives in the light of which we may more easily avoid the temptation to polarize corporate knowledge and individual criticism as opposites, and may see the complementary and positive ways in which the two poles interact and interrelate as contributions to the one ongoing dialectic.

First, light is shed on the nature of this interaction by the history of biblical interpretation. There has always been an emphasis in Christian theology on the 'givenness' of the biblical writings. The 1938 Doctrine Commission Report entitled *Doctrine in the Church of England* saw the Bible as the 'classical literature' of God's self-revelation, and viewed its authority as lying at least partly in its function of carrying us 'back to the concrete richness of the facts in which our religion is grounded'.[33] In the present volume Anthony Harvey has alluded to the givenness of the Bible, and discussed its authority partly in terms of its function. In current biblical studies, however, two further emphases can be found. In the first place, to the older recognition of the variety of literary forms which can be found in the Bible (noted in the 1938 Doctrine Report) is now added a further emphasis on the multiformity of its actual content or theological subject-matter. But this simply underlines the fundamental fact that the Bible embodies the corporate memories and corporate knowledge of a community, or (perhaps more accurately) of a community of communities. In the second place, increasing emphasis is laid today on the problem of biblical interpretation. How can an ancient text speak to our own times? The importance of both issues, the multiformity of the biblical writings and the problem of interpretation, was underlined in the Doctrine Commission Report of 1976, *Christian Believing*.[34] Both are of positive importance for the present discussion.

The connection between the authority of the Bible and the corporate foundations of Christian knowledge, memory and belief, was noted in fact many years ago by C. H. Dodd. It is worth quoting some of his sentences in full. There may be times, he wrote, 'when doubts are stronger than faith'.

It would not be honest at such times simply to silence our questionings with a text. Nevertheless, we may well turn away from the narrow scene of individual experience at the moment, to the spacious prospect we command in the Bible . . . Here we trace the long history of a community which, through good fortune and ill, tested their belief in God, and experimented too in varieties of belief, with the result that the 'logic of facts' drove deeper and deeper the conviction that while some ways of thinking of God are definitely closed, *this* way lies open and leads on and on.[35]

Dodd went on to stress the corporate dimension of faith by describing individual belief as being primarily a matter of 'living oneself into' the corporate experience and corporate memory of community. The very nature of the biblical literature draws attention to this aspect of Christian believing.

However, if one pole in the use of the Bible is that of the corporate knowledge of the community, the other pole concerns the Christian's understanding and interpretation of that knowledge in the present. We have already argued in the first half of this essay that 'understanding' depends on a context of 'effective history' or corporate knowledge. The two poles of the past 'givenness' of the Bible and its present interpretation do not (or at least should not) stand in opposition to each other. In this respect the history of biblical interpretation is the history both of false trails to be avoided and of insights to be developed further. Over the course of the history of the Church, different interpreters, and different eras of interpretation, have stressed the importance of each pole in turn. The Reformers urged that the Bible should not be made to wear 'a nose of wax', with the result that it could be made to say anything which the current generation wanted to hear, under the pretext of 'interpretation'. Others have stressed that meaning transcends the conscious intention of the original writer, and that meaning *cannot* remain unchanged when it is understood in a changed situation.

In an attempt to give some place to both the past and present aspects, an analogy may be suggested. The Bible may be compared to a musical score. What 'controls', or sets limits to the scope of, the present performance is the notation of the composition as it was composed at some time in the past. If it is not based on the score, the present performance is not a performance of *this* composition. Nevertheless, what the current audience experiences in the present is the actual *performance,* and no two performances will be quite the same. Wooden repetition may turn out to be less faithful to the score than the use of creative imagination. Yet the creativity of the performer still takes place within clear limits. For without faithfulness to the score, the performance would not be a *faithful* interpretation of *that* work. Indeed, to return to our earlier observations about the nature of the Bible, to offer an 'interpretation' which did violence to the text would be to substitute some narrower individual viewpoint for the breadth and range of successive layers of corporate memory, belief and knowledge, gained by a community, or by a community of communities.

We turn now to our second suggestion about a way of looking at the problem of corporate knowledge which allows us to see how the corporate and individual poles of knowledge interact positively together, rather than standing in a relation of opposition or contradiction. If we are tempted to view Christian belief as being primarily a 'mental state', or a matter of thinking certain thoughts, it may seem as if creeds, confessions or the corporate testimony of the community represent a threat to make the individual think what everyone else thinks. But this way of understanding belief is inadequate, mistaken, and, in the context of the present discussion, also misleading. Christian believing by its very nature carries with it the appropriation of certain attitudes and patterns of behaviour which are called into play only on the basis of the shared public world of interpersonal relations. Belief involves, or commits, the self who claims to be a believer not merely (if at all) to the acceptance of certain theoretical statements, but to ways of understanding and acting towards God and others

74

which transcend the limits of a strictly 'private' or individual
world. In this sense, Christian belief has been described as
'self-involving'. It has practical as well as theoretical
dimensions, and these practical dimensions make themselves
apparent, and indeed make sense, only on the basis of a setting
or context in the public world of *shared* attitudes and *shared*
patterns of behaviour. Christian beliefs are thus, by definition,
we shall argue, *shared* beliefs.

We have already seen that Christian belief entails more than
thinking certain thoughts in our earlier discussions about
expected patterns of behaviour and the significance of status
and (in the sociological sense) role. Christian belief entails not
so much theoretical assent to the possible existence or
relevance of such roles, as their actual acceptance, adoption
and appropriation. Here we enter the realm of 'performative'
utterance, which is later discussed in this volume by W. H.
Vanstone. To say 'I promise to do *x*', is not simply to give
information about myself; the utterance *commits* me to certain
subsequent actions. The utterance itself, therefore, is an act
which is *performed in* the saying of the words. I *make* a promise,
for the promise itself constitutes a pledge or commitment. But
this means that making a promise cannot, *by definition,* be a
merely *private* or *individual* matter. It would not make sense
(apart from the very odd and derivative notion of giving
oneself a promise) to speak of 'promising', except on the basis
of *public,* shared, interpersonal relations. Precisely the same
principle applies to Christian believing. One cannot believe
'privately', for belief involves commitment to shared attitudes
and patterns of behaviour. It is not simply a matter of an
individual having certain ideas in his head. To say 'I believe'
is to make a pledge, to make a commitment. It is like nailing
one's colours to the mast. Even in a situation of political
oppression where 'secret' discipleship might be thought
necessary in certain exceptional circumstances, the secrecy of
belief would not be 'private' in the full philosophical sense.

All these kinds of considerations have been carefully
examined in a number of philosophical discussions of these
issues.[36] Each discussion seems further to underline the
importance of the 'performative' character of confessions of
belief, even though it is also rightly asserted that belief is *more*
than a pledge or first-person commitment. It has been pointed
out, for example, that if I claim to believe, this cannot mean
that I have a certain mental state continuously; for I hardly

stop being a believer when I fall asleep or lose consciousness. It means that I am committed (at least in principle) to those actions and attitudes which are appropriate in circumstances which would call belief into play. If I 'believe' that Christ is Lord, what gives content to that belief is my acceptance and appropriation of the role of Christ's servant. Whether I show fear, joy, shame, courage or hope in certain situations is part of what my belief may be said to amount to. This is not to deny the possibility of insincerity or hypocrisy. For I can *claim* to believe in such a way as to deceive even myself; just as I may promise to do something and then fail to carry the promise through. What is being said is that a statement of belief that does not affect action or attitude is (like a promise which is later broken) without substance. The Epistle of James is of course at pains to make this particular point. This does not invalidate the Pauline insight that faith is a *response*. For it entails the *acceptance* or *appropriation* of attitudes or patterns of behaviour which are 'given' prior to individual thought, and which are lived out in the shared world of interpersonal relations. It would make no more sense to speak of 'private' Christian belief than it would to speak of being a doctor, teacher or servant 'privately'.

To be aware, then, of the practical or self-involving aspects of belief is to move some way towards seeing how the dialectic between the corporate and individual aspects of knowledge and experience comes to operate in practice. Christian believing is possible only on the foundations of corporate knowledge and experience. It operates within the framework of corporate memory. But it does not demand a merely second-hand or uncritical acceptance of 'what others have said'. For *critical* faith, far from being a 'private' or individual affair, depends on the capacity to employ concepts which are themselves embedded in a process of corporate experience and knowledge. Luther's 'Here I stand' is not in the end incompatible with the patristic dictum (understood in its broadest sense): 'There is no salvation outside the Church.' Indeed, Luther explicitly endorsed Cyprian's maxim: 'He cannot have God for his father who has not the Church for his mother.'[37]

'I must not saw off the branch on which I am sitting.'

NOTES

1 William Temple, *Nature, Man and God* (Macmillan 1940), p. 57. (Chapter 3 is called 'The Cartesian Faux-Pas'.)

2 W. Stark, *The Sociology of Knowledge: An Essay in Aid of a Deeper Understanding of the History of Ideas* (Routledge & Kegan Paul 1958), pp. 13–14.

3 H.-G. Gadamer, *Truth and Method* (Eng. tr., Sheed & Ward 1975), pp. 19–29 *et passim;* and Alfred Schutz, *Collected Papers.* 3 vols., The Hague, Nijhoff, 1962–6. Cf. also Ronald R. Cox, *Schutz's Theory of Relevance: A Phenomenological Critique* (The Hague, Nijhoff, 1978), pp. 1–32, for a useful summary.

4 Georges Gurvitch, *The Social Frameworks of Knowledge* (Blackwell 1971), pp. 27–8 and 53–4.

5 Anthony C. Thiselton, *The Two Horizons: New Testament Hermeneutics and Philosophical Description* (Grand Rapids: Paternoster, Exeter & Eerdmans, 1980), p. 137; cf. pp. 115–39.

6 John Ziman, *Public Knowledge: The Social Dimension of Science* (Cambridge University Press 1968), p. 103, *et passim.*

7 A mass of literature could be cited, but see especially Peter Berger and Thomas Luckmann, *The Social Construction of Reality: A Treatise in the Sociology of Knowledge.* Penguin Books 1966 and 1971. Cf. also Barry Barnes, *Interests and the Growth of Knowledge.* Routledge & Kegan Paul 1977; Keith Dixon, *The Sociology of Belief: Fallacy and Foundation.* Routledge & Kegan Paul 1980; Nicholas Abercrombie, *Class, Structure and Knowledge: Problems in the Sociology of Knowledge.* Blackwell 1980; and Georges Gurvitch, op. cit.

8 Gadamer, op. cit., p. 245.

9 op. cit., p. 248.

10 Thiselton, op. cit., pp. 293–326 *et passim.*

11 Ludwig Wittgenstein, *On Certainty* (Eng. and German, Blackwell 1969), section 211. (His italics.)

12 op. cit., sections 83, 105 and 110. (His italics.)

13 op. cit., sections 115, 128 and 160. Cf. especially sections 106–70.

14 Wittgenstein, *Philosophical Investigations* (3rd edn, Blackwell 1967), section 279.

15 Wittgenstein, op. cit., section 265. Cf. further *The Two Horizons,* pp. 379–85.

16 Wittgenstein, *Zettel* (Blackwell 1967), section 173.

17 Thomas S. Kuhn, *The Structure of Scientific Revolutions* (2nd edn, University of Chicago Press 1970), pp. 10–11.

18 op. cit., p. 7.

19 op. cit., pp. 51 and 62.

20 op. cit., p. 113.

21 Karl Popper, 'Normal Science and its Dangers', in I. Lakatos and A. Musgrave, eds., *Criticism and the Growth of Knowledge* (Cambridge University Press 1970), p. 56.

22 S. Kierkegaard, *Purity of Heart is to Will One Thing* (Collins Fontana), p. 163.

23 Kierkegaard, *Attack upon 'Christendom' 1854–5* (Eng. tr., Oxford University Press 1946), p. 127.

24 ibid.

25 Kierkegaard, *Concluding Unscientific Postscript to the 'Philosophical Fragments'* (Eng. tr., Princeton University Press 1941), pp. 181 and 221.

26 Kierkegaard, *Attack upon 'Christendom'*, pp. 24 and 34.

27 Wittgenstein, *Philosophical Investigations*, section 55.

28 R. P. C. Hanson, *Tradition in the Early Church*. SCM Press 1962.

29 Berger and Luckmann, op. cit., p. 91.

30 I have set out a few of the issues involved in *The Two Horizons*, pp. 53–63; 69–84; 205–92; 392–401 and 439–45.

31 This distinction is suggested by Ian Henderson, *Myth in the New Testament* (SCM Press 1952), p. 31.

32 Cf., for example, Graham N. Stanton, *Jesus of Nazareth in New Testament Preaching*. Cambridge University Press 1974; SNTS Monograph 27.

33 *Doctrine in the Church of England* (SPCK 1938), pp. 31 and 34.

34 *Christian Believing* (SPCK 1976), pp. 6–14; 21–31 and 43–51.

35 C. H. Dodd, *The Authority of the Bible* (2nd edn, Nisbet 1938), p. 298.

36 See especially H. H. Price, *Belief*. Allen & Unwin 1969; and D. M. High, *Language, Persons and Belief*. Oxford University Press, New York, 1967.

37 Martin Luther, commentary on the Psalms, *Weimarer Ausgabe,* iv. 239. 21.

4

Story and Liturgy

Introduction

Story

The last chapter has shown that 'myth', though potentially a
useful word for describing some aspects of the Christian
message, is also fraught with dangers and difficulties.
Especially now that it has become such a vexed issue in English
theology, it is more or less unusable unless hedged round with
endless explanations and qualifications. Recent theology,
however, has thrown up a new term which we might want to
use: 'story'. Story, like myth, is a word with many possible
meanings. On the one hand, it is hallowed in Christian usage:
'Tell me the old, old story'; on the other, it can be used in a
debunking way, as when people say that Christianity is 'only a
story' or 'only a collection of old stories'. In this chapter we
shall try to show that it can be used in a positive way, to
describe the way in which much of the Bible, and of other
traditions and formulations of Christian faith, actually
function in the life of the Church and contribute to the
corporate belief of Christians.

As Anthony Harvey points out in Chapter 2 above, one of
the features of the Bible that is particularly puzzling to anyone
who seeks to find in it explicit formulations of Christian
doctrine is that very much of it consists of *narrative*. Typically,
the Bible does not say 'This is what you must believe' but
'This is what happened'. Theologians have often spent time
in trying to find a route from the narrative to the doctrine, in
looking for the 'point' being made in a narrative text, or in
seeking 'themes' running through narrative books such as the
Old Testament 'histories' or the gospels and Acts. They have
also, quite rightly, been concerned with whether the stories
told in these narratives are true or historically reliable.
However, it is also important to take seriously the fact that
such texts *are* narrative, and not simply to try to reduce them to
something else. Narrative, after all, plays a vital part in human

life. It is, indeed, one of the most normal means by which people communicate with each other; for whatever reason, our usual way of laying ourselves open to each other is by reciting some version of our life-history. As a matter of fact it is only highly articulate people who regularly communicate in any other way; and it is hard to imagine any two people really getting to know each other without ever narrating sequences of action to each other.

Now it is only a very partial truth to say that in such narration 'historical information' or 'facts' are conveyed. For example, very many husbands and wives probably conclude many days by exchanging simple narrative accounts of what they have been doing; but so far from this being a substitute for some more elevated or less circumstantial form of communication, it seems to be generally found highly satisfying. It would not be better if they presented each other with a concise summary of the main points, under suitable headings: the narrative form is essential, and it can be long without being felt to be long-winded. Narrative is comforting, satisfying – emotionally irreplaceable. Whether a narrative is true or not is an important question: wives do not expect their husbands to construct ingenious but untrue accounts of how they have spent their day to narrate to them each evening; but it is a separate question from how the narrative 'works'. Narrative does not belong to the world of 'hard fact', like a bank statement; it belongs to the world of evenings with a photograph album, of reminiscences which unite a family, of meetings with friends in which one goes over old ground for the sake of the solidity and depth it gives to friendship.

If we are to understand the forces binding together friends or families, therefore, we need to attend to the stories they tell each other, the shared framework of narrative that gives their relationships shape and meaning. In the case of the Church, it seems that a similar function is to be found in what may be called 'the Christian story', which includes the Bible and some other expressions of Christian faith in narrative or story-like form. And just as, for a family, the 'family story' is told and reinforced when the family meets together, so in the Church the liturgy, the coming together of Christians to worship God, provides the natural context for the Christian 'story' to be told. So, if 'story' is to be a fruitful term in discussing the belief of Christians, and is not to degenerate into the sort of vagueness that has been the death of 'myth', it will be best to use it within this context. 'The Christian myth' is certainly understood by many people as a polite, theologians' way of saying that Christianity is not true, while trying to save appearances. It should be said quite clearly that 'the Christian story' is not being used for this purpose. The object of this chapter is to show how the idea of 'story' can help to elucidate the way the Christian community at prayer actually appropriates and is built up in the faith to which the Bible and other traditional formularies bear witness.

Liturgy

As will be shown in detail in Chapter 5, it has in fact been customary in the Anglican tradition to appeal not only to the creeds, to antiquity and to the councils of the Church as standards of Christian faith, but also to the Church's public liturgy, especially as enshrined in the Book of Common Prayer. It is clear that one can learn much about the beliefs of *any* given Christian community from both the forms and the content of the prayers that it addresses to God in its public worship; but if the *lex orandi* is important in other parts of the Christian Church, it is crucial in Anglicanism, which (as other chapters show) accords a rather lower place than many other communions to explicit definitions of doctrine, and has nothing obviously corresponding to the Confessions of the Reformed Churches or to the 'teaching office' of the Roman Church. It may truly be said of Anglicanism (as it often is said of Orthodoxy) that the best way to discover what Anglicans believe is not to read the works of their theologians, but to attend their services. But for our present purpose of studying the way the Church tells and reappropriates 'the Christian story', it will be important to concentrate on certain aspects of public worship more than on others, and in particular to examine some of the 'non-sacramental' elements of public worship that tend to attract rather less notice in traditional studies of liturgy. We shall be concerned chiefly with the use in the liturgy of material which is not ostensibly addressed to God in the form of prayer, but which forms part of what may broadly be called the 'liturgy of the word'; with dramatic, musical and other non-sacramental ways of telling the Christian story; and with some aspects of the Eucharist that are not normally handled in studies of 'eucharistic theology'. We begin by examining a widespread understanding of the difference between word and sacrament, and by trying to show that it fails to do justice to what is actually happening when the Christian liturgy is performed; and through this we hope to make clearer what is meant by saying that, in the liturgy, 'the Christian story' is narrated and appropriated, and becomes the focus for the Church's corporate belief.

Lesson or lection

The simplest way of drawing a contrast between the liturgy of the word, on the one hand, and the offering of prayer or sacrament, on the other, might well seem to be to say that the former is directed to the congregation rather than to God. One may see this contrast symbolized by a movement from the lectern, used for the Antecommunion, to the altar for the Eucharist proper. The most characteristic element in the liturgy of the word, on this view, is the sermon. In other words, one might think, prayer and sacrament are a matter of Christians addressing God; in the liturgy of the word, God, or his preacher, speaks to Christians, and tells them what they need to know.

But it seems likely that this contrast is greatly overdrawn, both as a statement of the actual historical development of elements such as the public reading of Scripture, the recitation of psalms or the singing of anthems, and as a description of how these are perceived by most worshippers. It is a severe distortion of the liturgy of the word to see it as purely didactic in function, as a kind of Bible class or catechism. The recitation of creeds is not undertaken primarily to provide the congregation with fresh information, or even to remind them of what they already believe; psalms and anthems and the ceremonial of worship are not simply audio-visual aids; and the reading of Scripture in the Christian liturgy is far from being merely a form of instruction. The liturgy of the word is indeed largely narrative and expository in its formal character; but the 'syllabus', so to speak, does not change from year to year, and no one may be excused from attendance at the first part of the eucharistic liturgy, or at the daily office, on the grounds that he has 'heard the story already' or holds a certificate of competence in biblical literature. Clearly narrative here is more than a didactic tool; and the act of narration in the assembly has a significance beyond that which is immediately evident.

Various arguments of a more or less didactic kind may indeed be adduced for the practice in both the contemporary and the ancient Church of reading the Scriptures according to a set order, year by year. It is perfectly true, for example, that one cannot exhaust all the riches of the text in one reading and one exposition. So, too, familiarity with selected passages of Scripture, before the days of universal literacy or not, is a strength to Christian holiness. Christians, it may be said, have to be regularly nourished with the word of God, and lection followed by sermon constitutes the staple element in this diet. Jewish Christians would probably be familiar with this pattern before their conversion. They would understand the reading of Scripture in course, and according to festival and fast. Indeed, it is sometimes argued that parts of both the Old and New Testaments are actually structured according to a pattern of liturgical readings or expositions: the historical books from Joshua to Kings, the work of the Chronicler, the Psalter, the gospels, Ephesians and 1 Peter have all been the subject of scholarly hypotheses of this kind. But the question still remains – for Judaism as for the Christian Church: does the reading of Scripture in the assembly serve an additional and different purpose? For example, does the rehearsing year by year of the same passages contribute towards the establishment of a portrait of corporate believing through which the community establishes and asserts its identity and enters into the mystery of its experience of salvation?

It seems that for both Jews and Christians the liturgical reading of scriptural (perhaps especially narrative) material does indeed have a function which is more than didactic. It may be called *kerygmatic* or proclamatory, since by publicly rehearsing its corporate 'story' the community proclaims its identity as the people of God; it may also be called *doxological*, in that the telling of the story is directed not simply to the congregation, as a word from God or from a teaching church, but also to God, as a form of worship. The blessing at Passover, like the consecration of the eucharistic gifts, is accomplished by a recital of the acts of God; and for the Jew, the public reading of Scripture, especially the Pentateuch, is similarly a kind of prayer, an exposition in God's presence of an ordered account of his deeds, demands and promises which becomes a vehicle through which he is worshipped. It is through publicly reading a portion of the Torah that one becomes a full member of the worshipping community in Judaism (*bar-mitzvah*). The community of the Torah is not simply the community that lives under certain *laws*; it is also,

83

and perhaps more importantly, the community in which certain stories are told: stories that add up to one story, running from the creation of the world, through the redemption of Israel from Egypt, to the entry into the Promised Land, of which the present experience of those who tell the story forms or can form a part. The story presented in the Old Testament is important for belief not primarily as a set of assertions about external reality that have to be affirmed, but as a narrative thread that has to be entertained and into which present religious experience or commitment has to be fitted. Now in the same way it might be said that Christians are those who tell the Christian story, who share in the corporate 'knowledge' that consists in knowing that story, belonging to the community that tells it and allowing its patterns to regulate their lives. And so it seems that the liturgical recitation of Scripture and of other classic texts, together with the various solemn ceremonies that accompany this in almost all Christian tradition, ought to be seen as having a function for the Christian similar to that which reading the Torah has for the Jew. The function we have in mind is well described by Alexander Schmemann:

> Western Christians are so accustomed to distinguish the Word from the sacrament that it may be difficult for them to understand that in the Orthodox perspective the liturgy of the Word is as sacramental as the sacrament is 'evangelical'. The sacrament is a manifestation of the Word. And unless the false dichotomy between Word and sacrament is overcome, the true meaning of both Word and sacrament, and especially the true meaning of Christian 'sacramentalism' cannot be grasped in all their wonderful implications. The proclamation of the Word is a sacramental act *par excellence* because it is a transforming act. It transforms the human words of the gospel into the Word of God and the manifestation of his kingdom. And it transforms the man who hears the Word into a receptacle of the Word and a temple of the Spirit.[1]

The rest of this chapter will trace the development of a kerygmatic and doxological understanding of the liturgy of the word, and will try to show that it has been, and continues to be, important within the Anglican tradition, providing us with a context within which Christian texts and their visual and musical accompaniments tell the Christian story, and build up the community of worshipping Christians in the faith which they share.

Story and liturgy in the Christian tradition

Our knowledge of the manner in which Scripture was read in the earliest centuries is both limited and fragmentary. Such glimpses as we have, however, are very revealing, and illustrate well the principles already outlined in the first section of this chapter. We begin with the readings at the Easter Vigil in second-century Asia Minor; we then move to fourth-century Jerusalem for a consideration of the readings for Holy Week; then to the Roman eucharistic lectionary for which we have evidence from the sixth century onwards; then to the office readings as represented in the Sarum Breviary of 1535. The influence of the calendar in the choice of lection and in the whole pattern of Christian 'storytelling', so prominent in the later Middle Ages, demands that the structure of this calendar should be briefly considered; and on the same theme of narrative, we examine the eucharistic prayer and a number of non-scriptural texts, including hymns.

Easter in the second century – Melito of Sardis

Two texts from the second century enable us to reconstruct a fragmentary picture of an early Easter Vigil. The Quartodeciman document known as *The Epistle of the Apostles* refers to the practice that on 14 Nisan the paschal celebration was begun with fasting which continued into 15 Nisan. During the night, vigil was kept; whereupon at cockcrow (3 a.m.) the fast was broken when the Eucharist was celebrated in the context of an *agape*. Parallels in the *Peri Pascha* of Melito of Sardis suggest that this was the ceremony to which the author refers. The Scripture reading is Exodus 12.3–32; it may have been in Hebrew (which was subsequently translated or paraphrased – so F. L. Cross) or in Greek (Othmar Perler). It is followed by the full text of what at first sight appears to be a homily but which may be more appropriately characterized as a Christian *haggadah*[2] (Cross) or *praeconium*[3] (Perler). The text expounds the Scripture reading, explaining in some detail, with dramatic use of imagery, how the events of the Exodus are fulfilled in the passion and saving work of Christ. Its *haggadah* or *praeconium* quality suggests that the same text may

85

have been read each year, perhaps by a lector and not by the president or one of the clergy; its preservation in written form may indicate that it had become an established part of the Easter ritual in the church of Asia Minor to which it owes its provenance.

But why the repeated reading and exposition? First, imagine the occasion. The congregation has fasted for a whole day. With their fast still unbroken, they gather in church as darkness descends on 15 Nisan (i.e. at 6 p.m.). They keep vigil all night and, during the small hours, the reading of Exodus 12 is begun. They hear that they are the New Israel, awaiting their salvation, that the dark days of Egypt are over, that the powers of darkness have no hold over them, that they have an identity as the chosen people of God. The first light of dawn breaks in as the newly baptized enter the assembly; as the daylight fills the sky, the fast is broken amid general rejoicing and the Eucharist is celebrated. Christ is risen, Israel has come out of Egypt; their salvation has been brought nigh. They have mystically identified themselves with the events told in the story; they have dramatically represented their passage from slavery to freedom, from darkness to light in the circumstances of the vigil; they will experience the actualization among them of the work of the redeeming Christ through the celebration of the Eucharist.

But there may be a further (and perhaps undesigned) purpose, namely, the establishment of the congregation in Christian truth. Here there is no dogmatic statement about the creation, the fall and original sin, the redemption and the resurrection (though there is some poetry about the Word of God in the creation). Nevertheless, the reality of the Christian experience is related in narrative and dramatic form in strict relationship to the historical events of salvation. One could argue that it might have been more appropriate on this occasion to read and expound the narrative of the passion and the resurrection from one of the accounts in the gospels; but it is precisely the typological reference of the Old Testament reading which gives the Christ-event a precision which it would otherwise lack. Through this interpretation Christians will know that sin enslaves and darkens, that the water of baptism cleanses, that the blood of Christ is powerful to cleanse from sin and to renew life, that God is provident and faithful, that the profession of faith in Christ leads from darkness to light and that salvation is a present reality. The whole is in a sense a creed in narrative form; and the corporate rehearsal of the narrative constitutes a proclamation and reassurance of the corporate faith of those who thus enter the mystery.

Holy Week in Jerusalem – Etheria

Etheria informs us about four distinct kinds of service at Jerusalem in the fourth century; services for pilgrims, the Eucharist, the office on Sundays and the office on weekdays. Only three of these include lections; the service for pilgrims has a reading corresponding to the place visited, the Eucharist on Sundays has a lengthy service of the word with sermons for presbyters and bishop, and on weekdays in Lent (Wednesday and Friday) is simply a synaxis at which bishop and presbyters preach in turn. The office on weekdays has no readings at all; but on Sunday there is a solemn reading of the passion and resurrection of the Lord by the bishop at cockcrow.

The majority of readings to which Etheria refers are from the New Testament. There is a distinct penchant for the historical, and the events of the Lord's passion are commemorated at the appropriate place and season by the reading of a passage from Scripture on whose suitability Etheria frequently remarks. There is, however, in her account of the reading of Scripture, reference to what one can only rather clumsily describe as an 'actualizing tendency' (the German *aktualisierend* is rather more admissible). For example, on the Saturday before Palm Sunday, the congregation assembles at Bethany where the account of the raising of Lazarus is read. Then after hymns and antiphons, there follows the reading of Mary's anointing of Jesus 'six days before the Passover', Easter is announced and the crowd returns to Jerusalem. On Palm Sunday, the 'Palm Gospel' is read (Matt. 21.1–11) at the Mount of Olives, and the event is then dramatically set forth[4] so that the congregation through reading and action enters into this mystery of the Lord's passion. Again on Sundays before cockcrow the congregation assembles in front of the anastasis, the bishop arrives and all enter the church, now brilliant with lights, the air filled with incense. The bishop alone enters the shrine itself[5] and emerges, like the angel of the resurrection, to read the gospel narrative of the resurrection. The people are visibly and audibly moved by this recitation and to the accompaniment of a hymn follow the bishop out of the church to the crux, where there is a psalm, prayer, blessing and dismissal.

87

As in the Paschal Vigil of Melito, so here in these dramatic readings of Scripture there is a strong element of 'making present'. The Scripture is read under such circumstances as to enable those present to sense the presence of the mystery that is being proclaimed. Are we to say also that they are thereby confirmed in their belief, and that this corporate reading and participation is an aspect of corporate believing? This would seem a reasonable inference, and indeed it is strengthened by one episode. For the vigil of the Ascension, the congregation moves to Bethlehem for a service with appropriate readings. The ascent of the Lord is hereby linked with his descent, and we seem here to be in the realm of the dogmatic. Christmas is non-existent in this account, and Epiphany is celebrated at Jerusalem (with suitable ceremonies at the other holy places). But though at this period the christological controversies have not reached their height, the basic elements of the creed concerning the person of Christ would seem to be represented in the liturgical round of Jerusalem. 'He came down from heaven . . . suffered under Pontius Pilate . . . on the third day he rose again . . . he ascended into heaven . . . and in the Holy Spirit . . .' What the worshippers at Jerusalem are concerned with is not simply the fact that these events happened, but that through their rehearsal in reading and drama the belief of Christians thus set forth may have a saving effect on those who take part in the Church's liturgy.

The lectionary and calendar

Apart from the sermons of the Fathers, there are two principal sources for our knowledge of the early lectionaries of the Western Church. The first is the compilation known as the *Capitulare Evangeliorum* with its companion volume, the *Liber Comitis,* evidence for Roman Mass readings from about AD 700 to AD 1100; the second is the text known as *Ordo Romanus* XIV, which gives an account of readings at the divine office in St Peter's, Rome, in the eighth century. The former of these is of interest here for two reasons. First, though basically a two-lesson system (unlike the three-lesson arrangement of Ambrosian, Mozarabic and Gallican lectionaries) such limited use of the Old Testament as is to be found confirms what we have already seen in earlier liturgies, namely, that (to quote J. A. Jungmann) '. . . the Old Testament . . . is not read for its own sake or as some sacred text, but has its place here in virtue of its prophetic content and the way in which it illuminates the New Testament.' Obvious examples are the choice of lections for the Paschal Vigil, the reading from Isaiah's prophecy of the return of the nations at Epiphany, the Lenten readings containing types of the Christian mystery of salvation or foreshadowings of Christian discipline, lessons from the Wisdom books on feasts of the Blessed Virgin Mary, etc. Second, it should be noted that despite some conscious attempt at *lectio continua*[6] (St John in Eastertide and the epistles in their canonical order, though headed by the catholic epistles, during Pentecost) the impulse to select according to circumstances and season is strong. Proper lessons for major feasts and the seasons of Advent and Lent are familiar to most of Christendom; but for the rest of the year at Rome during this period, the *Sanctorale*[7] has a very strong pull over the choice of lection, as does the system of Stational Masses (e.g. the Epistle for Lent 4 is not particularly Lenten but is chosen, in preference to an earlier reading, for its mention of Jerusalem, to suit the church of the Holy Cross in Jerusalem at which the Stational Mass was celebrated that Sunday). Needless to say, most of the Roman Sunday lectionary in its developed form with its reference to Roman dedications and Roman churches passed straight into the Book of Common Prayer.

The culmination of this selective procedure is a rich handbook of doctrine and devotion, particularly when the lections are supported by carefully selected psalms and neatly composed antiphons for introit, gradual, offertory and communion. The whole is very much a guide to Christian believing through liturgical participation in the mysteries of the Christian year.

The second of these Roman texts is a landmark in the development of a system of office lections which begins on the one hand with the cathedral office (e.g. the Sunday or occasional office at Jerusalem) and on the other hand with the two-lesson requirement for the evening office of the Egyptian monastic tradition. Undoubtedly the monasteries (the Benedictine foundations in particular) had a profound influence on the Scripture reading pattern for the hours of prayer, religious or secular, and the culmination of this may be seen, for example, in the Sarum Breviary of 1535.

As had become the custom well before the sixteenth century (at least as early as St Benedict) the bulk of Scripture reading was appointed for the night office, the number of lessons ranging from three to twelve. At first sight, an extremely limited selection of Scripture is appointed to be read at Salisbury. Isaiah is begun in Advent; from Christmas to Epiphany the lections are all proper to the season, feast or octave (there is not a single feria from 24 December to Epiphany). In Epiphanytide, Romans 1–5 is read in the first week, 1 Corinthians 1–5 in the second, 2 Corinthians 1–6 in the third, Galatians 1–4 in the fourth, Philippians 1–4 in the fifth, 1 Thessalonians in the sixth. Genesis is read selectively from Septuagesima to Lent 1, Exodus in the same way from Lent 1 to Lent 5, Jeremiah during Passiontide, Lamentations during the *Triduum Sacrum*, Revelation 1–8 from Easter 1 to Easter 3 and James from Easter 4 to Ascension Day. Lessons are again proper to the feast from Ascension to Trinity Sunday; and from Trinity to Advent a series of *historiae* is appointed, i.e. readings from Samuel, Wisdom, Job, Tobit, Judith, Maccabees and Ezekiel.

The whole gives an initial impression of a frustrated continuous reading of books of the Bible. Why, we say with Cranmer, are books begun and never finished? Predictably, the Old Testament lections are chosen to suit the season (following an ancient tradition) and those for feasts are frankly typological (e.g. an Old Testament dromedary is a *sine qua non* for the feast of the Epiphany). The closest attempt at *lectio continua* is the reading of St Paul in Epiphanytide (often frustrated by an early Easter) and of the *historiae* in Trinitytide. But the truth of the matter is that the lectionary for this breviary is dominated by the calendar. The main problem for the compilers was in the light of tradition to relate the table of fixed feasts (the Christmas/Epiphany cycle and the *Sanctorale*) to the table of moveable feasts. This is done in regular tables of great detail which, by reference to the Golden Number, the dominical letter and the bissextile variant, provide accurate guidance as to the precedence of one day over another. Sometimes, in some years, even the Sunday lapsed, and *lectio continua* suffered inordinately owing to the frequency of feasts and commemorations. Clearly, at Sarum, the mysteries of salvation are to be read in the cycle of feasts, and to these the witness of the Scriptures is integral, the whole constituting the round of prayer which sanctifies time and brings salvation to man, woman and child in medieval *Ecclesia Anglicana*. We have here, again, another rich book of doctrine and devotion which with antiphons and responsories and sermons from the Fathers is a profound guide to the corporate belief of the Church of that era.

In the light of this, we should now turn to the calendar.

The calendar

If we preserve the traditional division of the calendar into the *Temporale*[8] and the *Sanctorale*, then in a sense the *Temporale* speaks for itself as a locus of Christian corporate believing. Originating in the festival of Easter (with its weekly Sunday commemoration), now spread throughout the year, the events of our Lord's life and saving work from the mystery of his advent, through his nativity, baptism, passion, death and resurrection, ascension and sending of the Holy Spirit, commemorated in the calendar of the Church's year, proclaim the Christian understanding of salvation and involve Christian people year by year in the experience of this saving power. We could say: if you want to know what Christians believe, then see how they keep the feast.

The *Sanctorale* raises many questions. The Marian feasts on the one hand should perhaps be treated separately, since they are closely related to the mysteries of the life of Christ (e.g. the Purification of the Blessed Virgin Mary has recently been renamed, in the Roman Communion, the Presentation of Christ in the Temple). On the other hand, to continue our investigation into the choice of lections, both the 'proper' and the 'common' of saints (which includes not only the readings for the Eucharist but also the office lections, including the lives of the saints and the commentaries of the Fathers) are powerfully didactic and greatly beneficial in their frequent rehearsal. From the lections alone we know the virtues of the martyr, the wisdom of the doctor and confessor, the perseverance in prayer of the abbot, the constancy of virgins and widows, we know in other words who is a faithful and wise servant and who a virtuous woman. The festival is perhaps an expression on the part of the whole Church of how the Christian life is to be lived. We could say that this is how the Church talks about corporate living, based on corporate believing. But that is probably another subject.

Further considerations

We have so far confined our research to the Church's choice of lection and ordering of the calendar as a means of discerning the corporate belief of Christians. What of the liturgy as a whole?

To begin with the central prayer of the Eucharist. This, like the Scripture readings, is largely narrative. It is a prayer addressed to God by his people, telling what he has done in creation and redemption, supremely in the passion, resurrection and ascension of Christ, and asking that the benefits of Christ's redeeming work may be granted to all for whom they are entreated. Such prayers, originally recited extempore on the basis of what appears to have been a recommended thematic pattern, though varying from area to area, are remarkably long-lived and surprisingly consistent in their theology. Additions, adjustments and modifications there have certainly been – liturgy is always on the move – but one can say, for example, that the faith of the church of Edessa, knowing perhaps the earliest form of the liturgy of Addai and Mari, is substantially the same as that of nineteenth-century Christians in Kurdistan who were caught unawares by Anglican missionaries and persuaded to lend their copy of the Nestorian rite. Even the briefest acquaintance with the eucharistic prayer in history will confirm that the prayer is not a dogmatic statement of eucharistic theology, but an expression of the Christian's faith in God. In the course of the narrative, Christian conviction about creation, God in Trinity, the incarnation of the Word of God and his saving work, is unswervingly asserted. (The same is true of the liturgy of baptism, and is underpinned in the collects, with their carefully constructed endings, and in the doxologies following psalmody and canticle.) It is significant that variance between Christians in any central article of faith is frequently reflected in the sphere of eucharistic theology; and in the rejection of traditional rites and the construction of new liturgy, difficulties are most often encountered when there are differences among the compilers over central Christian doctrines (e.g. grace, the work of Christ, etc.). The eucharistic prayer is thus a sensitive area of Christian theological thinking and an important guide to the belief of those for whom it forms the centre of their act of worship.

Second, another way in which the liturgy becomes a medium for the expression of corporate believing is in the composition of non-scriptural texts for inclusion in the act of Christian worship. This phenomenon dates from a very early period. Though the psalter passed naturally into Christian

usage, it was not long before Christians gave expression to
their own faith and piety in 'hymns and spiritual songs' of
their own composition, and the rudiments of 'rhythmical
prayer'[9] may be discerned in the New Testament: these are
probably rightly called 'the sources and models of Christian
hymnography'.[10] The discernment of rhythm (one of the most
characteristic features of hymnody) enables us to trace the
same tendency in the writings of the early second century (e.g.
in the Epistle to Diognetus). Methodius of Olympus provides
evidence for a psalm with refrain, and from there we pass very
quickly to clear texts of the earliest known compositions (e.g.
'Hail, gladdening light').

The devil's claim to the best tunes, however, though
successfully challenged in late nineteenth-century England,
was an early inspiration for Christian hymnody. Gnostics and
Arians alike exploited the technique of popular and memorable
poetry (if such it can be called) to propagate their doctrines,
and orthodoxy promptly responded. Ephraim the Syrian,
author of the earliest known Syriac hymns, observes:

> In the resorts of Bardesanes
> There are songs and melodies
> For seeing that young people
> Loved sweet music,
> By the harmony of his songs
> He corrupted their morals.

It is recorded that, to counteract this 'poisoned sweetness',
Ephraim 'gathered the daughters of the Convent' and that he
then, 'like a spiritual harpist, arranged different kinds of songs
and taught them the variation of chant until the whole city was
gathered to him, and the party of the adversary put to shame'.
If Arius composed songs in the style of the local hostelry, then
Augustine will challenge the Donatists with a psalm having a
lusty refrain. Dogma and hymnody are immediately allied and
will remain so for many centuries to come, and not only in the
heat of controversy. Arian hymn singing at Constantinople in
the year of John Chrysostom's enthronement may have been
counteracted by orthodox hymns in procession under the
patronage of the Empress Eudoxia; Ambrose's congregation at
Milan may have been reassured in their siege not only by
antiphonal psalm singing but by the hymns composed by their
bishop (to the wonder of St Augustine); but the outcome is a
style of hymnody with a strong dogmatic content. Ambrose on

the creation, Venantius Fortunatus on the redemption, Prudentius on the incarnation, the communion of saints and the departed are but three among many witnesses to this tradition in the Western Church. In the East, it is of the greatest significance that the rebirth of hymnography (after a richly endowed beginning) follows the iconoclastic controversy. Those who burned the icons were answered by a burst of new hymns, not to speak of the flowering of *troparia* and antiphons. These last are again strongly dogmatic, not only, as in the West, pointing the meaning of psalms and Scripture readings (as do the responsories after the lections at the night office), but in themselves statements of Christian truth. The antiphons at Mattins for Trinity Sunday, for example, in the Roman Breviary are not extracts from the psalms nor paraphrases from Scripture but assertions of orthodoxy about faith in the Holy Trinity (e.g. *Te unum in substantia Trinitatem in personis confitemur*. And the Troparion from the Eastern liturgy, ascribed to the time of Justinian, runs: 'Let us who mystically represent the Cherubim and sing the thrice holy hymn [i.e. the Trisagion] to the quickening Trinity, lay by at this time all worldly cares, that we may receive the King of Glory, invisibly attended by the angelic orders.'

It is perhaps significant that in one contemporary hymnal, no less than seventeen translations from the Greek and 170 from the Latin are included. This may well be an important way in which the faith of antiquity is confirmed in a generation which at the very least gives its television vote to the broadcasting authorities on Sunday evenings or on Monday afternoons.

More, clearly, could be added about other features of the liturgy, of Christian iconography, of Christian liturgical drama and popular mystery plays, which would convey a similar understanding of the way in which the Christian story is proclaimed from generation to generation. We must look next at the Anglican tradition in particular, giving special consideration to the use of Scripture and then examining other aspects of the Anglican liturgical tradition.

Story and liturgy in classical Anglicanism

The liturgical reading of Scripture in the Prayer Book

The system of public worship set out in all Anglican prayer books from 1549 onwards enshrines three principles which have so far become second nature to Anglicans that they are rarely thought to be theologically significant, but which in fact find few close parallels within other Christian traditions until quite recent times, and formed the subject of violent controversy for the first 150 years of the Church of England's life after the Reformation. As we shall see, they are in some measure the result of accident rather than design; yet in their gradual assimilation into the structure of Anglican thought in the period of the Elizabethan settlement we can see important theological implications emerging. Incidentally this is a good illustration of the way in which the *lex orandi* often works in forming corporate belief: the influence of belief on liturgical practice is not a simple matter of cause and effect, but much more nearly a circular process.

The three principles referred to are:

1 A requirement that the whole of the Bible (with some concessive exceptions) shall be read publicly in the liturgy;

2 The lack of any requirement that the Scriptures read in the liturgy shall always, or even frequently, be expounded to the congregation;

3 A prohibition of reading anything other than the Scriptures liturgically in the public services of the Church, at any rate in the place assigned for 'the lessons', and the consequent 'cutting off' of non-scriptural lections and other post-biblical material.

One might sum up these principles as 'the Bible, the whole Bible and nothing but the Bible'.

The arguments in support of these principles adduced by Cranmer, as these appear in the Prayer Book and its Prefaces, do not at all suggest that he himself perceived them as forming a coherent system or as proceeding from a consistent theology of worship. The reading of the whole of Scripture is justified on the grounds of edification, no doubt with an eye to a laity who could not become familiar with Scripture at all unless they heard it read aloud in reasonably large quantities (thus in the

95

Preface to the 1549 book, now printed in our Book of Common Prayer as 'Concerning the Service of the Church'); and with the same object in mind it is directed that the reader shall read 'distinctly with an audible voice', 'so standing and turning himself, as he may best be heard of all such as are present'. But the lack of any requirement that Scripture shall always be expounded assumes that it is simply not practicable to direct otherwise: it is better to hear Scripture unexpounded than not to hear it at all, but one can hardly doubt that Cranmer would have preferred frequent exposition, had there been any chance of securing it. Again, the removal of much non-scriptural matter is justified on various grounds: the superstitious and false character of much that had been read in the medieval Church; the fact that in any case it got in the way of scriptural lections; the excessive lengthening of the service, and consequent loss of seriousness, that it frequently produced. But non-scriptural material 'agreeable to' the word of God is still permitted, only not (as it happens) in the form of lections. The concern for what is practical and will edify or instruct the congregation is apparent throughout.

In two ways, however, this overarching concern with edification seems to have been blurred even as early as Cranmer himself, and certainly in the architects of the settlement under Elizabeth I. Alongside the concern with *lectio continua* of the whole of Scripture in the daily office, which sometimes had the effect of producing lessons whose very length must have made them hardly more 'edifying' than parts of the medieval office, and of assigning material of striking inappropriateness to liturgical seasons in some years,[11] Cranmer's prayer books showed a curious conservatism in the choice of lections for the Holy Communion. The seemingly chaotic system of readings current in the late medieval Church was adopted with only quite minor changes. This would make it possible for later controversialists to argue that Anglican services were defective both (in the case of the office) because the scriptural readings were so long and hence unedifying, and (in the case of the Communion) because the lessons were in many cases so short and disjointed, and hence unedifying! Second, however, the extreme concern with continuous reading at the offices was modified as early as the Elizabethan Prayer Book by the provision of special Old Testament lessons for all Sundays and Holy Days (not just the few very special cases singled out by Cranmer), and this system has lasted until the present day. Furthermore these lessons, like the lessons at Communion, were chosen largely from the medieval service books, restoring the reading of Isaiah 1 on the first Sunday in Advent and of Genesis 1 on Septuagesima; and it is striking that this system does not produce a selection that we, at least, would be unlikely to regard as specially suitable for 'edification'. With these two features tending in a direction different from – in some respects opposed to – Cranmer's essential concerns in devising the prayer book services, the ground was prepared for an interpretation of these services and the principles exemplified in them, as forming a system with some internal coherence of a kind that was fairly certainly not in Cranmer's own mind. Such an interpretation is to be found in the replies formulated first by Whitgift, and then classically by Hooker, to the criticisms of the Prayer Book mounted by Cartwright and others, during and after the so-called Admonition Controversy in the reign of Elizabeth I.

These criticisms shifted the ground of opposition to the Cranmerian scheme very greatly from what it had been in Cranmer's own day. Instead of being confronted with Catholic opposition to lay bible-reading, and having to establish a system in which the laity could be enabled to hear the Scriptures at all, Hooker was fighting on the opposite flank, against opponents who were fully in agreement with him in wanting the laity to know the Bible, but opposed the Prayer Book on the narrower ground of *liturgical* reading, which they perceived (perhaps oddly to our minds) as 'popish'. Cranmer's contention, that the public reading of Scripture is *edifying*, was thrown back in the Church's teeth: how could the people be edified, it was asked, by vast chunks of uninterpreted Scripture read in liturgical tones? One hears the same argument today, and there is plainly some substance in it. But though both Whitgift and Hooker reiterated Cranmer's point, and argued that 'bare' reading could *be* a form of preaching, they necessarily shifted their ground in replying to this uncomfortable but (to Anglicans) familiar charge that half-hearted reform had only compounded the original abuse. They went beyond merely trying to show that the lections really were edifying 'lessons' – teaching – and began to take their stand on what could best be called a kerygmatic understanding of the lections, such as we have outlined. We have seen that this understanding underlay at least the eucharistic lections from early times, and that it constitutes the real difference between

97

an intentionally liturgical reading and a merely informative one. A contemporary example of the merely informative approach might be the practice, in some Reformed churches of the period, of reading Scripture before the service began, to acquaint the congregation with the passage which the preacher would later expound. The contrast is drawn explicitly, and with heavy sarcasm, by Hooker:

> Somewhat they are displeased in that we follow not the method of reading which in their judgement is most commendable, the method used in some foreign churches, where Scriptures are read *before* the time of divine service, and without either choice or stint appointed by any determinate order. Nevertheless, till such time as they shall vouchsafe us some just and sufficient reason to the contrary, we must by their patience, if not allowance, retain the ancient received custom which we now observe. For with us the reading of Scripture in the church is a part of our church liturgy, *a special portion of the service which we do to God*, and not an exercise to spend the time, when one doth wait for another's coming, till the assembly of them that shall *afterwards* worship be complete.[12]

Hooker here presents the lections not so much as teaching or instruction, but rather as part of the worship of God. And this is a very significant shift; for whereas the use of Scripture for teaching is, as Hooker's opponents wished it to be, essentially an activity directed from God to man through the medium of an accredited preacher (with all the dangers of clericalism, which Hooker never tired of pointing out), an understanding of the Scriptures read in the liturgy as 'worship' or 'proclamation' is not so simply described. 'Teaching' presupposes a prior ignorance in the hearers, but 'proclamation' is a more properly liturgical function, in which the congregation hears again and again, and reappropriates, a message or gospel that it already knows. Instead of a passive audience waiting for instruction, this assumes an actively worshipping community assenting to the words that express the common faith it shares with the biblical writers, as their words are read aloud by one who speaks as much *for* the congregation as *to* it. This might well be described as a *doxological* understanding of the reading of Scripture, in which the congregation is seen as reading with the reader, and using the scriptural text as a vehicle for presenting its praises to God.

98

Such a view is clearly present in Hooker's discussion of the psalms. He has been presented by his opponents by the claim that the psalms, read antiphonally, are not edifying to the congregation. He counters this claim *not* by trying to show that such reading is indeed some form of 'preaching' or 'instruction', but instead by pointing out that the psalms are being used for some quite other purpose than edification in any case: for the worship of God, and for the inculcation, by repeated use, of all the habits of heart and mind which the psalmists' words express. 'These interlocutory forms of speech what are they else, but most effectual partly testifications and partly inflammations of all piety?'[13] Of course it was never in doubt for Hooker that the Bible is addressed from God to man; but he was open to the possibility that, in its liturgical function, it can become a word spoken by man in the presence of God: a word by which the worshipping community sustains and transmits its faith as it confesses its identity with the people of God in the Scriptures. This is indeed 'edifying' in the sense that it builds up the Christian community, and helps to form the character of those who participate in it; but it is far more than merely *didactic*. By continually 'reciting' the story which the Scriptures tell, the Church at worship actually engages in dialogue with God – for, as we have seen, much dialogue even in human relationships takes the form of the recitation of significant narrative: people get to know each other by telling each other the story of their lives. So, in the system enshrined in the Prayer Book, it might be said that the Church reads over the Scriptures in order to tell God its 'story', to go over its formative years with him anew, to proclaim in his presence the salvation it has experienced. The accidents of the Elizabethan settlement throw up an approach to the Bible which sees it contextualized in liturgy, functioning as a focus for the Church's corporate belief not just by being an external norm of faith but by being itself a form of prayer, a text by which the worshipping community praises God. The reading of Scripture in church is far more than instruction in the faith, the 'lection' is more than a 'lesson'; it is both an announcement of Christian belief and an actualization of the mysteries of salvation. It seems right to claim that the establishment of the prayer book system in the sixteenth century preserved for Anglicans the insight into the 'sacramental' significance of the proclaimed word that Schmemann sees as characteristic of the Orthodox experience of liturgical reading.

Church music

The main emphasis of this section has, intentionally, fallen on liturgical reading of Scripture since it is there that the element of liturgical recital and 'story' may be most easily discerned. But it may also be seen clearly in an aspect of Anglican public worship which has appeared to many external observers to be one of its most distinctive strengths: the tradition of English church music. Its birth and early development are described as follows in a recent sermon by Mary Warnock, and it will be seen that her comments show a broad similarity of theme with what we have already said about other aspects of the liturgy:

> The revolution of the Anglican Church was as much musical as linguistic. The rough guide for the composers who were to set the new prayer book was *a note to every syllable*. Between the moment when alert composers realized what was going to happen and Pentecost 1549, when the services were due to be sung in English, there was an incredibly short length of time; but it was long enough for the birth of an entirely new style. And this style, gradually modified and becoming more relaxed, *is* the great style of the Anglican Church, of Byrd, Gibbons, and, later, Purcell and even of Handel. This tradition of church music is the result of a . . . flowering of imaginative genius, confronted by a particular challenge. The challenge was theological; and so the foundation of the tradition must be seen as essentially part of a religious, not just an artistic, renaissance. Centrally, and informing it all, was the idea of the Christian story, now to be rendered immediate and direct through the most purely imaginative of the arts, music. The consequence is that the music as much as the words is the bearer of meaning, is symbolic, as the words are. If this is doubted, let someone try to think of the *purely* musical impact of that greatest of all verse anthems, Gibbons' *This is the record of John*. No one could fully grasp the significance of such music without at least temporarily giving himself up to the meanings of the words.[14]

The Eucharist

Least promising of all aspects of Anglican worship from the point of view put forward in this chapter might seem to be the Eucharist. It is indeed arguable that the element of recital which we have seen to be clearly present in the public reading of Scripture within the prayer book system, and in the musical tradition that accompanies it, is largely lacking from our eucharistic prayer in the truncated form it had from 1552 until the recent revisions. It could even be said, with some justice, that this element has been *transferred* from the eucharistic action, now seen as a bare 'memorial' rather than as an actualization of the mysteries of salvation, to the lessons, and it may well be partly for this reason that the reading of lessons has continued in Anglicanism to bear a great weight of devotional and dramatic value.[15] But this is in fact only partially the case. While it is certainly true that the lessons have the story-like character we have described, the Eucharist actually lost less of its dramatic quality than might be supposed when the lengthy canon of 1549 was divided into three separate sections. The effect of administering communion immediately after the words of institution, and placing the prayer of oblation after all have communicated appears in theory to destroy the classical shape of the eucharistic prayer; but in practice it simply means that the communion is now included *within* that prayer, and this can serve actually to heighten the congregation's sense of taking part in the story which the Eucharist celebrates. It is true that this can lead, and has led, to an impression that the Eucharist is intended as a re-enactment or commemoration of the Last Supper, rather than as a celebration of the death and resurrection of Christ and a participation in the fruits of salvation. But it also conveys – and this in spite of the lack of congregational ritual or movement in the classic Anglican rite – a sense of being caught up into an action or drama: a sense that could be lacking in a liturgically more 'correct' rite in which the congregation simply waited passively while the priest spoke the consecrating formula. In 'drawing near',[16] in watching the manual actions performed in imitation of Christ's own acts at the Last Supper, in receiving the elements immediately after the words 'Take, eat . . .', and in hearing themselves offered to God in the prayer of oblation, the congregation at a prayer book Eucharist may well have had a greater sense of being incorporated into the retelling of the story of their salvation than they might have had as spectators at a medieval Mass.

Story and liturgy in Anglicanism from the seventeenth century to the present day

Since the age of Hooker the liturgy of the Church of England has developed and diversified enormously; but throughout its complicated history, and down to the present time of sweeping liturgical revision, the themes treated so far may still be discerned. The purpose of this section is not, of course, to attempt a complete survey of the development of the liturgy over the last 300 years, but to point to ways in which Anglican public worship has continued to be concerned with the recital and reappropriation of what we have called the Christian story – and especially to show that this is true in those parts of its structure which at first sight might appear to have some other purpose in view.

The divine office

One feature which is immediately striking to outside observers of Anglican worship is the continuing attachment to the divine office, whether in the form of cathedral Evensong or Sunday Mattins in the parish church, and a tendency on the part of many English laypeople to prefer the office to the Eucharist as the normal, week-by-week form of worship. Clerical reformers in every century have tried with more or less success to reverse this trend, but it is only very recently that communicating attendance at the Eucharist has become the usual form of weekly worship for a majority of Anglican worshippers; and a preference for Mattins and/or Evensong is still widely observable in many places. It is usual for theologians to be enthusiastic about the increasing tendency to accept the Eucharist as the normal Sunday service. But even if this is justified, it is important not to present the issue in such a way as to suggest that those who are committed to, say, sung Mattins are to be regarded merely as devotees of (on the one hand) a 'bare' preaching service or (on the other) a merely aesthetic exercise, whose purpose has nothing to do with that participation in, and appropriation of, the mysteries of salvation which is generally felt to characterize the Eucharist. This is a false contrast. On the contrary, once (in the last century) Mattins came to be regularly detached from the Litany and (Ante) Communion as a Sunday morning service in its own right, one could say that it acquired for many people a 'sacramental' character of its own. This was the vehicle by which the congregation was built up in its faith, and in moral allegiance to its God. In the singing of psalms and canticles and anthems, and (increasingly since the eighteenth century) hymns, the Christian mystery continued to be celebrated; and participation in such services, whether by singing in the choir or by reading the lessons, continues to be perceived by many laypeople as a form of liturgical ministry just as important as, perhaps even more important than, ministering in the sanctuary. In the light of the arguments of the previous section, it is perhaps not surprising that such a high status should be accorded to reading and singing; for whatever the historical origins of these elements of public worship, there can be no doubt that such means of recital of the Christian story are perceived by very many Anglicans to be themselves a form of prayer fully as important as eucharistic worship in the liturgical life of the Christian community. Any treatment of the *lex orandi* in Anglicanism must allow them their proper weight.

Popular observances

Second, we should not overlook the impact on the Christian consciousness of those enactments or representations of the Christian story that fall outside the regular and repeated round of Eucharist and office. Since the nineteenth century these have grown and flourished, and are for many people vital parts of the annual cycle of the Church's year. One might mention such activities as the performance by the church choir of the *Messiah*, the *St Matthew Passion*, or Stainer's *Crucifixion*; the Christmas carol service or Christingle, nowadays preceded in many churches by a service of Advent carols; the nativity play and passion play; some form of service or ceremony associated with the blessing of the crib and the unveiling of the Easter garden; the pageant which marks some milestone in the life of the local church; or the parish pilgrimage to some ancient and revered centre of Christian worship. It may be said that these are the points at which the *lex orandi* of the Christian community proper fades off into 'folk religion', and that we should be unwise to look for the Church's corporate belief in such ambiguous ground. Nevertheless, for most of those who take part in such occasions there is a definite desire, if not to 'confess' the Church's faith (an idea we have seen to be rather uncommon in Anglicanism in any case), then at least to stand in the Church's tradition, to be associated with the Christian

103

story and to assent to it as true and valuable, and as a context within which they would wish to make sense of their life. In such activities there is, indeed, a very evident exposure to the Christian story, and especially to the central and decisive elements in it; and it may be observed that members of a local community whose contact with Christianity is chiefly through such 'para-liturgical' activities, sometimes preserve a sense of Christian priorities, both in faith and morals, which can be of value to more 'committed' Christian congregations who can be carried away by temporary enthusiasms that, unchecked, might cut them off from the continuity of Christian tradition. 'Folk religion' is no guide to the essence of Christianity, but it can be a useful monitor against excessively exclusive or (perhaps especially) antinomian forms of Christianity. The sorts of activity we have mentioned have the strength of ensuring that those on the fringes of the Christian community are both kept in touch with, and in turn enabled to keep a watchful eye on, what the Christian faith is understood to be within the body of regular worshippers.

In certain other familiar, non-liturgical activities, elements of the Christian story are brought to mind rather less clearly and directly. The celebration of harvest, processions round the parish (on Good Friday or Rogation Sunday), even the visit of the bishop, may serve to bring the Church and its faith before people's awareness. A person who was exposed to no other activities of the Church but these would at least become aware of the Church as something more than an *ad hoc* association of likeminded people.

Activities such as those just discussed may 'tell the Christian story' with considerable power and effect. Because they happen relatively infrequently, they involve thought, preparation and even a measure of excitement in those who are directly participating in them; and since some of them require a good many participants, a large circle of parents, relatives and friends may become indirectly involved. Attention born out of sympathetic interest in the participants and performers may win for the Christian story a livelier, as well as a wider, reception than is often achieved through Eucharist and office: and for the participants themselves such activities may evoke new depths of interest, respect and understanding in their attitude to the Christian story.

The calendar and lectionary

Anglican revisions of the lectionary also show an underlying concern to ensure that the story continues to be duly told. At first sight Cranmer's insistence on *lectio continua* for the services of Morning and Evening Prayer would suggest that the thematic arrangement of Scripture readings in divine service was a principle he did not appreciate. The calendar was deemed to run with the civil year from January to December; Genesis was begun on 2 January and Matthew 1 on the same day; the Old Testament, with certain exceptions, was read once during the year and the New three times (with the exception of the Apocalypse). The eucharistic lectionary, however, remained virtually unchanged. The calendar was revised to reduce the number of feasts and commemorations, though the Tridentine reform of the *Sanctorale* a few years later was almost as drastic. It should be remembered, however, that the Sunday and Holy Day lections were revised in 1871, the entire lectionary in 1922, further proposals made in 1944, a lectionary authorized for experimental use in 1956, a revised lectionary in 1961, a new revision in 1971, and a further lectionary was approved by the General Synod in 1979. A new eucharistic lectionary was also authorized in 1971.

It is probably fair to say that the trend in Anglican revisions has been towards lessons appropriate to the season or feast. Notably in the recent revision of the eucharistic lectionary, care has been taken to include an Old Testament lesson and a gradual psalm, and to give each Sunday a theme which the selected readings characterize. So, for example, in the nine Sundays before Christmas, the Old Testament lesson is the controlling reading, and God's plan of salvation is set out, beginning with the creation and continuing through the Fall, the life of the 'Remnant', the covenant with Abraham, the promise to Moses, a slight hiccup for the traditional Advent 1 and 2 (the Advent hope, the Word of God) and ending with the forerunner and God's promise of redemption through the Blessed Virgin Mary on Advent 4. The Christmas and Epiphany cycle, so far as the feasts are concerned, required little adjustment as to theme. Septuagesima, Sexagesima and Quinquagesima become subtitles, and the sixth Sunday after Epiphany gives way to the ninth Sunday before Easter. For the period Christmas to Easter, each Sunday again has a theme related to the season and the Scriptures are appropriately chosen. Eastertide is devoted almost entirely to the theme of the risen life, Ascensiontide and Pentecost Sunday to the appropriate mysteries, and there is a careful attempt to schematize the remaining Sundays of the year after Pentecost in order to draw attention to essential truths of Christian belief and practice.

We instance this revised lectionary as an example of current Anglican consciousness of the need to link lection with belief. It is founded on traditional principles; its scheme may be original, but its purpose is both catechetical and confirmatory. Through the public reading of Scripture in the assembly there is both an announcement of Christian belief and an actualization of the mysteries of salvation. Is there after all so much difference between the Anglican waking up in a northern spring and going to church to hear the account of the appearance of the risen Christ to Mary in the Easter garden and the Mediterranean Christian waiting for the dawn an hour or so earlier to hear the same story in the Matthaean version? Do Anglicans with their complement of Morning Prayer, Eucharist and carol service feel less aware of the mystery of the Word made flesh than their Roman brethren with their lections for the three Masses of Christmas and that of the Sunday after Christmas? Surely, each, through the recital of the story enters more deeply into the mystery; and their common rehearsal of the sacraments of salvation points to their belief in a common redemption.

NOTES

1 A. Schmemann, *The World as Sacrament* (Darton, Longman & Todd 1966), pp. 37–8.
2 Hebrew for 'narrative': normally refers to the non-scriptural Jewish tradition of a non-prescriptive kind (as opposed to *halacha* – 'that by which one walks').
3 'Proclamation'.
4 *Episcopus eo typo quo tunc Dominus deductus est . . . omnis populus . . . infantes . . . pedibus itur . . . ramos tenentes . . . respondentes semper: Benedictus qui venit . . .*
5 *Spelunca, intra cancellos.*
6 The reading of books of the Bible in sequence.
7 The calendar of festivals of saints.
8 i.e. Sundays and moveable feasts.
9 Following Jean Leclerq, *DACL*, 'Hymne' sv.

10 ibid., loc. cit.

11 There were, for example, no special second lessons appointed for Holy Week in the Prayer Books of 1549 and 1552, and the date of Easter alone determined what was read. On Good Friday in 1550 worshippers at Matins will have heard Acts 1; in 1553, John 18, the first half of the Gospel that was to follow immediately at the communion; and in 1556, strangest of all, John 21, the account of the resurrection appearance at the lakeside, which was also the Matins lesson for Maundy Thursday in 1550. Indeed, Holy Week 1550 – the very first Holy Week after Cranmer's first book came into use – must have had an extraordinary effect on anyone who attended the full round of services, for after the resurrection narrative on Maundy Thursday and the Ascension on Good Friday, they were confronted on Easter Even with the story of the day of Pentecost (Acts 2). The worst anomalies were removed in the Prayer Book of 1559, though Maundy Thursday remained unprovided with proper second lessons for Evensong until 1871.

12 Richard Hooker, *Of the Laws of Ecclesiastical Polity,* v.xix.5.

13 ibid., v.xxxix.1.

14 Sermon preached before the University of Oxford, 9 March 1980.

15 See the next section, on the 'sacramentalizing' of the divine office.

16 In 1549, 'Draw near, and take this holy sacrament to your comfort', and the confession and absolution that follow, were the immediate prelude to communion, after the consecration was complete. In 1552 they were moved to their present place before the consecration, but the spiritualizing phrase 'with faith' was added only in 1661 – apparently from the Durham Book, which had in fact proposed that form of invitation which became the invitation to confession in Series 2 Communion ('draw near with a true heart, in full assurance of faith'). In the intervening years the interpretation of the formula 'draw near' became a subject of controversy, since it was now detached from its immediate connection with coming up to receive communion, and it was no longer clear whether it should be taken as prescribing physical movement (say, from nave to chancel) or not. See G. J. Cuming, *A History of Anglican Liturgy.* Macmillan 1969.

----- 5 -----

Where Shall Doctrine be Found?

Introduction

In a debate in the General Synod in November 1972, a lay member suggested that ordinary people in the Church of England needed to have some idea about 'what our doctrine is and where it can be found'.[1] Both parts of this question are harder to answer than might at first appear. Some will be disappointed that the first goes way beyond the brief of the present Commission. But, after the wide-ranging consideration of 'corporate believing' undertaken so far, we are now in a position to home in on the characteristically Anglican approach to doctrine, and to answer the second question: 'But where can our doctrine be found?' We will discover that what was said in the previous chapter about the typically Anglican setting of the Bible in the context of the total worshipping life of God's people applies equally well, *mutatis mutandis*, to doctrine. This leads us to divide the chapter into three sections, dealing respectively with the nature and characteristic role of declared, explicit doctrinal formulations; the typically Anglican characteristic of 'implicit' doctrine; and the typically English phenomenon of beliefs which are held by many on the fringes of the Church's life.

There is a danger in this approach which had better be faced at once. The respective titles of these three sections – Doctrine Declared, Implicit and Diffused – might be taken to imply that there are all sorts of things in the Church's life which are 'really' doctrine, or which have, as it were, a certain doctrinal cash value, and (moreover) that this is their real significance, as though everything from candles on altars (or flowers on tables) through to synodical debates only *matters* in so far as it implies, hints at, tacitly argues for, or merely assumes, points of doctrine which could in principle be stated in propositional form. Our whole book so far has been, in fact, arguing that this is not the case, and it is important that we should not, even by

108

implication, give the impression that in talking about explicitly stated doctrine we are reaching 'the real thing', the heart of the matter. If that had been our intention, we could equally well – perhaps more appropriately – have homed in on prayer, holiness, love or mission as the 'real thing' at the centre of 'corporate believing'.

We need, in fact, to distinguish between 'believing' and 'doctrine'. The former is a very wide term, the latter comparatively narrow. 'Doctrine' is not the be-all and end-all of 'believing', though we will suggest that it has a crucial and indispensable role within the larger entity. It is, in fact, a controlling factor – perhaps *the* controlling factor – within the total life of the Church, acting in relation to that total life like a combination of road signs, map, compass, dashboard warning lights and log book in relation to a car and its driver. The Church needs doctrine not because it is called to analyse God, and his ways with mankind, in a scientific or pigeonholing fashion, but because it is called to love God with the mind as well as with heart, soul and strength. Doctrine is the intellectual counterpart of prayer, holiness, love and mission, and cannot be ignored or played down without denying one highly important facet of our God-given, and God-shared, humanity. To embark upon the Christian way of life without regard for doctrine, and to attempt to examine corporate believing without showing the role of explicit doctrinal statements within that larger entity, is like setting out on a journey without a map or road signs, without a sense of direction, and in ignorance of the car's capabilities and roadworthiness. Thus, just as it is wrong to see doctrine as the 'real thing' to which everything else can in principle be reduced, the currency into which all else must be changed if its value is to be assessed, it is equally wrong to see non-doctrinal (or even anti-doctrinal) 'believing' as the 'real thing' and doctrine as a dangerous, perhaps divisive, luxury.

Doctrine declared

At this point we meet a familiar Anglican objection. It is often said (or, perhaps characteristically, implied) that Anglicans have no specific doctrine of their own. Bishop Hensley Henson once put the position thus: if a doctrine is true, the Church of

England believes it. We define things only when really necessary, and that often means that we define in practice, not theory. Thus, to take a small recent example, David Edwards' splendid little paperback *What Anglicans Believe*[2] states that 'the Anglican tradition preserves the essential beliefs which are held in common by all Christians'.[3] Moreover, the whole book is organized to express this point by expounding, not a 'specifically Anglican' viewpoint, but one which would be shared by a great number of Christians from many denominations, with only one chapter, mainly historical, on Anglicanism itself. In so far as Anglicanism has a distinctive position,[4] this appears to be not a matter of doctrine but rather the reverse, the 'belief in freedom' which allows 'any member of the Anglican Church . . . to disagree with his bishop or with any other teacher', and which encourages both laymen and priests 'to think for themselves . . . to seek truth and express it'.[5] Nor can it be denied that this, *de facto* at least, is the position of a great many contemporary Anglicans. Official doctrinal statements are, like the foundations of a house, thought of as important but seldom seen. It is characteristic of some contemporary Anglicanism to look with a sort of distaste on churches which, so to speak, seem to spend all their time digging away at their foundations and then shoring them up again.

At a more formal level, it is instructive to look back to the work of the Archbishops' Commission on Doctrine which, appointed in 1922, published its report in 1938. Its brief was wide ranging and eirenic: 'To consider the nature and grounds of Christian doctrine with a view to demonstrating the extent of existing agreement within the Church of England and with a view to investigating how far it is possible to remove or diminish existing differences.'[6] We will discuss this report later, in a different context. Here the point to be made is simply this: throughout the entire work, which occupies some 242 pages, there is almost no mention of specifically *Anglican* doctrinal positions, apart from a three-page note about the Articles (pp. 36–9, discussed below). Nor is this accidental. In the Introduction we read:[7] 'There is not, and the majority of us do not desire that there should be, a system of distinctively Anglican Theology. The Anglican Churches have received and hold the faith of Catholic Christendom, but they have exhibited a rich variety in methods both of approach and of interpretation. . .'

The report as a whole expounds a position consistent with this, attempting as it does to find common ground between the different emphases within that ecumenical-movement-in-miniature, the Church of England by law established.

There is, however, an oddity about this idea of having no specifically Anglican doctrine, of simply believing things if they happen to be true. It looks somewhat like Shaw's character who claimed that 'Right is right: and wrong is wrong: and if a man cannot distinguish them properly, he is either a fool or a rascal.'[8] If the play had been about our present topic, he might have written: 'Truth is truth: error is error: and if a man cannot distinguish them properly, he is either an unbeliever or a papist.' In other words, this position could be taken simply as a naive refusal to look objectively at one's own presuppositions and claims. In similar vein, C. S. Lewis once recalled pointing out to an elderly friend the fact that every race thought its own men the bravest, and its own women the fairest, in the world. Back came the reply: 'Yes, but in England it's true.'[9] Something of this tone can be heard in Bicknell's celebrated book on the Articles:[10]

> Our English Articles avoid the sweeping anathemas of the Council of Trent or the 'endless arguings and chidings' of contemporary confessions. They move on a higher level. If we compare them with other performances of the age, we must see in them an example of the special Providence that has watched over the Church of England.

This shows, of course, that if it really is the case that we believe ourselves to have no distinctive beliefs, this belief is itself sufficient to distinguish us from most others: and behind that superficial *reductio ad absurdum* there lies one clue at least to the peculiar nature of Anglicanism. But already the difficulty about declared doctrine within our Church of England has been exposed. Put crudely, the problem about Anglican doctrine, about answering the layman's question with which we began, is that you both can and can't 'go and look it up'. This statement is not just an indication that, today, some Anglicans think you can and some think you can't. It is an attempt to do justice to the (apparently) mainstream Anglican insight that doctrine – not just Anglican doctrine, any doctrine – must, if it is to be true to itself, be set in a wider context, that of the whole worshipping and witnessing life of the Church;

111

and must also recognize its own provisional and partial nature, its own need of restatement and rethinking.

Both of these last points were recognized clearly by the 1938 report, not least in a passage which anticipates many features of the present volume:[11]

> All Christians are bound to allow very high authority to doctrines which the Church has been generally united in teaching; for each believer has a limited range, and the basis of the Church's belief is far wider than that of his own can ever be. An individual Christian who rejects any part of that belief is guilty of presumption, unless he feels himself bound in conscience so to do and has substantial reasons for holding that what he rejects is not essential to the truth and value of Christianity . . . The Church should also recognize as necessary to the fullness of its own life the activity of those of its own members who carry forward the apprehension of truth by freely testing and criticizing its traditional doctrines.

Hence, not only Articles but also liturgy: and, not only doctrine and worship, but also Ordinal, Homilies and catechisms: not only thought, prayer, ministry and learning, but also canons (discipline and order), reports approved by Synod (the Church thinking on its feet) and official pronouncements by bishops, including the Lambeth Conference (the Church's official spokesmen clarifying and directing its mind and its course). All these form a sort of pyramid, with the Bible at the top, then the creeds, then the Articles, and the rest in a less definite order underneath – with, somewhere amongst them, important though unquantifiable, the writings of honoured saints and theologians, whether from our own church (Tyndale, Cranmer, Hooker, Andrewes, Herbert, Waterland, Simeon, Keble and many others) or elsewhere (the Fathers and, since their time, a great multitude which no man could number but to whom different sections of the Church of England have turned for help and guidance at various times). Not that Anglican doctrine, or even its corporate believing in general, is declared or even to be detected by putting all these into a pot and ladling out a dollop of the broth that results. A glance through the Articles, Evensong at King's and a day in the Synod will not necessarily give a completely fair picture. The 'doctrine' is still explicitly stated or pointed to in some places, principally the Articles, rather than others:[12] but within the 'doctrine' itself there are constant reminders that doctrine is not the whole story. And, as the Articles point to the liturgy, the liturgy itself insists that statements of belief are part of the air a Christian naturally breathes. At this point it is worth stating, without apology, that the Henrician and Elizabethan Reformations, to which Anglicanism owes so much (see page 115), began their outward life as statements of the statute book, and gradually became – with dialogue, and in co-operation with the episcopate – the believed faith of men's hearts.[13]

The fact that the Articles (and the liturgy) look back beyond themselves to the ancient creeds and ultimately, of course, to the Bible, indicates also that they are to be read in a geographical context wider than the borders of the Anglican Communion, and in a theological context wider than a list of things to be believed: for the creeds belong to others and not merely ourselves (and our use of them therefore makes an important ecumenical point, albeit implicitly), and the Bible is more (though not, I believe, less) than a set of (true) doctrinal propositions. Again, the references to the Homilies (Articles 11 and 35) remind us of another theological context, and of an historical one. In Elizabeth's reign, preaching licences were given but sparingly, even to presbyters (to say nothing of deacons), and the Homilies were what unlicensed clergy used instead. No doubt Trollope would have approved.[14] Theologically, this points to the belief, on the part of the framers of the Articles, that doctrine is not merely to be registered and assented to, but is to be preached, and preached in the belief that such preaching is a divinely appointed means of grace. The Articles belong in the context of the teaching ministry of the Church, and vice versa. They are more than a 'syllabus', but not less. So, too, they are more than an official boundary-marker, but not less. This point is also apparent in the existence of catechetical literature, though this has fallen out of favour in recent years, in contrast to developments in some other denominations.

It is thus characteristic of Anglicanism that it regards declared doctrine not in isolation, as it were in a test-tube under laboratory conditions, but rather as part – an essential part – of a wider whole, namely, the worshipping, teaching and witnessing ('confessing'?) life of the Church. When we say that 'Anglican doctrine', in a broad sense, is located in the Articles, the Prayer Book and the Ordinal, we are not lessening the importance of the first. Nor are we suggesting that the second and third are 'really' crypto-doctrinal statements. (There are, of course, some hymns which are just that.) Clearly liturgy embodies and thus reflects doctrine, and this is to be discussed in the second section of this chapter. But that is not its *point*. Its point is to be the vehicle for the true worship of God's people, and as such it sets the context for doctrine, by saying to the Church and the world that being a Christian, as far as Anglicans are concerned, is a total life of prayer and belief and learning and service. It is not what man does with his solitude, certainly not his intellectual solitude. It is, if anything, what God does with his family.

Within this understanding, there is a regular awareness within Anglicanism that 'doctrine' is more than the sum total of what Anglicans happen to believe at any given moment. Setting the Articles within the context of the Church's worship and teaching ministry indicates that the Church believes itself to have the responsibility for passing on truth (no doubt re-expressed and 'translated', in a way which will require fresh thought in every generation) from one generation to the next. This is made quite clear, for instance, in the Ordinal. Underlying that is the presupposition, which perhaps needs spelling out, that doctrine is not merely a boundary marker ('people who believe *this* sort of thing thereby define themselves as Anglican Christians, and people who don't thereby place themselves outside that grouping'), but has some organic connection – difficult though this is to state precisely – with the question of salvation itself. The setting of the creeds and Articles within the context of the life of the Church militant actually makes this point stronger, not weaker, than it would be if they were isolated. For it continually presents to the conscious and subconscious mind of the worshipper the fact that Christian living is not purely a thing of the moment, but is anchored in objective historical and theological truth. The Articles, like the creeds (to which they point back and to which, in some sense, they are supplementary), have the function both of establishing continuity from generation to generation, ensuring that Anglicanism remains Anglicanism and does not change into something else – at least, not without realizing what is happening – and of staking out the ground within which saving faith may grow and flourish.

The same is true, *a fortiori,* of the characteristically Anglican use of the creeds in the context of worship. While this is not unique, it may well be the case that the average worshipping Anglican actually says the creed(s) a good deal more than most other Christians. This, again, emphasizes *both* that explicit doctrine is not something outside the total life of the Church *and* that this total life is radically incomplete unless it has true doctrine at its heart. Articles and liturgy alike point back to the patristic formulations – and behind them, of course, to the Scriptures. In so doing they declare that the Church of England regards itself as part of a bigger whole, the one Church of Jesus Christ, and that therefore the Articles themselves have a relative, not an ultimate, status. They are not in themselves a new creed. Nor, of course, are they something quite other than a creed. They are, perhaps, best seen as the Church of England's confessional supplement to the Catholic creeds. We will return to this in a moment.

Creeds and Articles together thus form the heart of 'declared doctrine' in the Church of England. I say 'the heart' deliberately; they are not the whole, since one cannot simply divide up Anglican formularies and say which bits are 'doctrine' and which are not. For a start, creeds are *part of* liturgy. Nevertheless, they are the central, explicit part, the standard by which the rest is to be judged, the clear statements (in theory at least) by which the implicit doctrine found elsewhere is to be interpreted.[15] If we ask 'Where, within the Church of England, is doctrine to be found?' the answer is twofold. First, it is found precisely within the Church – not on its own, to be looked up and learnt in a vacuum, but as part of the life of God's people, to be believed and lived by. Second, it is found in a variety of written documents, which we have already listed. This life, and these writings, are incomplete in themselves, and must be seen together if we are to understand the nature and place of declared doctrine within Anglicanism.

The roots of a radical idea

How did the Church of England find itself in this position, when in so many other churches doctrine is more fully defined and more distinctly demarcated from other aspects of church life? The answer lies in the peculiar circumstance of sixteenth-century England. This itself raises an interesting general question. If the Anglican settlement, in all its phases from Henry's reign through to Elizabeth's, had an inescapably political context, how should we view the results? Ought we to be grateful for our own position, where we can discuss doctrine without feeling that the stability of the state, as well as of the Church, depends on the decisions we reach? Is our position 'normal', or is it in fact (in terms of the last 2000 years of world history) extremely abnormal? Does the sixteenth-century context relativize sixteenth-century theology (compare the occasional misguided attempts by Catholic apologists to suggest that the English Reformation was simply a political, then a theological, rationalization of Henry's desire for divorce), or does it mean that, like Johnson's man-about-to-be-hanged, the Reformers' minds were wonderfully concentrated? (Does this complexity itself perhaps arise because you cannot, ultimately, *force* men either to love God or to worship him in one way rather than another?) And does all this result in a difference between the position of the Church of England and that of other (non-established) Anglican Churches? What difference did seventeenth-century events make to the Settlement? Does our own situation within a modern parliamentary democracy under a constitutional monarchy lay upon us the obligation to think the whole thing out afresh? And this in turn raises the question: which is the more important? Is theology important *because* it can be either a glue to hold society together or a bomb to blow it apart? Or is a stable society (or perhaps a revolutionary one) important *because* it provides a good context for the Church to be itself in?

I suggest that the peculiarly Anglican shape of Church life and doctrine is not merely an *ad hoc* arrangement for the prevention of revolution – appealing though that motive clearly was in Elizabeth's reign. Its roots lie in the early years of the century, before the English Reformation was anything more than a set of disconnected discontentments – underground Luther-reading parties in the universities, lingering Lollard sympathies, renewed scholarly interests in original texts and sources as opposed to medieval systems, and, last but not least, a desire for moderate reform on the part of some clergy, particularly some of the bishops.[16] The crucial factor in all this seems to be that *the reforms that eventually came* owed their origins to men whose desire was precisely for a moderate and stabilizing change. In their different ways Colet, Erasmus, Thomas More and Thomas Cromwell were all working for a reformation without tears. And two men whose services in this task Cromwell had tried to enlist, but whom he and More eventually opposed, drew up plans for the future Church which (though their *direct* influence is difficult to quantify) bore more resemblance to the eventual settlement than did those of their opponents, clerical or lay.

During their continental exile, William Tyndale and John Frith worked towards two goals. First, reformation – a return to the Bible and the Fathers, to a personal religion of faith before works, to a non-magical view of the sacraments and a Pauline view of justification – must come, for the glory of God and the salvation of souls. Second, reformation must not produce a fissiparous Church, for the sake of the state and the welfare of its inhabitants – and also for the sake of the gospel, whose greatest theme is love. The effect on subsequent English church history of the Colloquy of Marburg (where, in 1529, Luther and Zwingli quarrelled irreparably on the nature of the Eucharist) is, perhaps, difficult to overestimate. Almost at once Tyndale and Frith were writing books and letters to urge the point which echoes through later Anglicanism that this sort of thing must not be allowed to happen in England. The Church is not to divide over secondary issues. Definition of doctrine is necessary to present the gospel to the current generation and to preserve it for future ones. But over-definition of doctrine produces tragic and unnecessary divisions between people who are really on the same side. Here is John Frith writing about the Eucharist: [17]

> First, we must all acknowledge that it is none article of our faith which can save us, neither which we are bound to believe under the pain of eternal damnation: for if I should believe that his very natural body, both flesh and blood, were materially in the bread and wine, that should not save me, seeing many believe that, and receive it to their damnation. For it is not his presence in the bread that can save me, but his presence in my heart through faith in his blood, which hath washed out my sins and pacified the Father's wrath towards me . . . *And so ought neither part to despise the other, for each seeketh the glory of God, and the true understanding of the Scripture.*

Frith expanded this position in his longer treatise on the Eucharist (1533), urging More that, since both accepted the basic doctrines of the creed, they should no longer quarrel over inessential matters. He stated the same position, with Johnsonian clarity, in his final section on the reason for his condemnation, written not long before he went to the stake (4

117

July 1533). He was not trying to save his skin. On the contrary, he and Tyndale came to terms early on with the likely outcome of their work. He was laying down a principle – not of 'toleration' as such, but of *adiaphora* (though he did not call it that), the doctrine that some matters are secondary; and it has often been recognized that this principle is close to the heart of the Anglican approach to doctrine.[18] His death was, of course, a pointer to the further problem: is the doctrine that some doctrines are secondary itself a primary or secondary doctrine? (Frith in his insistence on the point, and his judges in their condemnation of him, both clearly regarded it as primary.) And what about the decision as to *which* doctrines, if any, are secondary? These were questions which needed careful debate, for which the mood of the times allowed no opportunity. But the point of principle grasped by these Henrician reformers – who died long before their ideas bore fruit – has remained a characteristic of the Church of England ever since. It is therefore worth exploring it further.

It is not, of course, 'purely English'. We sometimes pride ourselves on the 'Anglican genius for compromise', perhaps on the analogy between our Church as a many-mansioned paradise and our state with its unwritten constitution.[19] But in fact the roots of the Henrician distinction of primary and secondary matters are found in those continental reformers whose ideas, unlike those of their English disciples, were never translated (except in England itself) into practical ecclesiology. Philip Melanchthon's *adiaphora* doctrine was regarded with suspicion by many fellow Lutherans. Martin Bucer (himself, of course, with a good claim to be considered an 'English reformer') anticipated Frith in teaching that love must act as a principle of theological debate, but no continental church was built on this foundation. Oecolampadius' patristic and semitic scholarship gave him a caution and a learned wisdom which was, sadly, ignored as Luther and Zwingli glared at each other over the table in Marburg, but which became the strongest influence not only on Frith but also on Cranmer. (The fact that Oecolampadius' treatises on the Eucharist remain untranslated goes some way towards explaining why so many Englishmen misunderstand Cranmer, placing him on the Procrustean bed of 'either Lutheranism or Zwinglianism'.)[20] Later, Peter Martyr made his pleas for a broadminded reformation not in his native Italy but from the regius chair at Oxford. The English Church, many of whose bishops and theologians had hoped for a moderate reformation, was able to profit from the experience of its continental cousins.

There can be little doubt that the direct heirs of this Henrician emphasis were, in Edward's reign, Cranmer and Ridley, and in Elizabeth's reign Parker, Jewel, Whitgift and Hooker. (There were, of course, other Henrician reformers, the ancestors of the Elizabethan Puritans, but their work is less substantial and influential than that of Tyndale and Frith.) The political pressures on Cranmer when he was Henry's archbishop joined forces with the theological influences listed above (his eucharistic doctrine matches Frith's closely) to produce a reformed Church of England which cannot be aligned with either Wittenberg, Zürich or Geneva. So, too, the returning exiles who led the Elizabethan church, and the great writers whose patient work gave it its intellectual foundation, had the same double motive as their Henrician predecessors, though now reinforced by the memory of the previous reign: the Church must be reformed, but the Church must not be split. Their continental experience had emphasized both points, and both, in historical perspective, are given depth by the events of the next century. We may note, for instance, the statement of the martyrologist John Foxe:[21]

> . . . friendly and prudent moderation in uttering of the truth, joined with a learned godliness . . . hath always so much prevailed in the Church of Christ, that without it, all other good gifts of knowledge, be they never so great, can not greatly profit, but oftentimes do very much hurt. But would to God, that all things in every place, were so free from all kinds of dissension, that there were no mention made among Christians of Zwinglians and Lutherans, when as neither Zwinglius, neither Luther died for us, but that we might be all one in Christ. Neither do I think that any more grievous thing could happen unto these worthy men, that their names so to be used to sects and factions, which so greatly withstood and strove against all factions. Neither do we here discourse which part came nearest unto the truth, neither so intermeddle myself by rash judgement that I will detract from either part, but I would to God I might join either part unto other.

We may smile at Foxe's protestation that neither Luther nor Zwingli were party men, but this only highlights his determination to present to his Elizabethan contemporaries an ideal of a Church both reformed and united. They did not seek a halfway house (certainly not, as is sometimes suggested, between Rome and Geneva; if anything it was between Rome and the Anabaptists), but rather a positive position of their own, leaning on the work of many continental reformers (among whom none of the 'big three', Luther, Calvin and Zwingli, were especially prominent), and thinking through an authentically English position, attempting to restate biblical and patristic theology in the light of the uniquely English situation and in continuity with earlier English insights.

It was in this historical and theological *milieu*, which we have, of course, greatly simplified here in order to highlight certain features, that the Thirty-nine Articles were born and developed, and given their distinctive place and role. The story of their origins is well known, and may be retold briefly with the help of an accompanying diagram. [22]

Attempts to state the official doctrine of the English Church begin with the Ten Articles which were published in 1536, two years after Henry's break with Rome. [23] These, issued with royal authority, represent the first stage of transition from the orthodox Roman position, a movement continued in the so-called 'Bishops' Book', *The Institution of a Christian Man*, published in 1537, which was prepared by a commission under the presidency of Cranmer. But progress towards Protestantism was not to be smooth. The *Six Articles* of 1539 reasserted a strong Catholic (albeit anti-papal) position, and the 'Bishops' Book' was superseded by the more reactionary 'King's Book' (1543), *The Necessary Doctrine and Erudition for any Christian Man*. [24]

At the same time, however, Cranmer had been engaged in a parallel project of a very different orientation. In 1538 a group of Lutheran theologians had come to England for consultations with a view to the drawing-up of a joint Confession of Faith. Though the Thirteen Articles which were drawn up by this group were not made public at the time, since the project itself fell through, they made a considerable contribution to subsequent formularies, and, since these Articles leant heavily in some respects on the Lutheran *Confession of Augsburg* (1530), an influence both of content and method, to be discussed below, can be traced from the earlier continental confessions to later English formularies. [25] The ground had thus been prepared for more definitely Protestant developments after Henry's death. By 1549 Cranmer was already using, as a test of orthodoxy, a draft set of Articles[26] which developed into the Forty-five submitted to the Privy Council in May 1552 and thence to the celebrated Forty-two Articles issued in the King's name on 19 June 1553.[27] These established a solidly Protestant position, over against Rome on the one hand and Anabaptism on the other.

Or, rather, it would have established such a position. Edward's death and Mary's accession in July of that year meant the reversal of this gradual change, and, of course, ultimately, the removal of the man who had worked for twenty years to bring about the English Reformation in doctrine as well as in the liturgy for which he is famous. But Cranmer's work was not lost. When Elizabeth appointed Matthew Parker to succeed Pole at Canterbury, it was on Cranmer's work that the new Archbishop built in drawing up his Eleven Articles of 1561, and then the Thirty-eight Articles of 1563[28] (both sets resting on the Statutes of Supremacy and Uniformity, themselves a compromise), which were duly approved by Elizabeth with minor alterations made, apparently, on her own initiative. It is important to note that these articles drew, in form and even in phraseology, not only on the 1553 Articles (themselves indirectly linked with the Augsburg Confession) but also on the Würtemberg Articles of 1552, which the Lutherans presented at the Council of Trent. Again, English writers borrowed continental material without being dominated by it.[29] Finally, the Articles underwent a further revision in 1571, bringing the number up to the eventual Thirty-nine by the restoration of one Article earlier omitted; and the requirement of clerical subscription to these articles passed on to the Statute Book, there to remain.[30] This requirement was further clarified, in 1583, by Archbishop Whitgift, whose Three Articles provided a precise form of subscription. The first Article deals with the royal supremacy; the second with the Book of Common Prayer, asserting it to contain 'nothing contrary to the word of God'. The third deals with the Articles, and includes the words '. . . and that he believeth all the Articles therein contained to be agreeable to the Word of God'. With minor alterations, these three Articles were incorporated into the Thirty-sixth Canon of 1604, which also provided the exact form of subscription:

> I, N. N., do willingly and *ex animo* subscribe to these three Articles above mentioned, and to all things that are contained in them.[31]

Henry 1509	
1530	Confession of Augsburg
1534	Henry's breach with Rome (Act of Supremacy)
1536	Ten Articles
1537	Bishops' Book
1538	Six Articles
1539	Consultation of Lutherans and English . . . Thirteen Articles
1543	King's Book
Edward 1547	
1549	Cranmer's early Articles — Würtemberg Confession
1552	Forty-five Articles submitted to Privy Council (May)
Mary 1553 (8 July)	
1553	Forty-two Articles, given royal mandate, 19 June
Elizabeth 1558	
1559	Acts of Supremacy and Uniformity
1561	'Declaration of Doctrine' prepared by returning exiles[32] — Eleven Articles (Parker)
1563	Thirty-eight Articles
1571	Thirty-nine Articles
1583	Details of Subscription (Whitgift)
James 1603	
1604	Subscription to Three Articles

The same set of canons also forbade public dissent from the Articles, so that the laity were forbidden to speak against them while the clergy were obliged to subscribe to them.

So much for the genesis of the Thirty-nine Articles, and the origins of the legal requirement of subscription to them. If we reduce this complicated little story to diagrammatic form, we will be in a position to observe in particular the links, and the contrasts, between the Articles and the formularies current in Lutheran circles at the time.

We are now in a position to look at one of the most vexed questions about declared doctrine in the Church of England. Are the Articles a 'confession', or even a 'creed'? If not, what are they? Recent Synod debates have made it clear that there is no generally accepted answer to this.[33] It all depends, of course, upon what you mean by a 'confession'. If we are thinking of such documents as the Westminster Confession (1646), the Articles stand out in contrast both by their location within the wider context of the Church's life and by their consequent role, which is very different from that of the continental, and Scottish, 'confessions', which in some sense are held actually to create and define the churches which 'confess' them. Moreover, they do not now have identical status throughout the Anglican Communion. In Central Africa and the West Indies, for instance, the Articles are not specifically mentioned in the formularies, and in some other provinces they have been revised or replaced.[34] Most important, they attempt to be exhaustive neither in scope (several important matters go unmentioned) nor in substance (no attempt is made to tie down precisely what is to be believed, or to state Christian doctrine in a complete or balanced way). The Articles rule out extreme options, leaving believers, clergy and theologians elbow room to work things out for themselves within the wide limits laid down. Though the Articles of 1571 are a good deal more detailed, and more permanent in intention, than those of 1533,[35] the general point holds true for both sets. The Thirty-nine Articles do not set out to define and delimit Anglican doctrine at every point or in every detail. They illustrate in themselves the openness of, as well as the necessity for, 'corporate believing'.

But when we consider the genesis of the Articles as described above, and inquire as to the motives and methods of their compilers, it appears too simplistic to say that they are *in no sense* a 'confession', or at least a 'confessional document'.

Cranmer, as we saw, drew indirectly on the Augsburg Confession, and Parker more directly on that of Würtemberg, both retaining the form of the German confessions even though some of the content, particularly in the area of the Eucharist, is closer to the doctrine held in Switzerland. If these two archbishops had in no sense thought they were drawing up an Anglican Confession, they appear to have been singularly incautious in their method of working. At most, we may say that the Articles appear to have a different role and function from their continental cousins. (It is perhaps misleading to attribute this, as is often done, to the lack of any single presiding genius in the nascent Church of England. It is precisely because Thomas Cranmer's genius lay in eirenic and discerning compilation, combination and lucid restatement of a wide range of theological viewpoints, not least patristic, that the Articles, not to mention the liturgy, are what they are – documents which put the worshipping and witnessing life of the Church above the theological schemes of any one brain.)[36]

Different though their role may be, the Articles have been generally regarded as *in some sense* a confession from that day to this. The Elizabethan writer Thomas Rogers can even refer to them as a 'creed',[37] in the sense that, though not replacing the Apostles' and Nicene Creeds (any more than the latter did the former), the Articles are designed as a supplement to the Catholic creeds, adding precision and detail at points of more recent controversy,[38] with the same aim of preserving order and of 'confessing' the true faith. Writers as diverse as Lancelot Andrewes, Burnet and Geoffrey Lampe[39] refer to them as a 'confession', and they were included in the *Harmony of the Confessions of Faith of the Orthodox and Reformed Churches*, published in 1581 at Geneva (though the later Reformation monument in that city gives Oliver Cromwell, rather than Thomas Cranmer, the credit of the English 'Reformation').

In particular, we should note that the Articles were drawn up with a view to the unity and harmony of the Church in England (by contrast, as we saw above, with some more precise, and hence more divisive, continental formularies). This both distinguishes the Articles from other confessions (by their brevity and latitude, by their distinction of primary and secondary material), and gives them a parallel function to the others – in that they are Articles of faith designed to facilitate the creation, and feed the life, of the sort of Church which their compilers wished to see. (This also sheds interesting light on modern questions about declared doctrine: see page 134.) The real distinction is thus not so much between the Articles and their continental near-equivalents in themselves, but between the varied intentions of those to whose lot it fell to guide the early life of the very different European churches of the Reformation.

We may conclude this section as follows. If by a 'confession' we mean a document in which the Church says to God, to the world, to itself and to the next generation, '*This* is where we stand, and what we stand for', then the Articles are indeed a confession. But there are two ways in which they differ from other 'confessions'. First, they are drawn up in such a way that these functions (doxological, declarative, disciplinary and didactic)[40] are seen to take place within the total life of a worshipping and witnessing ('confessing'?) sacramental Church. Second, the brevity and latitude of the Articles when compared with some continental formularies is itself a point of theological substance. It is saying, by implication, that there are several widely debated theological issues on which a loyal Anglican is not enjoined to take up a particular stance. It implicitly sets out categories of primary and secondary truths. In both of these ways we are led to the conclusion that the Articles are the peculiar Church of England confessional supplement to the Catholic creeds. This is the sense in which Henson was right: the doctrine peculiar to the Church of England is that there is no doctrine peculiar to the Church of England. The founding fathers of Anglicanism, with good reason, drew up the Anglican formularies in such a way as to reflect that theological position for which the major Henrician reformers and their successors had worked. The Church of England was to be reformed, but not fissiparous. Its doctrine was to be neither Roman nor Anabaptist, but was to embody Reformation insights while remaining true to the continuing heritage of the Bible and the Fathers. It is this intention which invites us to ask: how has the Church of England faced up to these questions since the sixteenth century?

On living with declared doctrine: four centuries of debate

The Articles did not stifle doctrinal debate in the Church of England. They merely gave it a focal point. From the first, the (so-called) 'Puritans' objected to what, in their view, was the insufficiently *reformed* character of the Articles (and, for that matter, of the Prayer Book and Ordinal), and this position was held by many until the rise of legal independency towards the end of the following century.[41] It was pressure along these lines that led to the 1688 Act of Toleration, which allowed nonconformist clergy to be licensed with only a formal assent to the Articles, allowing for exceptions to be made. This formality was removed altogether in 1779. At the same time, pressure was applied to do away with subscription for Anglican clergy too. This was the purport of the unsuccessful 'Comprehension Bill' of 1689, which would have substituted the following declaration for the existing one:

> I do approve of the doctrine and worship and government of the Church of England by law established, as containing all things necessary to salvation, and I promise, in the exercise of my ministry, to preach and practise according thereunto.[42]

Equally unsuccessful was Archdeacon Blackburne's fight for the removal of subscription in the 1770s.[43] The Church of England remained of the opinion that its clergy should be able to subscribe to its Articles, problematic though that in some cases was. The work of such apologists as Hooker and Jewel laid foundations for a long period in which the Elizabethan Settlement was regarded by most churchmen as the norm by which they were happy to abide.[44]

Alternative solutions to the problems of subscription in the seventeenth century were found by those who were happy to subscribe but who meant by 'subscription' something less than total, wholehearted and glad affirmation. Taking their starting-point from the clear intention of the compilers that the Articles should be a means of holding together a potentially fragile church and settlement, Laud and his followers,[45] and such subsequent writers as Bramhall, Stillingfleet and Bull, put forward the view that the Articles were *only* 'Articles of Peace' – i.e. not so much to be affirmed as not to be contradicted.[46] The same period also witnessed William Chillingworth's celebrated changes of mind, after his reconversion from Rome, which first prevented him from taking a living because of scruples about subscription, and then allowed him to proceed on a different, and looser, understanding of the required declaration. Two passages from his works indicate not only his own state of mind, but the sort of arguments about subscription current at the time. The first is from his letter to Dr Sheldon, written in September 1635:[47]

. . . For though I do verily believe the Church of England a true member of the Church; that she wants nothing necessary to salvation, and holds nothing repugnant to it; and had thought, that to think so had sufficiently qualified me for a subscription: yet now I plainly see, if I will not juggle with my conscience, and play with God Almighty, I must forbear.

In other words, Chillingworth at this stage felt that anything short of total *ex animo* agreement was dishonest. But, by 1637, these scruples had been overcome:[48]

For the Church of England, I am persuaded that the constant doctrine of it is so pure and orthodox, that whosoever believes it, and lives according to it, undoubtedly he shall be saved; and that there is no error in it which may necessitate or warrant any man to disturb the peace, or renounce the communion of it. This in my opinion is all intended by subscription; and thus much if you conceive me not ready to subscribe, your charity I assure you is much mistaken.

Chillingworth was no doubt not untypical of many during this period whose consciences wavered on the matter. At the same time, however, there were some who, by the end of the seventeenth century, took their subscription in such a loose sense that they were able to hold blatantly Arian views, justifying their stance by declaring that the Articles did not have to be understood in the sense originally intended by the compilers, but could be taken in any sense which the subscriber could square with (his understanding of) Scripture. Against this challenge Daniel Waterland, who had already debated the subject as part of his examination for the BD degree at Cambridge in 1714,[49] wrote his pamphlet *The Case of Arian-Subscription Considered: and the Several Pleas and Excuses for it particularly Examined and Confuted,* which went through two editions in 1721. Waterland was at once attacked by A. A. Sykes, and wrote a further pamphlet to refute the objections and restate the original position.[50] Waterland argued (pp. 11ff.) that the sense intended by the 'Compilers and Imposers' was all-important, and suggested (as has been done more recently)[51] that dangerous results would follow if the casuistry of the Arian subscribers were to be employed in, say, the legal profession.[52] He summed up his case in several propositions, of which the first three are especially striking:[53]

1 The Church of England requires Subscription not to Words but Things: to Propositions contained in her Publick-Forms.

2 Subscribers are obliged not to Silence or Peace only, but to a serious Belief of what they subscribe to.

3 Subscribers must believe it true in that particular sense which the Church intended . . .

In his book on the Declaration of Assent, Bishop Gibson comments favourably on the fact that Waterland's case was won without recourse to legal action. The appeal to conscience which he put forward was sufficient of itself – as Gibson no doubt hoped his would be, at least in his own diocese.[54] But consciences continued to be flexible. Dr Johnson remarked that the subscription to the Articles required by Oxford and Cambridge meant simply that subscribers would 'adhere to the Church of England'.[55] Later the question of what sense the Articles could bear was raised again, though in a form very different from that attacked by Waterland in the Tract 90 controversy. In the latter work,[56] Newman argued that the 'Catholic' sense of the Articles, though not that intended by the authors, was an admirable interpretation of their words. To the obvious objection that 'it is an evasion of their meaning to give them any other than a Protestant drift', Newman replied *(inter alia)* that

> in the first place, it is a *duty* which we owe both to the Catholic Church and to our own, to take our reformed confessions in the most Catholic sense they will admit; we have no duties towards their framers . . . [the Declarations] enjoining the 'literal and grammatical sense', relieves us from the necessity of making the known opinions of their framers, a comment upon their text; and its forbidding any person to 'affix any *new* sense to any Article', was promulgated at a time when the leading men of our Church were especially noted for those Catholic views which have here been advocated.[57]

This very selective slice of English church history has made it clear that there have been, broadly, three approaches to the doctrine which has been officially declared to be ours since 1571. First, there have been those who, like Waterland, insisted on the necessity both of taking the Articles in the sense intended by the compilers, and of subscribing them *ex animo*. Second, there have been those, like the Arians of Waterland's day and the author of Tract 90, who maintained a firm subscription but did so in relation to their idiosyncratic understandings of the Articles. Third, there have been those who recognized the originally intended meaning, but who regarded subscription as something less than full *ex animo* assent to every last detail. Such were Chillingworth, Johnson and others. And it was the third view which eventually prevailed, causing a succession of changes in the formula of subscription between 1865 and the present day. It is this sequence of events which we must now briefly describe.

Pressure for change in the form of subscription came to a head in the early 1860s, not least because of the fear that over-scrupulousness was holding back worthy ordination candidates.[58] A. C. Tait, then Bishop of London, backed proposals for reform despite warnings of possible dangers, and the Royal Commission appointed to look into the matter successfully recommended that the relevant canon (no. 36) should be revised, thus, incidentally, simplifying the complex procedure of subscription necessitated since 1604.[59] The resulting formula of subscription reads as follows:

> I, A. B., do solemnly make the following declaration: I assent to the Thirty-nine Articles of Religion, and to the Book of Common Prayer and of the ordering of bishops, priests and deacons. I believe the doctrine of the Church of England, as therein set forth, to be agreeable to the Word of God; and in public prayer and administration of the sacraments I will use the form in the said book provided, and none other, except so far as shall be ordered by lawful authority.[60]

This form of words has been interpreted and commented on in various ways. It is beyond question that the *effect* of the change over the following century was to enable many who could not have subscribed to the Articles in detail to give the required 'assent'. This is expressed by Bicknell when he says:

> We are asked to affirm today, not that the Articles are all agreeable to the Word of God,[61] but that the doctrine of the Church of England as set forth in the Articles is agreeable to the Word of God. That is, we are not called to assent to every phrase or detail of the Articles but only to their

129

general sense. This alteration was made of set purpose to afford relief to scrupulous consciences.[62]

But the idea of a 'general sense', and the corresponding notion of 'general assent', are decidedly unclear. The 1938 report of the Doctrine Commission understood the word 'assent' as signifying 'general acceptance', but 'without implying detailed assent to every phrase or proposition thus employed' (i.e. in formularies and liturgy).[63] However, a good case can be made out for saying that the Royal Commission whose work resulted in the 1865 Act, and the Parliament which passed it, did not intend a difference of *substance* from the older forms of subscription;[64] and Bicknell's distinction quoted above, between 'the Articles' and 'the doctrine of the Church of England as set forth in the Articles', looks shaky on closer examination.[65] Thus, though the idea of 'general assent' became an influential one, allowing many to 'assent' who formerly might not have done so, this may have been the result of a misunderstanding. The 1968 report, *Subscription and Assent*, is quite clear on the matter (p. 12):

> Some people appear to have thought that a wider meaning of 'assent' was being legitimized, though it was clearly pointed out at the time that the proposed modifications would not in fact alter the meaning of the declaration. The Act of 1865 retained the word 'assent', and it is this, rather than any intentions expressed by individuals in the debates, which has legal force. *Thus in law the situation remains* [i.e. in 1968] *essentially what it was.* (My italics.)

The same report, however, went on to argue for a new form of the Declaration of Assent. This argument was based on two presuppositions. First, many have long felt that the demand for subscription 'tends to tyrannize the conscience in a way that destroys intellectual integrity'. Second, the equation of the Bible with the word of God (to which latter, of course, the Articles are declared 'agreeable' by the canon and the Declaration), and the assumption of traditional Augustinian categories, are both felt to be at least questionable.[66] In the light of this, the report asked, and answered, two questions. First, do the present forms of subscription and assent make adequately clear what theological affirmation should characterize the commitment required by the Church today from its accredited ministers? Second, if they do not, can any

· change be made in the present arrangements which might give more reality and significance to the act of subscription than many can find in it at present? In the light of the wide varieties of 'Attitudes to the Articles and Varieties of Assent' (pp. 29–37), the Commission considered various courses of action open to the Church – to abolish subscription altogether, to revise the Articles either lightly or intensively, or to revise the formula of subscription and assent (pp. 38–45). In the end, they proposed a new departure: a brief form of assent, preceded by a preface 'which could spell out the context within which the formula was to be understood and given its meaning and implications'.[67] Interestingly (in the light of the last decade of Anglican theology) the Commission resisted pressure to reduce the number of occasions when the Declaration should be made, on the grounds that 'it seems to us important that doctrinal trust should be fostered between clergy and laity'.[68] They deliberately devised a form of assent 'which can be made with a good conscience',[69] though, since they did not specify whose conscience was being referred to, it is not clear that this proviso has any real force (what, for instance, about an Arian or a Baptist who wishes to make the Declaration?). The recommended Preface and Form of Assent were as follows:[70]

> The Church of England is part of the Church of God, having faith in God the Father, who through Jesus Christ our only Lord and Saviour calls us into the fellowship of the Holy Spirit. This faith, uniquely shown forth in the holy Scriptures, and proclaimed in the catholic creeds, she shares with other Christians throughout the world. She has been led by the Holy Spirit to bear a witness of her own to Christian truth in her historic formularies – the Thirty-nine Articles of Religion, and the Book of Common Prayer, and the Ordering of Bishops, Priests and Deacons. Now, as before, she has a responsibility to maintain this witness through her preaching and worship, the writings of her scholars and teachers, the lives of her saints and confessors, and the utterances of her councils.
>
> In the profession you are about to make, you will affirm your loyalty to this inheritance of faith as your inspiration and direction, under God, for bringing to light the truth of Christ and making him known to this generation.
>
> (Form of Assent)
> I, A. B., profess my firm and sincere belief in the faith set

131

forth in the Scriptures and in the catholic creeds, and my allegiance to the doctrine of the Church of England.

In the time between the publication of the report and the Church Assembly debate on it, an ambiguity was noted in the preface.[71] To remove this, the sentences beginning 'Now, as before, . . .' were amended to read:

> . . . through her preaching and worship, the writings of her scholars and teachers, the lives of her saints and confessors, and the utterances of her councils, she has sought, through her history, to further this witness to Christian truth. This responsibility remains.[72]
>
> You will, therefore, in the profession you are about to make . . . etc.

This report was generally welcomed by the Church Assembly, though several speakers made it clear that their reason for approving of it was their serious dissatisfaction with the Articles both in general and particular, and their feeling that, by requiring assent not to the Articles explicitly but to Christian and Anglican doctrine in general, many who would be forced otherwise to strain their consciences and appear casual and insincere at solemn moments would find welcome relief.[73] One speaker went so far as to regret the new Canon A2, which now officially declares that the Articles 'are agreeable to the Word of God, and may be assented unto with a good conscience by all members of the Church of England'. At the same time, the report was warmly welcomed by Evangelicals who felt more at home with the Articles and hoped that this would mean a less flippant approach to them.[74] The Bishop of Durham concluded his summing-up with a paragraph that could have been taken from the discussions of our present Commission:

> We are anxious that [the Articles] should be set in their full context along with other elements in the Anglican tradition, and in the act of subscription we should be declaring our loyalty, and allegiance, to that community which was structured by these several elements of authority to which assent was then asked. I hope in discussing the matter further we will have as comprehensive a view as the Church of England itself, and see emerging from this kind of discussion a new coherence, and reasonableness, and a new concept of authority.

Having been agreed to in principle by the Church Assembly, the proposals were then incorporated into a 'draft canon' (presented to the General Synod as GS 116), to which was appended an explanatory memorandum summarizing the theological and legal arguments and proceedings. The draft canon was then amended by the Revision Committee, which omitted entirely the previously amended sentence of the preface, and altered the preface's concluding sentence, and the Declaration of Assent, as follows:[75]

DRAFT CANON *(based on 1968 report)*	FINAL VERSION *(submitted for Royal assent, February 1975)*
You will, therefore, in the profession you are about to make, affirm your loyalty to this inheritance of faith, as your inspiration and direction under God for bringing to light the truth of Christ and making him known to this generation.	In the declaration you are about to make will you affirm your loyalty to this inheritance of faith as your inspiration and guidance under God in bringing the grace and truth of Christ to this generation and making him known to those in your care?
I, A. B., profess my firm and sincere belief in the faith set forth in the Scriptures and in the catholic creeds, and my allegiance to the doctrine of the Church of England . . . etc.	I, A. B., do so affirm, and accordingly declare my belief in the faith which is revealed in the Holy Scriptures and set forth in the catholic creeds and to which the historic formularies of the Church of England bear witness . . . etc.

The purpose of this final revision is clear both from the Synod debate which preceded it and from the changes in the wording. The phrase 'the doctrine of the Church of England' is not to be prized apart from 'the historic formularies' (which have already been enumerated in the preface). It is, of course, possible to drive a wedge, similar to the one Bicknell tried to drive in the 1865 Declaration, between the faith 'witnessed' in these various documents and the actual statements of the documents themselves. This is helpful in reminding us that all our formulations are approximations to the truth and not the truth itself, and in allowing for the fact that words and phrases change their meanings and that, to borrow Waterland's distinction, assent is given to things, not words. At the same time, the distinction can of course be exploited by treating the Articles and other formularies as the sort of witness whose

133

testimony must be taken with a large pinch of salt. But the natural sense and meaning of the now canonical Preface and Declaration is still that the Articles, together with the Book of Common Prayer and the Ordinal, remain as the standard of declared doctrine in the modern Church of England. If this causes problems, they are problems that the Church has declared that she intends to live with.

On living with declared doctrine: current questions and clarifications

We do not now theologize by Article, and the loss of this particular theological idiom does not fill us all with equal regret. Some may regard this fact as a theological impoverishment, even perhaps as evidence of a lack of theological seriousness. The point is that we are not at home in this field. But a genuinely corporate attempt to work out an Anglican dogmatic or systematic theology remains an urgent need, and might well prove a starting-point for the wider task of constructing an ecumenical dogmatic for which Christendom is still waiting.

So wrote H. E. W. Turner,[76] shrewdly summarizing the current problem of declared doctrine in the Church of England – a problem which remains current even despite the new canon. In the same volume, the late Professor Geoffrey Lampe commended the same task of attempting to state the common mind of the Church in an ecumenical context, aiming ultimately at 'a new confession . . . more broadly based than the Articles'.[77] Whether or not we agree with his further proposal that this confession should function as a test neither for membership nor for office in the Church, since fellowship 'must be based on a common devotion rather than on any standard of orthodoxy', the vision of long-term doctrinal study and debate, leading to a clarification of the Church's corporate believing, and to possible ecumenical advances, is a fine one. The strange thing is that an attempt has already been made, this century, to state the common mind of the Church of England in an eirenic and positive way: and yet the attempt – the 1938 report of the Doctrine Commission, which set dauntingly high standards for future commissions – is scarcely mentioned in recent official statements of Anglican theology. It is worth looking briefly at the aims and scope of the Commission's work, and learning one or two lessons from it.

Perhaps the most interesting feature of its work, which

lasted from 1922 to 1937, is the surprising parallel between its aims and those of the compilers of the Articles. Both went to work at times of different theological debate which threatened to tear the Church apart, against a background of political and social upheaval. Both saw their task as being so to state the explicit doctrine of the English Church as to provide clarification of points whose lengthy dispute had been damaging to the Church's life, and emphasis of points which were of such central importance that their denial could not be sanctioned as carrying the Church's authority.[78] That being so, it is a little surprising that the 1938 report itself does not, apparently, notice the parallels, and, more surprising, that later discussions of declared doctrine in Anglicanism have not pointed them out. In effect, what the 1922–37 Commission was doing was going back behind the Articles to take a long run at the same problems, attempting the same task for a new day. In his Introduction (p. 8), Archbishop Temple notes the lack of prominence given to the Articles, and, having explained this as resulting from their comparatively slight *de facto* influence in the Church (this would, of course, be even more so today), comments:[79]

> The Church of England is a living community, moving, as we trust, under the guidance of the Holy Spirit. We have, therefore, not supposed that it could be the function of a commission, appointed as we were, only to see what bearing the Articles or even the Prayer Book might have on the questions that chiefly divide Anglicans, but rather that we were called upon to handle these questions as best we could in the light of reason, of modern knowledge, and of that universal Christian tradition to which our Reformers themselves appealed.

Within the report itself, the note about Anglican formularies consists of three interesting sentences on the status of the formularies and the task of creative theology within the Church, pointing forward to some of our own discussions:[80]

> Anglican formularies represent the doctrinal, ecclesiastical and historical position of Anglicanism in relation to the rest of Western Christendom in the sixteenth century, and the position of the Church of England in relation to other Christian bodies is still defined by the retention of those formularies.

135

These formularies should not be held to prejudge questions which have arisen since their formulation or problems which have been modified by fresh knowledge or fresh conceptions.

Nevertheless, if an Anglican theologian thinks a particular formulary not wholly adequate, he has a special obligation to preserve whatever truth that formulary was trying to secure, and to see to it that any statement he puts forward as more adequate does in fact secure this.

Similar though the general aims of the sixteenth-century Articles and the twentieth-century report may have been in other ways, Archbishop Davidson made it quite clear, when the Commission was set up, that their work should not aim in any way at replacing the Articles. Bishop Bell, summarizing the moves that led to the Commission's appointment, highlighted 'a desire for something fresh in the way of exercising authority in matters of faith', which could be realized through a carefully pondered book:

When the book appeared, the bishops might, if they found themselves able, make some kind of pronouncement to the effect that the doctrine therein contained was, in their view, generally agreeable to the word of God and expressive of the general mind of the Church of England, but must not be taken as binding individuals. This body of doctrine would then (it was suggested) stand as a general norm of Anglican teaching, with a general episcopal approval. Appeal could be made to it by all clergy who desired, while it would also serve to check and test the teaching of those clergy who were so fond of individual initiative that they were apt to claim the Church's sanction for what were in fact their private and quite unauthorized views. No one would be silenced or made liable to heresy hunts, but no one would be able to claim the authority of the Church of England for what was opposed and contradictory to this statement of doctrine thus generally agreed and approved.[81]

Davidson came down firmly against the idea of a commission producing a book to be in any way an 'expression of the Church's official teaching',[82] and the commission's first chairman, agreeing that such a book was not contemplated, wrote that 'it is for the bishops to consider how far further action might be desirable in regard to any agreed conclusions which such a commission might reach'.[83] This suggestion was written into the commission's terms of reference,[84] but (so far as I can tell) no such subsequent action was taken.

Indeed, it is hard to see precisely what sort of action could have been taken that would have been any more than hollow words. The advantage of brief Articles is that it is possible to see at least what *assent* to them might mean. It would be extremely difficult to command, or even to commend, assent to a sophisticated theological book of over 200 pages. It may well be, as Archbishop Davidson suggested at various times, that the proper way forward in such controversies is for the Church's best theologians to write books that would persuade men of the truth, rather than for its bishops virtually to add to the formularies by signing a statement compelling assent.[85] We have noted already the satisfactory way in which Waterland's arguments about Arian subscription won the day by a reasoned appeal to conscience rather than by a heavy-handed and unpleasant legal process. There can be little doubt that the Church should hope and pray that its doctrine may be declared, and defended, in the former way rather than the latter whenever possible. But at the same time the 1938 report itself stresses that authorized teachers of the Church must be subject in certain ways to doctrinal standards:

> The Church has a right to satisfy itself that those who teach in its name adequately represent and express its mind. No individual can claim to receive the teacher's commission as a right, and the commission itself involves the obligation not to teach, as the doctrine of the Church, doctrine which is not in accordance with the Church's mind. If any authorized teacher puts forward personal opinions which diverge (within the limits indicated above [i.e. under the rubric of 'general assent', etc.]) from the traditional teaching of the Church, he should be careful to distinguish between such opinions and the normal teaching which he gives in the Church's name; and so far as possible such divergences should be so put forward as to avoid offending consciences. In respect of the exercise of discipline within such limits as the above resolutions recognize, great regard should be paid to the need for securing a free consensus, as distinct from an enforced uniformity.[86]

However we are to interpret the final sentence, the preceding ones make it clear that 'the Church's mind' needs to be something which can in principle be ascertained reasonably easily. When we ask how this is to be done, something like the Articles – in the context, to be sure, of Scripture, creeds and liturgy – is still the only resource that can credibly be offered. If today we do not theologize by Article, that may be an indication that we do not, after all, conceive of the place of declared doctrine in the same way as our forefathers, not only of the sixteenth century, but also of more recent times.

It is a false economy to suggest, as many have done when faced with this *impasse,* that the Church would be better off without declared doctrine at all. A more relaxed family, perhaps, more easygoing, certainly, but not nearly so much like a church. As we said earlier, declared doctrine is part of the Church's struggle to *be* the Church, to be holy in its thinking as well as in its living, not least because it recognizes that those two are in fact ultimately inseparable, that if we conceive of God in ways that are fundamentally wrong-headed, we will end up attempting to serve him in a manner which in fact dishonours him. God is not honoured when the Church fails to appropriate and enjoy the great truths that form its doctrinal heritage, in need of constant rethinking though those truths may be. The Church is engaged in a battle, and its formularies are its weapons, its plans of attack, its iron rations, laid up by former generations. Old weapons may need polishing, or even replacing. Iron rations may taste a bit musty when dug out of a cellar at sudden need. But to throw them away is sheer folly, as well as apparent disobedience and disloyalty. The Church has always believed that, in some sense and in some ways, it has been entrusted with truths to be passed on to subsequent generations. If it is true that 'God has still more light to break out of his holy word' (and why else do we have theologians at all?), it is wise that doctrine should not be *too* tightly defined. But if it is also true that God has already, in the past, allowed 'more light' to break out, a failure to be illuminated by, and in turn to reflect, that light within the living context of the Church, under the guidance of the Spirit, is to risk throwing some of God's good gifts on to the rubbish-heap.

A subsidiary, but very important, argument for the continued existence of declared doctrine in the Church is the urgent quest for true visible unity among professing Christians. It has been well said that 'without creeds or confessions, [visible unity] could only be held to lie in some secondary matter such as a certain form of church polity. But this would provide a unity essentially sectarian. Genuine catholicity requires unity of faith, and for this unity of government is no substitute.'[87]

In particular, declared doctrine must be allowed to function, as the 1938 report clearly stated, as a check on those who wish to teach things which the Church as a whole would disagree with. This matter will be dealt with again in the closing chapter of the present report. But for our present purpose we must note that this has certain implications for the nature of declared doctrine. To the extent that unrevised, or unsupplemented, Articles are a blunt instrument when it comes to functioning in this way, a good case can be made out for their revision. Otherwise – and this is very important in the light of the historical background surveyed above – they are not able to perform for the twentieth century the task for which they were designed in the sixteenth. They were not, after all, drawn up as an archaic indication of the Anglican ethos. To resist revision or supplementation on the grounds that that is what they are and should remain is in fact to suggest that the Anglican ethos is something different from what it was for two or three centuries at least. It is to suggest that, for Anglicans, *all* doctrines are *adiaphora*, and that the Church can, in the last analysis, get on just as well without them. But one only has to look at the noble witness – undertaken largely for *doctrinal* reasons – of the 'confessing church' in Hitler's Germany to see the two alternatives starkly posed. A doctrinal vacuum will quickly be filled by ideas from other sources. The battle for doctrine is not merely about truth in the abstract.

That is why, today, the question is often pressed both by members of the Church of England and by outsiders (Christian and non-Christian) looking in: are there *any* effective controls today over what ordained and licensed teachers of the Church may say and write? The answer to this question is an essential part of the *meaning* of 'declared doctrine', since if that doctrine is not adhered to in some recognizable fashion, the word 'declared' has become meaningless. This is not merely a question of challenging the right to teaching office of those who cannot, even 'generally', give assent to the formularies. It is equally about the tender consciences of those who believe passionately that truth matters, and that the Church has a responsibility to stand for truth, and that if a church does not do so in some way or other it is wrong for serious Christians to

139

remain within it. One can envisage the possibility that, in the not too distant future, a bishop may be faced with a choice: either to withdraw his licence from someone whose deliberate and considered teaching cuts directly against the Church's formularies in general as well as in detail, or to fail to do so, and thus actually to 'unchurch' those who find it in conscience as good Anglicans intolerable to stay in a place where such teaching flourishes unchecked. Indeed, one fears that the latter alternative, though less dramatic, shocking or headline-catching than the former, may have been happening in some quarters already. (It should be emphasized that the former option does *not* involve 'unchurching' the person concerned. It does not imply that he is not a Christian. It is simply to declare effectively, as the 1938 report implied should be done, that his teaching is not that of the Church.)[88] Comments like this will, of course, raise hackles. But the underlying issues will not go away, and the problem of two dogmatisms, the one in favour of declared doctrine, the other opposed to it, may well be our modern version of problems faced by our forefathers ever since the Reformation. At its heart, this is a question about the nature of the Church.

That, after all, is what this chapter, and indeed this report, is about. It is not true – though some may try to suggest it – that doctrine commissions have now given up discussing actual doctrines, and have taken instead to writing about second-order questions. To ask about the nature of corporate believing, and particularly about the nature of declared doctrine, is to ask about the Church, the people of God, viewed from one perspective in particular as the people marked out by that faith in Jesus Christ which, set in the context of a corporate life of worship and witness, love and service, is stated explicitly in creeds and formularies. It is to ask about the health and vigour of the Body of Christ. It is a study in ecclesiology.

It is, moreover, a study which forces us to face hard questions about the future of explicit doctrinal teaching in the Church of England. If we let the Articles sink even further into obscurity; and make no attempt to fill the vacuum which they leave, we shall have abandoned those controls, those boundary-markers (to use John Bowker's phrase), through which the Anglican Settlement of the sixteenth century achieved its identity and helped to create a careful balance in the total life of the Church and, for that matter, of the nation – a balance which succeeding generations have maintained, albeit precariously. There may be other ways of doing the same job. As we have seen, the 1938 report was an attempt of one sort. But if we simply do nothing, we are thereby actually altering the character of Anglicanism. We are implicitly shifting the weight of doctrinal authority more and more on to either the bishops or the Synod, placing an unwarranted strain on both, inviting flagrant inconsistencies and creating new anomalies.[89]

These unattractive alternatives pose again the problem: what are we to do with our declared doctrine? If we were to update the Articles, or rewrite them from scratch (and if the Synod can scarcely agree new liturgies, how would new Articles fare?), there would be a danger of distorting the balance in the other direction – of setting them up *de facto* as *the* standard, outside the old and essential context of liturgy, Ordinal, and so on. Nevertheless, if the Articles are in fact conditioned by their time (not in their theology and language – though some would say that too – but in their reference to social and political circumstances now no longer obtaining), and if some modern controversies are adjudged of equal importance to some of the sixteenth-century ones, and if a church without a confession has a vacuum at its heart, so that a 'confessing church' is simply a way of talking about the Church doing its proper job, then a case for revision, perhaps even for supplementation, could be made. But before such an attempt would be viable in the present mood of the Church, it may be that, as a prior task, the case for having Articles at all needs first to be set out, particularly in relation to the place of such Articles within the total life of the Church, and the correlated place of other statements of doctrine, not least the reports of doctrine commissions. The present chapter is, in fact, one step towards this difficult and necessary task.

Doctrine implicit

Doctrine revealed through worship

But explicit formularies and statements like the Articles, the Catechism and the Doctrine Report of 1938 are not the sole means by which the Church of England establishes its corporate belief. It is, in fact, more typical of Anglicanism to rely upon custom, ceremonial and, above all, its forms of public prayer, to reveal its doctrine by implication. Jeremy Taylor states this unashamedly:

> Public forms of Prayer are great advantages to convey an article of faith into the most secret retirements of the spirit, and to establish it with a most firm persuasion and to endear it to us with the greatest affection.[90]

Bishop Burnet (*Pastoral Care* VI) defends this reliance upon the witness of our external acts of worship to confess our faith on the ground that these are more often and widely proclaimed than any formal statement.

> The truest indication of the sense of the Church is to be taken from her language in her public offices; this is that which she speaks the most frequently and the most publicly. Even the Articles of doctrine are not so much read or so often heard of as her Liturgies are . . .[91]

In the eyes of other churches Anglicanism may appear to be peculiarly limited in confessional dogmatic statements and even casual in its use of them. We are certainly liable to be misunderstood in this respect unless the central significance of our regulation of public prayer is grasped. *Lex orandi lex credendi* is, in fact, a reputable and well-accredited principle throughout the history of the Church. St Basil defended the divinity of the Holy Spirit with reference to the doxology and to the rite of baptism. St Cyril and Nestorius debated the Person of Christ in the light of their own belief in the Real Presence in the sacrament.

In the doctrinal disputes of the Church of England the authentic verdict of the Church has accorded with the familiar words of its liturgies even when legal opinion has supported a minority. In the nineteenth century the Revd G. C. Gorham was upheld by the Judicial Committee of the Privy Council in his argument that, though the form for the Baptism of Infants in the Book of Common Prayer declared the child to be regenerate, this was no more than a charitable hypothesis conditional upon a subsequent response of faith. But *The Times* of 9 March 1850 commented:

> The decision of the Privy Council has altered nothing in the policy of the Church or in her teaching . . . As the matter stands the orthodox doctrine of the Bishop of Exeter will be preferred by the majority of English churchmen without suffering any disparagement from the fact that a minority in

the Church continues . . . to lay peculiar stress on a clause in the Articles . . .

A leaderwriter of *The Times,* even in the heyday of its pontifical prestige, carries no more authority in the Church than the Court of Arches. Yet it may be said that, while the latter administers the Canon Law, the former may have the better ear for that undercurrent of inarticulate conviction which, for all its lack of definition, can most truly claim to be the corporate belief of any church.

It is, perhaps, important to notice that it is the phrasing and content of the prayers themselves that carries this peculiar power of expressing the voice of the Church concerning its belief. Dogmatic assertions in the prefaces or rubrics of the prayer books do not have the same permanence. Few theologians today, for example, would uphold the claim in the preface of the Ordinal of 1661–2 that 'it is evident unto all men diligently reading holy Scripture and ancient authors that from the Apostles' time there have been these orders of ministers in Christ's Church: Bishops, Priests and Deacons'. It is now the received view among most scholars that in the New Testament period presbyters and bishops were the same, that the distinction between them became general only during the second century and that, even then, the emergence of diocesan from congregationally based bishops was gradual. Yet despite all this, the words and actions of the consecratory prayer, the exhortations and the choice of Scripture reading, in both the older and the revised Ordinal, declare a firm contemporary consensus about the historic continuity of the gift of Orders!

Actions speak louder than words

Those beliefs that take possession of people's minds by implication and insinuation have greater persuasive power than direct assertions. Once a change in routine behaviour has become habitual, the view of the world which this change embodies has already become deeply rooted in the consciousness of those who have been affected. Though the historical evidence is not conclusive, it is interesting to compare the ways in which Islam and Christianity arrived in West Africa. Islam drifted, as it were, down the caravan routes of the Sahara. Its only missionaries were traders whose forms of prayer and rules of abstention were noted and associated with their success in business and attractiveness of demeanour.

Little by little parts of the new way of life were adopted without conscious conflict. There was a decisive moment for each individual convert, when 'idolatry' had to be given up, but that step was not felt to be necessary until a whole corpus of new belief had already infiltrated the tribal life and laid hold upon it. In contrast to this, Christianity came by sea. It was unloaded, whole and entire, as a foreign import. It was a hard-sell evangelism calling for an immediate conscious choice. It made its dramatic conversions, widespread all around the coast. But because this faith was adopted, if at all, *in toto,* it is equally liable to be discarded neck and crop, whereas Islam, though practised inadequately, has become inextricable where it has taken root.

The more profound and basic the doctrine, the more likely it is to be preserved implicitly in the myths, symbols, rituals and behaviour-patterns of the believing community, rather than being placarded explicitly in formal propositions. It is in the way they do things, in the values they attach and in their innate sense of what is appropriate or sacrilegious, that believers reflect their corporate recognition of the mystery of humanity, the grace-bearing experience of Christ and the nature of the God they have encountered. So changes in liturgy or squabbles over a new clause in Canon Law often conceal a struggle between conflicting emphases in people's idea of God.

Not only is doctrine that is implicit stronger in winning and keeping adherents, it also proves to be more enduring. What has been made explicit dates more noticeably than what is implied. As Bishop Montefiore said in the final essay of *Christian Believing*, 'dogmas are written in the language and the thought forms of the age that defined them . . . every formulation of faith is "imperfect, incomplete, partial and fragmentary". Usually they have a polemical bias; they are responses to questions which may be framed very differently today.' But beliefs that are expressed only by implication are less exposed to incredulity or correction and, on the contrary, are invested with the mystique of custom and ceremony, and so outlast the changes that take place at the level of argument and knowledge. Doctrines that are gently commended by implication or by praxis are less open to rejection because they do not assert themselves so specifically or in terms that can be so easily challenged. By allowing a measure of ambiguity, they embrace a greater diversity of consent. This may be the reason why priests of the Church who teach a Unitarian doctrine of Christ continue still to find meaning and satisfaction in celebrating an unchanged Eucharist. The doctrine implicit in the traditional praxis outlives the explicit denials of that tradition. So Bishop Hensley Henson asserted that 'Controversy determines the Articles and Devotion the Prayer Book. Controversy is ever relevant to factors which have no intrinsic permanence, but Devotion is timeless and universal'.

Precisely because beliefs that are not verbalized but are left to be inferred are so powerful, there is all the more need for explicit formulations of doctrine which have been thought out and examined. Inasmuch as the charismatic movement, for example, has revived a more conscious belief in the Third Person of the Trinity, released greater spontaneity and generated more unity among Christians, it has been widely welcomed. But its development in practice has doctrinal implications, and therefore it needs to be accompanied by more deliberate study of the doctrine of the Holy Spirit which will, on the one hand, reflect the Church's own more vivid experience and, on the other, correct the vagaries of teaching which experience alone may give rise to. This is the point that 'protestants', in every generation and whatever their 'colour' may be, have been trying to make, and it explains their perennial concern to anchor the Church with the right prescriptive definitions. But this also explains the irony in which they are always bound to find themselves. Their proper preference for words and their suspicion of everything that may imply doctrines without stating them puts them always into the lighter side of the balances. Bishop Stephen Neill makes the contrast in his book, *Anglicanism*:

> In the seventeenth century the Puritans were prepared to suffer imprisonment and worse, because they would not wear as much in church as the bishops thought it suitable that they should wear. In the nineteenth century the Anglo-Catholics were prepared to go to jail because they regarded it as essential to wear more in church than the bishops were prepared to allow them to wear. In each of these periods good men made a principle out of something indifferent in itself, and were prepared to die rather than surrender what they had come to regard as a principle.

Over the years the Tractarian martyrs have succeeded where the Puritan martyrs failed. Saying no to the actions sounds so much more negative than saying yes to the words. There is no way of avoiding this imbalance: actions have always spoken louder than words, religious actions most of all. But at least, by recognizing the nature of this dilemma, we might avoid the injustice of insisting that what has become a matter of principle is still doctrinally neutral. If the wearing of a stole, for example, has once been something worth fighting for, it may be both bland and blind to declare that it has no doctrinal significance – bland because, while controversy can eventually cool to indifference, this takes a deal of time and toleration; and blind because it overlooks the fact that corporate belief may be moulded and affirmed as much by implication as by direct statement.

Many outward forms imply doctrine

Those responsible for the revision of the Church's forms of worship have been keenly aware of the power of liturgy to convey and entrench a doctrinal position. A careful analysis of the successive drafts of the series of services offered for experimental use in the Church of England between 1960 and 1980 reveals a prolonged scoring of points, tempered by a general and more truly Anglican determination to secure a balance of emphasis. It is difficult, for example, to use the various eucharistic prayers in Rite A without being made aware of the tug-of-war between those who want to bring to the fore the doctrine of the eucharistic sacrifice and those who do not. Similar scuffles between 'realized eschatology' and 'a personal return of Christ' have left their marks in the sand. In any study of the composition of liturgical texts, however, it is important to distinguish between the deliberate or 'planted' indicator of doctrine and the liturgical change which is extensively adopted not because it is without doctrinal significance but because it reflects a substantial though inarticulate shift in corporate belief. The widespread acceptance of the 'westward-facing' position for a celebrant at the Eucharist is an instance of the latter. The very fact that not all could give the same reasons for making the change suggests that it was one of the signs of a mutation in the corporate conviction of the Church as a whole which lay below the level of conscious argument. It seems to have been a reflection of a general movement towards a more participatory worship, the shared action of the community as a whole. For better or for

146

worse these changes of direction do take place in the consciousness of people who share a common culture and there is no gainsaying them. This new emphasis in worship is closely related to a change in people's understanding of God's transcendence – an interjacent or intermediary transcendence. The *laos* now feels itself to be not merely 'people of his pasture and the sheep of his hand', but the people in the midst of whose relationships God is pleased to dwell. The same new awareness underlies the tension between synodical and episcopal authority in the Church of England, since monarchical structures witness implicitly to a monarchical God. The same change reverberates in the small innovations that admit lay people into the sanctuary, or coffee urns into the nave, and build a dual-purpose church. There are losses as well as gains in this change, and we are not arguing here either in favour or against it. Our point is to show that the deeper the level at which such changes of attitude take place, the more likely they are to be expressed by implication rather than overtly.

Again, what the Church builds certainly reflects what the Church believes. And what the Church believes about God cannot be unaffected by the new perspectives within which mankind as a whole surveys its existence. The awful vistas of geological and cosmic time and the insecurity of the atomic age and the virtual abandonment by scientists of the mechanical model of the universe have produced a new awareness that Man and his works are ephemeral. Churches, or even vicarages, which were a rhetorical assertion of the temporal triumph of Christendom seem pretentious now, unless they are valued as monuments of past faith. The pilgrim tent of Abraham seems more fitting than a tower of Babel. Some of this, no doubt, is a rationalization of financial stringency, but it is hard to deny that church architecture now, as always in the past, is a non-verbal affirmation of the corporate belief of the Church.

Is it cause or effect?

In the nature of things, however, it is impossible to be certain whether belief has dictated the usage, or whether the usage has generated the belief. Does the wider acceptance of cremation instead of interment, for example, betoken any change in popular convictions about personal survival after death or, having been introduced, is it beginning to modify those convictions? The fact that the Roman Catholic Church has fairly deliberately set its face against this change in practice indicates that it recognizes that there is more to the matter than expediency. Burial customs are very central to the beliefs of any society concerning the nature of human existence, and the Church's doctrine of man is not exempt from this interplay between practice and belief. Owing to the great distance of crematoria from people's homes, there is a growing tendency to ask whether the journey is really necessary, and quite often the words of committal are spoken in the church porch. If the ritual disposal of the body ceases to be part of the experience of most people, including most Christians, we are likely to find ourselves faced not only with psychological but also doctrinal consequences. Closely connected with these developments is the modification that has taken place in people's attitudes towards graveyards and what may be done in them. In the Middle Ages bishops tried to ban dancing and fairs from the churchyards, and in these days there are regular individual protests against every sort of tampering or supposed disrespect. The law, in fact, specifies in detail what must be done with human remains whenever a burial ground is included in a building or road-widening scheme, and under what conditions tombstones may be removed from original positions to allow for the churchyard to become a garden or park. Yet, for all the legal safeguards and individual protests, the tide of opinion moves steadily towards a relaxing of scruples in this matter, and this may indicate, or perhaps may be helping to bring about, a change in the inarticulate beliefs of our society concerning personal survival.

All of this lies in the area of uncertain speculation. We must be careful not to see doctrine necessarily implied in every case in which it *could* be implied. Change may be no more than an experiment with a variety of options. Yet, while admitting the uncertainties, we would be foolish to disregard the power of common usage both to express and to mould corporate belief. A church which still values establishment, in the sense of a conscious responsibility for the nation, must inevitably express its beliefs more by implication than by explicit confessional formularies and be singularly disinclined to excommunicate or deprive for heresy. Our public prayer and practice has long been the real test to our inner convictions. This is perhaps how we are best understood.

148

Doctrine diffused

Our broad constituency

The Church of England still possesses, in legal theory, a very broad constituency. Every resident in England lives in a parish of the Church of England; and every resident above a certain age in every parish possesses certain rights in relation to his parish church. He has the right to raise his voice and give his vote at least once a year on matters of church government; he has the right to be married in the church; and he has the right to expect certain services from the clergy of the church -- that they will, for instance, 'seek out' his children for baptism.

Relatively few people exercise these rights to the full. But the rights exist, and many people are at least vaguely aware of their existence. Many people are aware of the parish church as, in some rather indefinite sense, 'available' to them; and the availability of the church generates in a good many a certain loose and distant sense of responsibility for it. Those parishioners who form the active and worshipping core of the church are surrounded by, and in contact with, a much larger number of parishioners who, while distancing themselves from regular worship and active involvement, will still speak of the church as 'their' church; will comment freely on its present policies and practices; will feel themselves well or ill served by its clergy; and will give to it, regularly or occasionally, some measure of financial support or material service.

Many parochial clergy are acutely aware of the existence and importance of this broad constituency. Much of their time is spent, and much of their pastoral care exercised, within this constituency -- that is to say, among people whose attitude to organized and structured Christianity could be described in terms of 'good will' rather than 'commitment', of 'respect' rather than 'involvement' and of 'acquiescence' rather than 'activity'. Few clergy, and no theologians, would regard such attitudes as normative of 'what the Church believes'; but it can hardly be denied that they have some influence on the 'corporate believing' of the Church. For those who take such attitudes appear to be, and usually feel themselves to be, 'on the side of' the Church. They are glad that their children should be associated with the Church, and they often show a warm and moving friendliness to the clergy and to anyone else who calls on them 'in the name of the Church'. It is possible, of course, to regard such attitudes as 'antibodies' which inhibit the 'catching' of authentic Christianity, but it is also possible to regard them as a cultural medium in which faith may take root and begin its growth towards maturity. It seems, therefore, worth while to attempt a brief and highly impressionistic account of what may be called 'popular religion' in this country, of the ambiance of 'sympathy' and 'good will' which immediately surrounds the active and self-conscious core of the Church, and to try to detect whatever doctrinal presuppositions or convictions may underlie those attitudes which are so familiar to many of the parochial clergy.

A very personal God

The God of popular religion is unambiguously personal. He is so personal that he may be called, almost indifferently, 'God' and 'Jesus'. One may, when talking about Jesus of Nazareth, find it 'hard to believe that He was God'; but one has no doubt that God is 'just like Jesus'. God is certainly not 'It' or 'Creativity' or 'the Life Force'. On occasions when one doubts 'whether there is a God', it is the existence of a personal God that is doubted: whether or not 'Creativity' or 'the Life Force' exists, is a matter of no interest or importance. That God is 'a Person' is made plain by the value attached to intercessory prayer in popular religion. It is felt entirely appropriate to 'ask Him' for particular benefits in times of difficulty or crisis, and it is quite often claimed that these benefits have been 'granted'. It is believed that the affairs of the world are very directly 'in the hands of God' and no theoretical difficulty is felt about the possibility of his direct and decisive 'intervention' to avert a crisis, to ease pain or to save a life. It is also believed that 'something beyond this life' is in the hands of God, and, despite the emotional and existential difficulties of bereavement, no theoretical difficulty is felt about the possibility that the beloved dead are 'with God' or have 'gone to Jesus'.

No difficulty is felt either about the manner in which God is to be approached or addressed in prayer: to know 'a good prayer' may be helpful, but, provided one is sincere, one may pray in one's own words, in any place and at any time. It is recognized that 'we ought to pray more often than we do'; and that there is something of personal discourtesy in praying to God only when one is in particular need. Casual references to certain things that happened 'just as I was saying my prayers' suggest that a considerable number of people do this day by

150

day; and it seems that daily prayer usually includes an element of thanksgiving as well as of intercession – both thanksgiving and intercession being focused principally on the welfare of children, family and friends. It is also to be noted that, in times of particular crisis, what may loosely be described as 'the prayer of the Church' is often requested and invariably welcomed.

A good and righteous God

God is personal; and God is also – if the phrase may be permitted – 'morally sensitive'. 'We cannot all be perfect'; and God 'understands' our commonplace sins and shortcomings. But anything that stands out as 'immoral' is offensive to him and should, as it were, be kept at a distance from him. Some people 'stay away from church' through a genuine sense that 'they are not good enough to go'; and, by the same token, 'immorality' in someone who does 'go' is seen as particularly flagrant and improper. God is morally sensitive; but he is not sensitive to the propriety or impropriety of cultus or ritual. Protestantism has left its mark on the popular religion of our country in a relative poverty of outward forms of expression and a scarcity of 'procedures' to be followed at the major crises and turning-points of life. Whereas a certain moral standard is a requirement in those who would approach God, their 'procedure' is irrelevant. 'It is all a matter of how you were brought up'; and the ritual and cultus of the Church itself is of interest to the wider circle of sympathetic parishioners only when some change in it threatens the 'stability' which is felt to be a very necessary quality and characteristic of the Church.

God is morally sensitive because he himself is 'good'. His goodness ought to be reflected in his 'entourage' – the clergy and others who form the inner circle of the Church; and his goodness 'rubs off', as it were, on to certain objects which are closely associated with him, and makes them 'sacred'. A church building, its contents and the Bible are sacred. So also, to a slightly lower degree, are the resting places of the dead. It is noticeable that theft from, or damage in, a church, vandalism in a churchyard or cemetery, and any kind of obvious disrespect either to the contents of the Bible or to the book itself tend to cause even greater indignation among sympathetic parishioners than among the active and committed members of the Church; and churches and

151

vicarages are often used by people from this wider circle as repositories for family Bibles and other 'sacred' objects which one 'hasn't room for but cannot bear to see treated with disrespect'. The neglect and eventual closure of a church building often causes ripples of distress and anger which spread out far into the circle of those who rarely entered it when it was open and cared for.

The good God, who understands our weakness but is affronted by 'wickedness', is expected to bring retribution upon wickedness, and retribution is expected within the boundaries of his life. That the wicked should 'suffer for it' is seen as entirely proper; and when an apparently 'innocent' person suffers to a marked degree, the suggestion is still sometimes heard that 'he must have done something' – that his life must contain some kind of 'guilty secret'. It is only when the 'innocence' of the sufferer cannot be doubted – when he or she is a child or a member of one's own circle or in some other way thoroughly 'sympathetic' – that the suffering is felt as an acute problem and the question is raised: 'How can God allow such things?'. Sometimes the questioner finds some kind of answer in the thought that God was not immediately responsible for the suffering – that the 'cause' was 'heredity' or 'pollution' or someone's carelessness or error, but not infrequently one hears some such remark as, 'Well, He suffered Himself, didn't He?', and some reference is made to the figure of Jesus on the cross. That the good God may be the 'sharer' rather than the 'cause' of suffering is an idea by no means alien to popular religion.

A Christian God

As we noticed earlier, the words 'God' and 'Jesus' are used almost interchangeably in the popular religion of this country. To this extent, popular religion is unambiguously Christian, and, beyond this, is distinctively and even exclusively Christian in its 'orientation' or points of reference. The book which one 'ought to read more often' is, without question, the Bible; the days on which 'one ought to go to church' are the days – Christmas, Good Friday, Easter – which commemorate the decisive events of the Christian story; one refers to an outstandingly good person as 'what I would call a real Christian'; and though one may say, with reference to one's Muslim neighbours, 'Well, we all believe in the same God', one would certainly hesitate to attend a ceremony or make use of a symbol which was clearly identified with a religion other than Christianity. Most importantly, perhaps, it is to the Christian Church which one 'turns' on certain occasions which transcend the scope or compass of popular religion.

The need for something more

Popular religion, with its confidence in a good, understanding and approachable God, is felt to suffice for ordinary times and circumstances. But it is not a pretentious form of religion. It recognizes, often in a rather gracious way, its own provisionality. At times when the world discloses its dimension of mystery – when a hoped-for child is born or when adolescent love achieves maturity, when familiar landmarks are removed or familiar associations broken, when suffering arouses pity or terror, when bereavement takes away 'a part of oneself' – on such occasions the need is often felt for a more structured, more objective and more corporate form of religion. Then 'the services of the Church' are often sought and almost invariably welcomed; and they are welcomed, in general, *in toto*, without dilution or qualification. What is more, the probability that such need will some day arise is often recognized, especially among people of mature years, before it actually arises: one wants 'the Church to be there' even if one does not need it yet. It is no doubt partly for this reason that 'good will' towards the Church exists in so wide a circle of parishioners, and that 'scandals' or 'changes' in the Church give rise to such widespread comment, anxiety and resentment in a parish. The Church is 'wanted' – and, for that reason, often 'helped' or 'supported' – as a potential resort or resource in the dark days. For it is recognized that the-religion-of-every-day will not suffice always or in all eventualities.

Popular religion is not ultimately complacent. It appears complacent because it does not exhibit either the commitment or the self-questioning of fully Christian awareness. But it defers rather than denies the necessity for such commitment and self-questioning; it recognizes its own provisionality. It does not set itself up as an alternative to committed Christianity, but only as an everyday approximation. It is for this reason that many parochial clergy regard the ambiance of popular religion within which they live and work with a good deal of respect, and feel themselves supported rather than frustrated by it. Its acceptance of the good, understanding and approachable God is by no means antithetical to what they themselves would teach. Its recognition of its own provisionality offers at least a bridgehead for the introduction of deeper reflection, more urgent self-questioning and more positive commitment to the implications of the Christian gospel and of membership of Christ's Body in this world.

NOTES

1 See *General Synod: Report of Proceedings* 3 (CIO 1972), p. 800.
2 Mowbray 1974.
3 p. 94.
4 loc. cit.: 'It also contains many treasures which are its own.'
5 pp. 62, 100.
6 *Doctrine in the Church of England: The Report of the Commission on Christian Doctrine appointed by the Archbishops of Canterbury and York in 1922* (SPCK 1938), p. 19.
7 p. 25.
8 G. B. Shaw, *Major Barbara* (Penguin Books 1960), p. 59.
9 *The Four Loves* (Collins Fontana 1967), p. 29.
10 E. J. Bicknell, rev. edn. by H. J. Carpenter, *A Theological Introduction to the Thirty-nine Articles of the Church of England* (Longmans 1955), p. 17.
11 *Doctrine in the Church of England,* p. 36.
12 Explicit statements can often also be found in the preambles to certain reports commissioned by the bishops or Synod. But the status of such documents, even when accepted or approved by Synod, is very unclear.
13 See M. Bowker, *The Henrician Reformation.* Cambridge University Press 1981; and W. P. Haugaard, *Elizabeth and the English Reformation.* Cambridge University Press 1968.
14 See A. Trollope, *Barchester Towers,* first published in 1857 (World's Classics edn., 1925), pp. 47 ff. Trollope complains of long worthless sermons from young preachers, and comments: 'Nay, you yourself would be acceptable, if you would read to me some portion of those time-honoured discourses which our great divines have elaborated in the full maturity of their powers.'
15 See, for example, G. W. H. Lampe, 'The Revision of the Articles', in H. E. W. Turner, ed., *The Articles of the Church of England* (Mowbray 1964), p. 96.
16 See Bowker, op. cit.
17 *A Christen sentence and true judgment of the moste honourable Sacrament of Christes body and bloude* . . . London, circulated privately in 1532 and eventually published *c.* 1545, folios A2 recto-3 verso. See N. T. Wright, ed., *The Work of John Frith* (Sutton Courtenay Press: forthcoming), pp. 54 ff.; 75 ff.; 477 ff.

18 See H. Chadwick, 'Anglikanische Kirche', in F. Heyer, ed., *Konfessionskunde* (Berlin, de Gruyter, 1977), pp. 575–94.

19 See ibid., p. 573 and Bicknell, loc. cit.

20 See Oecolampadius, *De Genuina Verborum Domini, hoc est corpus meum, iuxta vetustissimos authores, expositione liber,* 1523; *Quid de Eucharistia Veteres tum Graeci, tum Latini senserint, Dialogus,* 1530.

21 *Acts and Monuments,* 1563 edn. (being a translation of the Latin version of 1559), p. 500.

22 For fuller details, see E. C. S. Gibson, *The Thirty-nine Articles of the Church of England,* 2nd edn. (Methuen 1898), pp. 1–47; C. Hardwick, *A History of the Articles of Religion,* 3rd edn. (Deighton, Bell 1876); Bicknell, op. cit., pp. 7–18; W. H. Griffith Thomas, *The Principles of Theology: An Introduction to the Thirty-nine Articles,* 3rd edn. (Church Book Room Press 1945), pp. xxix–xlix; J. C. de Satgé, 'The Compilation of the Articles', in H. E. W. Turner, ed., op. cit., pp. 1–24; C. W. Dugmore, 'Foundation Documents of the Faith: VI. The Thirty-nine Articles', in *Expository Times* 91 (1980), pp. 164–7. Dugmore's article does not mention the developments of the last fifteen years.

23 See Gibson, pp. 3 ff.; Dugmore, p. 164; Bicknell, pp. 8 ff.; Griffith Thomas, pp. xxxvi ff.

24 See Gibson, pp. 5 ff.; Bicknell, pp. 9 ff.; Griffith Thomas, pp. xxxviii ff.

25 See Gibson, pp. 7–9; Bicknell, pp. 10 ff.; Griffith Thomas, pp. xl ff.

26 See de Satgé, p. 9; Gibson, p. 13, with references.

27 Gibson, pp. 13 ff., discusses the details in full. Cf. also Bicknell, loc. cit. An important and closely related area of Cranmer's work at this time was the catechism: see D. G. Selwyn, ed., *The Catechism Set Forth by Thomas Cranmer* (Sutton Courtenay Press 1981).

28 Gibson, pp. 30 ff., compares these in detail with the 1553 articles. Cf. Griffith Thomas, pp. xliii ff.; Bicknell, pp. 14 ff.

29 See de Satgé, p. 13: Gibson, pp. 9, 38; Griffith Thomas, loc. cit.; Bicknell, loc. cit.

30 13 Elizabeth c.xii. Details in Gibson, pp. 42 ff., and H. Gee and W. J. Hardy, *Documents Illustrative of English Church History* (1910), pp. 477–80. See Griffith Thomas, pp. xlvi ff.

31 Gibson, pp. 59 ff. See *Subscription and Assent to the Thirty-nine Articles: A Report of the Archbishops' Commission on Christian Doctrine* (SPCK 1968), p. 11; Griffith Thomas, pp. lii ff.

32 Details in Dugmore, op. cit., pp. 166 ff., esp. note 12.

33 See Church Assembly, *Report of Proceedings,* vol. 49, no. 2 (CIO 1969), pp.189, 190 and particularly the exchange in *General Synod: Report* (as above, n.1), pp. 799–802.

34 See R. T. Beckwith, 'The Problem of Doctrinal Standards', in J. I. Packer, ed., *All in Each Place: Towards Reunion in England* (Marcham 1965), pp. 125–7; *Subscription and Assent,* pp. 19–22.

35 See Gibson, pp. 20 ff.; 25 ff.; 38 ff. Also Bicknell, pp. 14 ff. and Griffith Thomas, pp. xliii ff.

36 See Packer, 'The Status of the Articles', in Turner, ed., op. cit., p. 31. Compare Cranmer's own statement of his intention, quoted in Griffith Thomas, p. liv.

37 T. Rogers, *The English Creede*, 1585. See Packer, op. cit., p. 28 and Chadwick, op. cit., p. 584.

38 See, for example, Packer, op. cit., *passim*; Griffith Thomas, pp. xxiv ff.

39 The latter in Turner, ed., op. cit., p. 95. See too *Subscription and Assent*, pp. 10 ff.; Chadwick, op. cit., p. 583; Bicknell, pp. 18 ff. The present argument shows that, historically and legally, it is misleading to say that 'we do not have that kind of precise definition over and above the catholic creeds and Scriptures which some other Churches possess' (*General Synod: Report*, as above, p. 799).

40 See Packer, *Towards a Confession for Tomorrow's Church* (Church Book Room Press 1975), p. 4.

41 See Hardwick, pp. 212 ff.; 216 ff., concerning Richard Baxter in particular. Cf. Herklots, p. 71, in Turner, ed., op. cit.

42 Full discussion in Gibson, pp. 61 ff.; cf. Herklots, p. 64.

43 Hardwick, pp. 217 ff.; Gibson, pp. 62 ff. The story is retold in full by Herklots, pp. 76 ff.

44 See Richard Hooker, *The Laws of Ecclesiastical Polity*, 1594–7; John Jewel, *An Apology for the Church of England*, 1562.

45 See Gibson, pp. 66 ff.; Chadwick, op. cit., p. 582.

46 See E. C. S. Gibson, *The Declaration of Assent: An Appeal to Conscience* (SPCK 1918), pp. 29 ff.

47 Printed in the *Life* which prefixes the (3-vol.) 1838 edn. of his *Works*, pp. xxv ff.

48 From the Preface to his *The Religion of Protestants a Safe Way of Salvation*, 1638. See the discussion in R. R. Orr, *Reason and Authority: The Thought of William Chillingworth* (Clarendon Press 1963), p. 42.

49 See R. T. Holtby, *Daniel Waterland, 1683–1740: A Study in Eighteenth-century Orthodoxy* (Thurnan 1966), pp. 1 ff.

50 See Sykes, *The Case of Subscription to the XXXIX Articles Considered: Occasioned by Dr. Waterland's Case of Arian Subscription*, 1721; Waterland, *A Supplement to the Case of Arian Subscription Considered . . .*, 1722.

51 See *Church Assembly Proceedings*, as above, pp. 190, 193.

52 p. 14.

53 pp. 67 ff. Holtby (op. cit., p. 36) conveniently summarizes the issues in the Sykes–Waterland controversy.

54 Gibson, *Declaration*, pp. 37, 44 ff.

55 ibid., p. 23. Cf. also the case of F. D. Maurice, related by Herklots, op. cit., pp. 80 ff.; and see Gibson, pp. 65 ff. and note. This requirement was dropped by the universities in 1871 (Dugmore, p. 167).

56 Tract xc, *On Certain Passages in the XXXIX Articles*, 1865 edn., pp. 83 ff.

57 loc. cit.

58 See Herklots, op. cit., pp. 84 ff. For the full story, see R. T. Davidson, *Life of Archbishop Campbell Tait, Archbishop of Canterbury*, 2nd edn. (Macmillan 1891), vol. 1, pp. 487 ff.

59 For details of the debates in Parliament and Convocation, see Beckwith, op. cit. (above, n. 34), pp. 119–24.

60 See *Subscription and Assent*, p. 11; Gibson, p. 64; Dugmore, p. 167. The original text also refers to the Irish Church, which was subsequently disestablished (1869). The other provisions of the Clerical Subscription Act of 1865 are printed in *Subscription and Assent*, pp. 11 ff.

61 Though the canons still, in fact, state this: see *Subscription and Assent*, p. 12; Packer, in Turner, ed., op. cit., p. 53.

62 Bicknell, p. 21.

63 *Doctrine in the Church of England*, pp. 38 ff.

64 See Beckwith, op. cit., pp. 121 ff.; Gibson, *Declaration*, pp. 25 ff.

65 See Beckwith, op. cit., p. 123: and compare the discussion in *Church Assembly Proceedings*, as above, pp. 180 ff.; see also W. R. Matthews, *The Thirty-nine Articles: A Plea for a New Statement of the Christian Faith as Understood by the Church of England* (Hodder & Stoughton 1961), pp. 17 ff. Matthews's little book is the more interesting in that he had been a member of the 1922–38 Doctrine Commission.

66 *Subscription and Assent*, pp. 15–17.

67 p. 73.

68 p. 74.

69 p. 76.

70 p. 74. The preamble would, of course, be adapted for different types of occasion. The Form of Assent was the proposed first half of a longer statement whose second half would deal with forms of worship to be used in public.

71 See *Church Assembly Proceedings*, as above, pp. 169 ff.

72 This short sentence was designed, according to the Bishop of Durham, to 'bring all those people sitting at the back of the church at an institution up with a start' (loc. cit.).

73 See the discussion, loc. cit., pp. 173 ff.

74 ibid., pp. 185 ff.; 187–9; 190 ff.; 193.

75 The debate which influenced these revisions (9 November 1972) is recorded in *General Synod: Report*, as above, pp. 789–804.

76 Turner, op. cit., pp. xiii ff.

77 ibid., p. 112.

78 For details, see G. K. A. Bell, *Randall Davidson*, 2nd edn. (Oxford University Press 1938), pp. 1134–50.

79 *Doctrine in the Church of England*, p. 9.

80 ibid., pp. 36 ff.

81 Bell, op. cit., pp. 1136 ff.

82 ibid., p. 1147.

83 ibid., p. 1148.

84 ibid., p. 1150; see *Doctrine in the Church of England*, p.19.

85 Cf., for example, Bell, op. cit., pp. 396–8; 1141 ff.

86 *Doctrine in the Church of England*, p. 39.

87 Beckwith, op. cit., p. 143.

88   The doctrinal standards required of the laity are of course the creeds –
     since they occur within the liturgy, and are an absolute *sine qua non* of
     the baptism service in particular – and, for communicants, the
     catechism (*de jure* at least: its general disuse today raises again the
     question of whether we are preserving the careful balance of
     Anglicanism as well as we might be).

89   It is strange, for instance, that those entrusted with this responsibility
     are themselves, *qua* members of the Synod, under no obligation to
     declare assent to any of the Church formularies at all (a possible way out
     of this dilemma is indicated in *Subscription and Assent*, p. 22, para. 33).
     Compare the (inconclusive) discussion in *General Synod: Report*, as
     above, pp. 779–88, 795 ff. The possibilities for new style and method in
     Anglican doctrine, if the Synod really were to take on a more
     significant role in defining doctrine, are extraordinary: as lawyers daily
     consult law reports, so future theologians might be found anxiously
     scanning Synod reports for new rulings, interpretations and precedents
     – and might end up looking to a theological Lord Denning for a final
     verdict.

90   *Works*, 7, p. 375.

91   *Pastoral Care*, 6.

Religions as Systems

The mistrust of systems

Why do we mistrust so much the institutions, the systems, the
bureaucracies – the Juggernauts, as the title of a recent book
described them[1] – which control our lives? Because we know
only too well – only too frequently, not least in the last fifty
years – what the highly organized system is capable of doing to
individuals: the rise and fall of Hitler, the ruthlessness of
Stalin, the catastrophe of Kampuchea, the continuing
exploitation of one part of the world by another, and whatever
else one can bring oneself, with a heavy heart, to add to the
catalogue of organized and systematic evil: how is it possible to
be alive at such a time and not be deeply protestant against the
abuse and exploitation of power? Indeed, the very term 'the
system' has acquired overtones of an enemy to be opposed and
defeated. 'Screwing the system' is the blunt phrase through
which this protest has come to be expressed.

But it is not simply a case of 'them' against 'us'. Max
Frisch, in his play *Andorra,* put all of us on trial, in what he
called 'a model' of our responsibility in the destruction of
Andri, who is, as the underlying Greek suggests, Everyman –
as victim:

> *The Soldier, now in civilian clothes, enters the witness box.*
>
> SOLDIER
>
> I admit I never liked him, I didn't know that he wasn't a
> Jew, everybody said he was one. I didn't like him from
> the start. But I didn't kill him. I only did my duty. Orders
> are orders. What would the world come to if orders
> weren't carried out? I was a soldier.[2]

What would the world come to if orders were not carried
out? The problem is that the world would not come to
anything – indeed, the world could not have come into being
in the first place – if there were not a systematic, constrained
and organized transmission of energy and information, an
ordered process, organizing available energy, against the tide of

entropy, into regular and eventually self-replicating systems. It is that which creates the paradox and the tension between the individual and the system.

That may, of course, seem a rather different sense of 'orders' and 'control', but there are connections between the elementary and the complex organizations of energy which make it clear that no matter how much our sympathies may (and often must) be with the individual in relation to the system, organized systems are *necessary* for the continuity and transmission of information. That is as true of religious systems and religious information as it is of anything else (bearing in mind that both expressions are being used in a technical sense, and that the concept of information in this technical sense includes much more than verbal information). That is an important reason why there are religions, and why also, within Christianity, there is both the Church as the Body of Christ and the churches as the sub-systems which help to constitute that Body, enabling and continuing its life. And that, too, is why there *must* be 'corporate believing': it is necessary and inevitable in a universe of this sort.

Once we grasp this with sufficient understanding, then we are in a wiser position to be on our guard against the exploitation and abuse of this necessity. The institutional churches, as organized systems, are just as capable as any other system of making, not a virtue but a vice out of a necessity – of being, as Geddes MacGregor once put it, 'a Scarlet Woman, Devil's Harlot, Satan's Whore' – on which he commented, 'The language is sixteenth-century in its robustness, the phenomenon is twentieth-century, at least equally and perhaps even *par excellence.*'[3] The purpose of this chapter is to give a brief indication of the ways in which religions can be understood as systems, processing and making available information which humans have regarded as being of fundamental importance – more important, potentially, than any other information, since it transmits from life to life, and from generation to generation, 'the Way, the Truth and the Life'.

Since this way of gaining insight into the nature and necessity of organized religions is not extensively known, and since also (unhappily) it is laden with technical terms, not all of which can be eradicated, it may be helpful to offer a brief indication of the ground to be covered:

1 *Systems and the Organization of Life:* Human lives are now frequently understood as organized systems through which energy flows and is put to work in many different ways. One of the forms which energy takes in a universe of this sort is that of 'information': thus human beings are often now described as 'information-processing systems'. This is, at first sight, a strange sense of information, and an unfamiliar way of gaining insight into the complexity of human nature. So in this section a *brief* indication is given of why this approach is helpful and necessary.

2 *Systems and the Process of Information:* The process and transmission of information, in the human case, is *so* important that it has never been left to chance: it is channelled, protected and organized, in ways which require systems for those purposes.

3 *Religions as Systems:* Religious information is no exception to this, and thus organized religions appear as systems to protect information which is believed to be of vital (indeed, saving) importance.

4 *Religions and Boundaries:* The maintenance and continuity of a system demands some sense of a boundary – some way of marking what the system is, who belongs to it and who does not, who controls it and makes decisions within it, how the system is related to its environment (to whatever lies outside the boundary). Some examples are given of the problems this raises, and attention is drawn to the *limitations* of this method and style of analysis.

5 *The Appropriation of Resources in Religious Systems:* One limitation is that a systems analysis of religions cannot place sufficient emphasis on the fact that it is *individuals* within such systems who appropriate and internalize (make their own) the resources which religious systems mediate or make available. A fundamental reason *why* religions emerge as systems to protect 'saving knowledge' is precisely so that what is offered in and through the systems can be taken up by individuals and can lead to the transformation/transfiguration of life, and thus to the ultimate goals of salvation (or the equivalent) which are pointed to in any religious system.

161

6 *The Individual and the System:* But that leads to a potential (and often actual) conflict between the individual and the system. How can this conflict be handled? And how can it be made creative and liberating, rather than destructive and threatening?

Systems and the organization of life

Let us suppose that you and I have never met before, and that we first encounter each other in the way of business or inquiry, as did Mr Pickwick and Samuel Weller over the top of a pair of boots, the personal property of a farmer who was refreshing himself with a slight lunch of two or three pounds of cold beef and a pot or two of porter after the fatigues of the borough market. Much may then ensue in the way of further acquaintance. But even at the first moment of encounter, I already know a great deal about you. Indeed, *superficially* I could claim to know almost everything about you. I know that you have one or two feet (or conceivably none), but certainly not four trotters like a pig; I know that you have one or two arms (or conceivably none), but not eight tentacles like an octopus. I know that you were conceived and born in much the same way as other human beings were conceived and born. I know that given sufficient time you will grow to a height between two feet and eight feet, and I know it is highly likely – though not absolutely certain – that one day you will die.

All this I know about you because our lives are set within very clear *boundaries* of possibility; and the codes of information, which run particularly through our genetic inheritance (through the genetic code), ensure that we will be constructed within these boundaries. I know, therefore, that you will have to construct a lifeway, so long as you remain alive, within those boundaries, in which you will attempt to hold your life together and bring it to whatever outcomes you believe or hope are possible, from day to day, and from year to year. Obviously, there will be many problems and limitations, many things which threaten the continuity and success of your lifeway, not least death. But you have the intelligence to scan and understand what is going on around you, and you are able to plan and project a lifeway which will keep you in being; though for many people it is a mockery to talk of 'plans' and 'projects', when their lives are so close to bare subsistence, or when they are crippled by a ravaging accident or disease.

Still, the basic fact remains that we are all consequences of the transmission of information through the genetic code, and that is why it is possible for me to know a great deal about you, even though we have never met. And yet, when I have listed all these items, like legs and chromosomes and arms and toes, you may well feel that I hardly know you at all. Such generalities hardly say anything about what you are as a person. And that is indeed a curious and important thing: you are a *person,* not a parcel of matter being posted from birth to death. So what is it that contributes this added dimension, of which I can know very little – indeed nothing – unless I meet you or read about you or hear someone talk about you?

It is, of course, the fact that you are informed by much more than the genetic code; or to put it the other way round, the genetic code constructs you in such a way that you are eventually capable of incorporating energy (transacting energy through your own body), not only in the form of breakfast but also in the form of signals which you are able to interpret as a fairly reliable indication of what is happening all around you – in your environment. The genes constructed you as a trans-action of energy capable of processing information: the complicated accumulation of atoms and molecules inside your head, genetically coded into a non-random arrangement – the almost unbelievable complexity of chemistry and electricity which functions in that very tiny space – creates in you a consciousness of yourself and of your environment; a consciousness which because it has through time achieved a code of words, is able to interpret itself to itself, and is also able to share its interpretations, its hopes, its feelings, its under-standings with other people. Therefore, in a way which we are far from fully understanding, you are able to transcend the material analysis of what you are, in the way you live and move and have your being: in imagination you can go to the moon, or fly with Peter Pan through the nursery window, where in fact your body is gravitationally anchored to the bed. From your genetic inheritance and from your interaction with your surroundings when you are born and as you grow, you become an informed subject.

The human organism, then, is constructed genotypically, like other living organisms, but phenotypically it is diversified; or to put it more simply, we are all very similar in the general way in which the genes construct us, but we are very different as individual examples of human being. One source of diversity obviously occurs in the 'shuffling' of the chromosomes in sexual reproduction; but an equally important source of diversity is more *cultural* than *genetic*, and it lies in the capacity of a human being to become an informed subject. How does that happen? That question can be answered on two levels: the first is the investigation of how the brain functions as a receiver, storer and transmitter of information (remembering, as will be stressed again, that information in this technical sense is not confined to verbal communication); the second is the recognition of the many resources from which coded information flow is derived in the human case – such things as parents, family, school, friends, television, newspapers, pop concerts – or in other words, whatever can be specified in the environment in which a person actually lives and grows:

> Now I am old and wait
> Here in my country house in quiet Greece.
> What have I gathered?
>
> I have picked up wisdom lying
> Disused about the world, available still,
> Employable still, small odds and scraps of wisdom,
>   A miscellaneous lot that yet makes up
>   A something that is genuine, with a body,
>   A shape, a character, more than half Platonic
> (Greek, should I say?), and yet of practical use . . .
>
> I have learned another lesson:
> When life's half done you must give quality
> To the other half, else you lose both, lose all.
>
> Select, select: make an anthology
> Of what's been given you by bold casual time.
> Revise, omit: keep what's significant.
> Fill, fill deserted time. Oh there's no comfort
> In the wastes of empty time. Provide for age . . .
> Set up the bleak worn day to show our sins,
> Old and still ageing, like a flat squat herd
> Crawling like sun on wall to the rim of time,
> Up the long slope for ever.
>
> Light and praise,
> Love and atonement, harmony and peace,
> Touch me, assail me; break and make my heart.[4]

In the anthology which is our life, it is important to

remember that we also pick up cues of information directly from the environment – directly from experience of the universe, as we interpret it through the patterns we have built up and through the language we have acquired; and much of this information flow may be entirely without words. In discussing this in *The Religious Imagination*, I quoted a poem by Wordsworth to illustrate this point, but it is not difficult to find other examples. Here is a poem by Tennyson:

> Tears, idle tears, I know not what they mean,
> Tears from the depth of some divine despair
> Rise in the heart, and gather to the eyes,
> In looking on the happy Autumn-fields,
> And thinking of the days that are no more.
>
> Fresh as the first beam glittering on a sail,
> That brings our friends up from the underworld,
> Sad as the last which reddens over one
> That sinks with all we love below the verge;
> So sad, so fresh, the days that are no more.
>
> Ah, sad and strange as in dark summer dawns
> The earliest pipe of half-awaken'd birds
> To dying ears, when unto dying eyes
> The casement slowly grows a glimmering square;
> So sad, so strange, the days that are no more.
>
> Dear as remember'd kisses after death,
> And sweet as those by hopeless fancy feign'd
> On lips that are for others; deep as love,
> Deep as first love, and wild with all regret;
> O Death in Life, the days that are no more. [5]

In that poem by Tennyson, signs or cues of information arrive from his experience of the universe – the autumn fields, the ship's sail, the sunset – and those cues remind him of the deep and underlying consciousness of the passing of time, and of all that might have been and cannot now come to pass. The actual inputs are non-verbal, although of course they are immediately verbalized and interpreted in the existing brain state. As I summarized the point in *The Religious Imagination*:

It must be emphasized that transmission does not necessarily occur in verbal forms alone. Often, in the religious case, it is least of all in these. Consider the Bishop, in Chekhov's story of that name: his emotions are evoked in the opening pages through a whole succession of informational inputs which do not occur in discernible words at all, although the background murmur of prayer is one of them. In some forms of Zen Buddhism much emphasis is given to 'transmission outside the Scriptures', in the silent relation between teacher and disciple; but it is not denied that transmission is taking place.[6]

Systems and the process of information

So non-verbal information flow should not be underestimated. Nevertheless, words are clearly of supreme importance in the building-up of the human mode of being, and in consequence human beings have not usually left the process of information entirely to chance. They have not allowed the transmission of information from one life to another, or from one generation to another, to be entirely accidental. Contexts of information process have been elaborated, or sometimes have simply developed, because of the inherent necessity for information process to be non-random. These elaborations or developments may be gradual (as in the long development of an educational system) or they may be more sudden and deliberate (as in the introduction of a propaganda ministry in Germany in the 1930s).

What is certainly the case is that, whether devised or developed, means of information process can be of very considerable complexity. Schools and universities are an example of the way in which human beings have devised contexts in which information flow and information process can occur, and in which children or adults can become 'informed consciousness' in particular areas of human knowledge and understanding. Religions equally are systems of information process. They are contexts in which information flow, and in this case primarily religious information, is intended to occur. Each religion is a system – or more often a complex of sub-systems – in which fundamental resources of information are designated and are linked to a set of goals which lives may attain (usually lives informed from those resources). As Emerson observed, 'A man is a bundle of relations, a knot of roots, whose flower and fruitage is the world.' The goals may be near at hand or far-reaching, or, in other words, they may be proximate or ultimate. They may be proximate in the sense that more immediate goals may be held out as attainable

– such goals as the forgiveness of a particular offence or sin, the securing of a better harvest, the death of your malignant neighbour's cow, an act of love and charity towards your neighbour; or they may also be ultimate, in the sense that salvation, *moksha, nirvana* and the Elysian fields are held out as attainable – as also are such goals as Gehenna, the *pretaloka* and the cheerless fields of Asphodel.

The basic point which underlies all this is simple and important: *information (whether verbal or non-verbal) does not slop around in the universe in a random or arbitrary manner*. It is channelled and protected, coded and organized; and precisely for that reason the construction of complex organisms and highly complicated behaviour is possible. At the social and cultural level, information is not left to chance, either. It is not simply religions which have to be systematically organized in order to protect and transmit (make available) fundamentally important opportunity and information which, in so far as it is incorporated or internalized in any individual life, changes the character of that life, or changes what happens in the actual living of that life.[7] Trade unions, political parties, professional football, Marks and Spencer's, the Royal Air Force, British Leyland, the United Nations, as well as the Church of England (or a province, or a diocese, or a deanery or a parish) have to be *systematically* ordered if continuity is to be assured (or at least attempted), and if decisions affecting the organization are to be made and implemented; and there are effective and ineffective ways of achieving this.

We can see a comparable process at work in the case of the natural sciences. The information which constitutes the understanding of the universe (and the means to that understanding) which we refer to as 'natural science' is not shared and transmitted in a wholly random or haphazard manner (no matter what it occasionally feels like in a particular classroom). Nor can we possibly understand 'the whole of the universe' in a single act of comprehension (except in the non-science holistic experience of a mystic). The sciences are necessarily broken down into sub-systems of technique and understanding; and the community of (say) physicists has its own systematic means of continuity and communication, including its own control systems and systems of value and approval. Books like that of Daniel Kelves (*The Physicists: the History of a Scientific Community in Modern America*)[8] or of Horace Judson (*The Eighth Day of Creation: Makers of the Revolution in Biology*)[9] make the

167

organization of the control and transmission of scientific information abundantly clear. As Barnes summarized the point,
with reference to scientific education, 'transmission of the
current paradigm is the key point': 'Science is not a special
kind of knowledge source; it has to face the problem of
credibility, and the technical constraints facing the transmission of culture in any context.'[10]

Religions as systems

Religions, too, have to face the problems of credibility and
transmission. Different religions (or to be more precise, the
authorities or operators of a particular system) solve the
problems in different ways: some draw clear and strong
boundaries in order to designate who is in and who is outside
the system, what counts as orthodox believing, and what
counts as appropriate or inappropriate behaviour, with a
strong hierarchy of decision and control (examples are Roman
Catholicism and Sunni Islam); others draw loose boundaries
and are less concerned with the clear determination of who is
in and who is outside, or with the specification of orthodoxy
and unorthodoxy (examples are Anglicanism and Mahayana
Buddhism; though note that in both cases there may be
extremely strong *sub*-systems – highly organized and
hierarchical – within the more general system; and note also
that the general system designates *some* boundary markers, as
the chapters of this report make clear in the case of
Anglicanism).

But even in religious systems which are less boundary-
minded or boundary-concerned, the fact remains that in
Christianity, as (*mutatis mutandis*) in any religious system,
resources are offered and are made available (word and
sacrament, community, inspiration and judgement) which do
not 'slop around in the universe', but which are channelled
and protected (particularly in ritual); and goals are offered,
both to those within the system/church and to those outside,
which are both proximate (changing life by love) and ultimate
(the realization of our redemption and the vision of God). This
immediately illuminates why adherents to religions are so
passionate – not only in the ways that can be illustrated from the
contemporary political scene, but also in the long history of
religions which made Winwood Reade include them very
firmly in the Martyrdom of Man. They are passionate because
many of the goals held out in religions as attainable are indeed

of ultimate importance: they have to do, not only with life, but eventually with the possibility of life beyond life.

This also makes it very clear why religions as systems of information process necessarily produce mechanisms of transmission and control. It is necessary for there to be, both a connection between the fundamental resources and the lives that have to be lived, and also some means of monitoring the appropriation of the resources into life, and the appropriateness or otherwise in terms of outcome. The resources may be strongly defined in terms of content (as in the case of Scripture, the Torah, the Quran or Sruti) or loosely defined (as in the case of a guru, the words of an oracle, the Holy Spirit). At the furthest extreme there may be 'transmission outside the Scriptures', to quote again the Buddhist phrase, and there may be transmission by association, without any observable communication taking place: but transmission is still, by definition, claimed to be occurring.

Monitoring what is going on – that is, trying to ensure, both the process of information flow into other lives and other generations, and also the appropriateness of the actual outcomes when matched against what the resources themselves designate as appropriate, is served by an enormous range of different means, depending very much on the geographical extent of the system in question. It is much easier to ensure transmission and appropriateness in an African or an Indian village than it is to ensure it in the Roman Catholic Church. Yet what we know for certain is that, in the history of religions, what we are always observing are repeated attempts to enhance the formality (and effectiveness) of the system. We may be observing much else beside that, but *that* we are certainly always observing, just as we are always observing its counterpart, the protest against it – and to that highly important protest we shall return. But before doing so, we may ask: How can such a diffuse reality as Christianity be systematized? In other words, how can it function as a system in this formal sense? The answer is that it cannot do so. Christianity may be defined as *Quod semper, quod ubique, quod ab omnibus creditum est*, but in fact from the same resource (Scripture and tradition) have been derived innumerable sub-systems; and the same is true, *mutatis mutandis*, of Judaism, Islam, Hinduism, Buddhism, Shinto and any other complex religious system.

There are two points to notice here: first, the phrase, 'derived from the same resource': but it is characteristic of sub-

169

systems that they add other legitimating resources. They may add the interpretation or teaching of a founding figure or of a contemporary teacher; and that teaching may supplement or even displace the basic resources of the system; thus the Moonies claim to be Christian in the American courts, by associating the teachings of Mr Moon with Christian Scripture.[11] Or again, they may add tradition as a supplementary and authoritative interpretation of the fundamental resource; and that may be done formally, as when in the Roman Catholic Church a dogma is defined which finds at best only tenuous justification in Scripture – like the Assumption or the Immaculate Conception; or it may be an informal association, as in the Muslim association of *hadith* with Quran, in which Quran remains absolutely distinct and more fundamentally authoritative. Or yet again, they may add the inspired utterance of an ecstatic or charismatic figure or of an oracle. In other words, although the designation of fundamental resources is characteristic of religious systems, in the sub-systems the connection with those resources may be very loose, or indeed non-existent; but connection with *some* designated resource remains basic.

The second point is this: it is also characteristic of sub-systems that some of them will claim nevertheless to be the whole system – or at least to be the authentic representation of what is meant to be the case. Sunni Muslims believe themselves to be the authentic continuity of Islam derived from Muhammad and the Quran; but so also do those many sub-systems referred to collectively as Shi'ites and what is clearly at issue there is the *means* of continuity: *does* it have to be through the family of Muhammad and his descendants as Imams? Or again, Roman Catholicism has claimed to represent the authentic continuity from Christ and his apostles. With that claim has gone the construction of a strongly bounded system, with effective means of transmission and control: clear hierarchies of authority; the inquisition and the index; a heavy investment in education; the priesthood as father, and the confessional; the strong definition of the intermediate goals of behaviour; a common central ritual with (until recently) a common language of Latin.

Religions and boundaries

So potentially religious systems or sub-systems are strongly bounded open systems. The concept of 'boundary' does not in

170

the least mean that such systems are literally isolated. The concept of 'boundary' is a means of analysing action within a system, and interaction with its environment. To give a simple example, let us, à la Mrs Beeton, take one egg. A bird's egg is a bounded self-contained system whose 'action' is to support life for the developing embryo. All the necessary energy sources, the nutrients, minerals and water, are present in the new-laid egg; the parent bird or birds have nothing further to contribute beyond keeping the egg warm and occasionally turning it over so that the embryo does not adhere to the shell membranes. Yet even so, the strongly bounded system of an egg lacks one essential requirement, the fuel to drive the metabolism of the embryonic cells, and that fuel is oxygen. Oxygen has to be taken in through the boundary (through pores in the shell, first demonstrated by John Davy in 1863) from the atmosphere, and carbon dioxide has to be discharged. In fact it has been calculated that 'over the 21 days of its incubation a typical chicken egg weighing 60 grams will take up about 6 litres of oxygen and give off 4.5 litres of carbon dioxide and 11 litres of water vapour'.[12] Even then the interaction across the boundary will not be sufficient to meet the goals of the system (the hatching of the chick), and on about day nineteen the chick penetrates the air cell at the blunt end of the egg and begins to ventilate its lungs; about six hours later it uses its increased energy to make a small hole through the actual boundary, the shell.

In that example, the concept of 'boundary' clarifies the analysis of both the internal process of the system and the interactions with its environment. This means that the concept of 'boundary' is usually an operational definition in systems theory – an important definition, since, as H. R. Bobbitt *et al.* argue, 'without a boundary we do not have a system, and the boundary or boundaries determine where systems and sub-systems start and stop'. They then suggest:

A *boundary* of a system is a closed line placed around certain objects so that there is less intensity of interaction *across* the line or among objects *outside* the line than among objects *within* the closed line. *Less intensity* means an intensity below some level, this level being a function of the problem under consideration. For example, we might consider communication, influence or work flow as the interaction variables.[13]

That means that *different boundaries can be drawn with the same organization,* depending on which interaction one is studying. It follows that the defining of a system or of a sub-system is to a great extent a matter of opinion and decision on the part of the systems *analyst*; and in his analysis he must always be on his guard against reifying (turning into real objects) the interactions or the organizations which he is studying. What he isolates as a system or sub-system depends on what interactions, or what flow of information or of decision-making (or whatever) he wishes to understand more clearly. (It also follows that no single model of interpretation will ever be adequate.) Thus if one wishes to analyse the hierarchical flow of authority in a system, one will detach and schematize the authority figures and draw the boundary around the functioning of authority in the system. But if one wishes to analyse the process of research and development in a company, or the process of maintaining machines and buildings, then different boundaries will be drawn. But what is common to all of them is that they specify, not only particular functions within the organization, but also the interactions and interrelationships which obtain across the boundaries. Thus if a whole company is understood as a system, the boundary of the company relates what goes on inside the organization to what goes on outside it – its relation, for example, to its customers, its competitors, its shareholders, its suppliers, the Inland Revenue, and so on.

Such analyses can very easily be applied to religious systems and can help us to understand why and how religions continue themselves through time as they do. What sometimes emphasizes the concept of boundary maintenance in the religious case is the fact that in some religious systems there is a concern with literal, geographical boundaries – with their own parish or territory. Until recently, for example, an orthodox Indian was not supposed to travel out of India, or even out of his province; as Walker puts it, 'The brahmins of Panchala could not visit Vanga and those of Chedi could not journey to the land of Vidarbha. If they did so they were regarded as unclean until they had undergone the *prayaschitta* ceremony of purification.'[14] Or again, a hermit in his cave, or Simeon Stylites on his pillar, or a Dead Sea community in geographical separation, all exemplify an attempt at literal boundary maintenance.

Yet even they interact with their environment: even Simeon

Stylites let down an occasional basket for food; and in that sense of interaction, such systems are open to systems analysis. It scarcely needs to be said how directly applicable this is to Paul, and to his understanding of Christianity as a system on the analogy of the body, with one obvious operational boundary being drawn around the hierarchy of God, Christ, man, woman in 1 Corinthians 11.3. The practical necessities of church organization and management, traceable through the Pastoral Epistles and into the period of the Apostolic Fathers, led to the emergence of bishops, presbyters and deacons as the contingent hierarchy.[15]

It follows that the study of any complex system introduces *a necessary artificiality* if anything is to be learned about the behaviour of the system – what one might call a self-imposed limitation. To give an example: it is possible to study the energy flow through an individual organism, treating the organism as a thermodynamic unit, and observing the conservation and degradation of energy. In that case, the activities of its components, such as cells, can be ignored in detail. Exactly the same study of energy flow can be made – or attempted – for a whole ecosystem, because an ecosystem can be regarded as an 'individual'. In that case, the activities of its components, for example species populations, can be ignored in detail. That is already one level of restriction. But the complexity of the ecosystem introduces further artificiality. As Phillipson put it, 'Generally speaking, studies of energy flow through ecosystems do take into account the different trophic levels: but this approach, although a simplification, has the disadvantage that many animals are omniverous and cannot be assigned to any one level.' He therefore commented: 'The enormous task of studying energy flow both through, and within, a complex ecosystem restricts the research worker to an investigation of trophic levels as the components of the system, and the limitations of this approach will affect the overall study.'[16]

The complexity of systems means that we cannot understand the whole of a complexity in one large, single gulp of comprehension, like a Gollum attempting to swallow a Hobbit. The universe is intelligible only because it is highly redundant and reducible, not because we have to understand 'all or nothing'. Similarly, religions are highly complex systems which cannot be understood as a whole. Provided that we are not alarmed by the kind of restriction which is introduced into the study of any systems, then we can certainly gain understanding of the behaviour of religious systems, and of why they behave as they do, without claiming that we are thereby understanding 'the whole of everything' about religions.

So the behaviour of a *system*, as opposed to the behaviour of participants *in* a system, is to be discerned in its functions, in its maintenance of its structure, in the efficacy with which it transforms inputs into outputs, and in its ability to identify novel stimuli, both internally and externally derived, and to take action which is appropriate in relation to the goals of the system – remembering that 'goals' are elusive: what are designated as goals in the system (in its theoretical construction mediated through such artefacts as teaching or texts) *may* scarcely coincide at all with an individual's proximate or ultimate goals (and in the Christian case there is an inherent contradiction in any case in talking of goals: the Christian's engagement with God and with his neighbour cannot be undertaken in order to reach 'goals'); nevertheless, descriptively, there are 'goals' or ends, such as the love and worship of God, which can be discerned.

But that immediately means that a system which endeavours to change the nature of itself *in via* – which attempts, as Neurath put it, to repair the boat while still at sea, is going to come under great strain. We see this (or used to see this) commonly when unions hear that an operations research team or business efficiency expert has just come through the factory gates; but we see it also, to go back to an earlier example, in Roman Catholicism at the present time. I gave examples of the highly efficient system which was developed in the process of Roman Catholicism through time. But many features of the system are being dismantled: the virtual disappearance of the Latin Mass, the collegiality of bishops in relation to the pope at the Vatican (at least theoretically; not evidently in practice with the present pope, appearances notwithstanding), the erosion of sacramental and individual confession, the removal of the altar from the east end to the centre of the church, are simple and random examples of what is happening.

Such things may be highly desirable – and may be designated as desirable by reference to the legitimizing resources of the system in question (in other words, by appeal to Scripture and tradition), but that does not alter the extreme disturbance caused to those, who, like the present pope, realize (even if only intuitively) that the transmission of information does not occur randomly in the universe, but mainly through systematic means. What is at issue is not a particular piece of teaching, or a particular example of bureaucracy, but the continuity and maintenance of the system as a whole. It is very difficult for those formed in and through one system, and for whom that system is still resourceful in their own case, to imagine what could conceivably take its place and have the same effect in transmission and control. So when we observe that the pope's advice in *Humanae Vitae,* now reinforced by the recent Synod of Bishops in Rome, says one thing, and that the birth statistics of Roman Catholic parents say another, the consequences for the system and for the bonding of individuals to it far outweigh in importance the actual arguments about that particular issue.

However, the picture is not wholly gloomy. It is not a necessary condition of religious continuity that it should be boundary-minded in a strong sense. Anglicanism has notoriously infuriated Roman Catholics by its apparent unwillingness to draw its operational boundaries (for example, its means of determining doctrine) with formal and exclusive precision, though in fact there are very strong sub-systems within Anglicanism. Great virtues have accrued to Anglicanism by way of toleration and great virtues to Roman Catholicism by way of the disciplined and systematic pursuit of sanctity. But there is a price to be paid for each virtue.

What poses a great dilemma for *all* religious systems is that the human animal is increasingly becoming multiply resourceful – that is, drawing on *many* sources for its life. It may be the case that in an African or South American village there is still a single and integrated system. But even in such villages the transistor radio is frequently planted as carefully as the corn or the maize. Men and women are deriving information from a wide range of resources, some of them highly inimical to religious claims. There is nothing new in the multiplicity of resources. To give just one example, Lévi-Strauss coined the term *bricolage* to draw attention to this multiple resourcefulness at the most elementary level of myth-making: Lévi-Strauss derived the term from the verb *bricoler,* which referred originally to a movement out of the ordinary – to a horse swerving to avoid an obstacle, or to a ball rebounding or to the ricochet of a bullet. *Jouer la bricole* means to play off the cushion in billiards. So a *bricoleur* is a 'jack-of-all-

175

trades', someone who improvises and uses whatever comes to hand, rather than employing purpose-built parts. *Bricolage* in myth-making and myth-using refers to the fact that the components have been used before and will be used again, and also to the fact that the myth-maker draws on whatever happens to be lying around that will suit his purpose. So human beings, or at least some of them, have always been openminded. But what *is* new is the extremely wide practice and acceptance of multiple resourcefulness, combined often with an emphasis on the restrictive and incapacitating consequences of being bound to a single system.

To some extent, this is a consequence of the revolution in communications and in the expansion of information. We are saturated by possibility – and there is a price to be paid for that as well. The world has become a bit like the famous Fred Hoey broadcast, which began with a kind of semi-Spoonerism, 'Good afternoon, Fred Hoey, this is everybody speaking.' There are very real problems for religious systems as a consequence of this revolution, and ones which demand extremely clearheaded analysis of their implications for the continuity of transmission within such systems.

But for the moment at least, the systems remain in being – and in the case of at least one, Islam, we can see a religious system going through a process of re-enhancing its formality, by the reapplication of Islamic law in Iran and Pakistan. In others, for example Christianity, it seems likely that there will be continuing and (in some parts of the world increasing) diversity of interpretations derived from the same resource (Scripture and – with differing degrees of authority – tradition), believing themselves to be legitimate in relation to that resource; and it is predictable that these will develop their own means of continuity. The critical question will be how to establish a positive interrelationship of communication and trust between the parts (and this, from a systems point of view, is already a clear issue in covenanting), if it is to be held that they are sub-systems of the same system (Christianity) and are not new, independent systems (new religions or sects). To take the example of a different system, the human family: various parts of the system (uncles, aunts, grandparents, children as they grow up) will pursue their own lifeways with considerable diversity, yet still remain part of the same family. If the family is geographically restricted (living in the same area or even house) the expression of its life is more likely to be interactive;

if it is dispersed, less so. But in either case issues may arise which create disturbance in the system. Some may be 'family rows' which affect attitudes and behaviour but which do not disintegrate the system. But others may seem, to at least some of the participants (family members), to be so disruptive that the system cannot contain the expression of them. 'Go, and do not darken my door again' may seem melodramatic but it has occurred (and still does) when certain behaviour contradicts fundamental beliefs, practices or values which have previously obtained.

In religious systems there may be similar 'family rows', issues which affect attitudes and behaviour but which do not disintegrate the system. There is considerable disruption in the sub-systems of Christianity at the present time about grants made by the World Council of Churches to guerrilla organizations, but the dispute is not likely to create systematic schism. On the other hand, there are *other* issues where the disagreement is more profound – where, that is, a particular proposal seems to others to be so mismatched when judged against the fundamental legitimizing resources that it cannot be contained in the system. For example, where it is proposed in a sub-system of Christianity that women should be ordained, others within that sub-system and in other sub-systems believe that that proposal cannot be matched and thus legitimized in the fundamental resource (Scripture and tradition). So serious does this kind of mismatch seem that it creates systematic separation, a breakaway church in the United States and a warning from Roman Catholics and Orthodox Christians that such a move will set back or prevent explorations towards reunion.

This, then, is a classic problem of boundary analysis, of analysing the necessary (or what are believed to be the necessary) conditions of continuity, and of the kind of interaction which obtains or fails to obtain within what formally appears to be a whole system; and it is this kind of analysis which is required if an ecumenical ambition is ever to be realized, both within a system, such as Christianity, and between systems, such as religions. But whatever the future may hold, it is in such systems – or, rather, in the sub-systems which constitute such systems – that human beings become (if we can use these odd phrases) Hinduistically informed, or Islamically informed or Christianly informed – bearing in mind that those adverbs are broken up into many different forms of expression, and bearing in mind also the belief in all religions that their words, symbols, people, institutions, buildings and so on may be agents in the transmission of inputs derived from resources external to the system, such resources as God, or Brahma, or the Holy Spirit. But the general point is that from and within these systems there can occur an internalization of available resources which then acts, or can act, as a constraint in the continuing construction of life.

The appropriation of resources in religious systems

For the participant in a religious system, what is offered as resourceful in the system is internalized, at least in part, and is expressed in the outcome of life – or should be, if the participant is not to be hypocritical in his or her allegiance: '"A what, my good sir?" demanded Mr Pecksniff', when Mr Anthony Chuzzlewit told him bluntly not to be a hypocrite. '"A what, my good sir?" . . . "A hypocrite." "Charity, my dear," said Mr Pecksniff. "When I take my chamber candlestick tonight, remind me to be more than usually particular in praying for Mr Anthony Chuzzlewit, who has done me an injustice."' The real harm in hypocrisy lies neither in the prayer nor in the candlestick. If we all waited to pray until we were free of fault, the word 'prayer' would cease to exist in any human language. The real harm lies in the distinction in the *nature* of hypocrisy which Chuzzlewit made later on, when he encountered Pecksniff in the stagecoach, and when Pecksniff protested that while he may be a hypocrite, he is certainly not a brute: '"Pooh, pooh!" said the old man. "What signifies that word, Pecksniff? Hypocrite! Why, we are all hypocrites. We were all hypocrites t'other day . . . The only difference between you and the rest was – shall I tell you the difference between you and the rest now, Pecksniff?" "If you please, my good sir; if you please." "Why, the annoying quality in *you* is," said the old man, "that you never have a confederate or partner in your juggling; you would deceive everybody, even those who practise the same art; and have a way with you, as if you – he, he, he! – as if you really believed yourself."'

The distinction here is a critical one, because it emphasizes the obvious, that the human appropriation and expression of religious resources or inputs is nothing like so simple or mechanical as the input, storage, retrieval and output system of a constructed information system, such as a computer. It is perfectly accurate, and with reference to many social and psychological issues, extremely helpful to regard the human form of energy transaction as an information-processing system. But the complexity, speed, efficiency and 'regular irregularity' (effective rule-breaking) with which that is done in the human case creates the awkward reality of diverse character – awkward, that is, from the point of view of the system or design theorist, not from the viewpoint of the artist, the poet or the person who has to live.

Heroic attempts are made in the design of organizations to eliminate what are known technically (or jargonistically) as 'unanticipated mean behavioural patterns': as early as the work of Taylor and Fayol – the inventor of Fayol's bridge, which designates levels of cross-reference in hierarchies – attempts were made to determine what an average man could and could not do, and to judge what he would and would not do, and then to build into the control system in the organization, mechanisms which would constrain actual workers to work at the optimum level. But obviously the estimates of mean capacity were not an exhaustive set. It is the other variables which constitute the unanticipated mean sources of emergent behaviour. The analysis of these, although it has advanced greatly in sophistication since the time of Taylor and Fayol, remains necessarily incomplete, partly because of the huge range of variables, and partly because such analysis becomes a part of the set of possible behaviours and thus demands inclusion in the set of those possible sets; and since we can never arrive at the set of *all* possible sets, the analysis remains fruitful but incomplete. In practice, *what* is designed works back on those for whom it was designed, modifying their behaviour in unpredictable ways as they react to the design or programme.

But however much we rejoice that the human rat escapes from the experimental maze and dances its idiosyncratic pirouette on the grey hairs of the management design team, we must not lose sight of the equally fundamental truths that systems behave systematically; that religions are no exception to this; and that when we try to understand this, we are in a much better position to demand or to ensure that they function more effectively and less oppressively. But the point of stressing diverse character and the idiosyncrasy of human behaviour is to raise the question, what is the *purpose* of a religious system? For this question brings us back on to characteristically religious ground. What is the purpose or the

179

goal? Obviously not to increase exports or to improve profits – though occasionally the drive in a particular parish to pay for the new church hall, or to pay for the church schools, seems almost to have become the goal of a parochial system. But that is a proximate, or intermediate, goal. What is the overarching purpose, or ultimate goal, of a religious system? Certainly not to build bigger and better systems, though it is familiar in every religious system that some people *do* always emerge for whom the system is an end in itself: they become commissars, or they become inquisitors, or indeed some of them become university professors. But none of that is the purpose; it is the product of the systematic nature of systems. What is the purpose?

The purpose of the Christian system, and of the sub-systems which constitute Christianity, is to enable individuals to love God and to love their neighbour as themselves. The purpose of the system is to enable the worship and the adoration of God, in himself and in the service and stewardship of his creation. The purpose of the system is to make real among us forgiveness, redemption and atonement. The purpose of the system is to be the sign and way of salvation.

It follows that what Christianity offers and mediates into human life is not created simply or solely within the system. Some of the particular resources which are, so to speak, on offer, *are* generated within the system. But some of the institutions and protected channels of communication in Christianity (for example, prayer and the sacraments) are believed to mediate a direct input or constraint into life which is derived from outside the system – which is derived, in other words, from God. It is precisely for this reason that in general Christianity has refused to be casual about the sacraments, and has, for example, 'protected' the special character of the Eucharist and the consecration of the elements, in its restriction of who may be the president or celebrant, in its caution about appropriate liturgy, and in its care to ensure that any remaining consecrated elements shall not carelessly be discarded ('shall not be carried out of the church', as the Prayer Book puts it, but shall be reverently consumed). The sacrament is a 'protected channel' of communication, in which the initiative comes from outside the system, and is then mediated through it. Ritual and sacrament are indispensable for the Christian system (in other words, for Christian life), given that this is the sort of universe in which we live, and which we believe is itself derived from God as 'the unproduced producer of all that is'.

So the first purpose of the Christian system is to draw us into the worship and adoration of God. But that implies a second purpose – to draw *us* into that vision; for it is also a goal in a religious system that we or any other human subject can be informed, can receive into the construction of a lifeway, those constraints of information which if they are appropriated and realized in life, can lead that lifeway to what the system in question counts as an ultimately successful outcome – to salvation, to the worship and love of God, and to the service and care of his creation.

The individual and the system

It is true that human systems have a history and a life of their own, which is independent of the particular individuals which constitute them, even though *some* individuals *must* constitute them. Thus there is a history of Parliament, a history of nursing, a history of higher education, a history of synodical government, which is more than the stories of the people who participate in these activities. Yet the fact also remains that an important locus for the process and transaction of religious information and resources *is* the individual. And this creates precisely that tension and paradox with which this chapter began: on the one hand, religious systems have to be organized if they are to mediate what they believe to be the words of life, or of salvation, or of truth, to individual lives; yet the individual appropriation of what is offered or mediated through the system *may* lead to a rejection or criticism of the organization of the system – particularly if it leads, with impeccable internal logic, to the setting-up of inquisitions. The problem for the authorities or operators of a strong religious system is that the individuality – say, the individual's conscience – while in one sense being the point of the system, cannot be allowed to destroy the system, or even, too seriously, to disrupt the system, since otherwise the simplest form of continuity is threatened; and the importance of continuity, for participants in a religious system, is not because continuity is an end in itself, but because of a hope that other and future lives may have the opportunity of being similarly informed from the resources which are believed in all systems (with very different identifications of content) to be 'the words of life'. Thus in virtually all religious systems, and certainly in

181

Christianity, there is an emphasis that it may be necessary to die in order to live, to lose one's self in order to find it, and *not* in fact to set up targets and goals, and 'strive officiously' to reach them. Not surprisingly, this may well lead to serious conflicts between the individual appropriations of what is mediated through the system, and what the operators of a system believe is required for the successful continuity of the system.

Here is the real challenge to corporate believing. What sort of priority and status must be given to the means of a system's continuity, and how much divergence and individual creativity can the system encourage and tolerate, particularly when or if that individuality seems to be disruptive of the system? For the paradox is that while the systems *enable* us to be human (we are all born in particular cultures and languages and belief systems), it is often the aberrant individual who turns back on a system which has given him life and breathes new life into the system. Thus, while sometimes the individual turns against the system, and from that tension a new system is eventually derived (Jesus and Jerusalem, Luther and Rome, Gautama and Benares), it is not always so: it is often the individual appropriation which justifies the system, by exhibiting, in the transformation of life, the truths and possibilities towards which the system points, and for which, at least in part, it exists.

And there is a further paradox: sensitive as we are to what we take to be the oppressive nature of systems (restricting individual liberty and curtailing freedom of expression), we sometimes overlook the extent to which systems *enable* creativity and freedom. In a strongly bounded system, where individuals know where they are and what counts as appropriate or inappropriate behaviour, they can get on with the business of living, without being preoccupied with the foundations of what they are doing. It is in this way that strongly bounded systems may produce, not only mindless conformity (which sometimes happens) but, at the other extreme, powerful and creative explorations of the implications of the system in art, music, iconography, architecture, self-sacrificing lives and the like.

These themes of creative, though potentially and sometimes actually oppressive, interactions between the individual and the system, have been explored, with reference to examples in the history of art, in my article 'Art, Theology and Religious

Systems: A Case for the Inquisition?'[17] The same point can be seen in Stravinsky's plea on behalf of dogma and for the acceptance of the constraint of discipline as necessary conditions of musical creativity – what he called 'the necessity for order and discipline'.[18] In a passage which recalls what was said earlier about the positive and liberating nature of constraint (see note 7), Stravinsky wrote:

> As for myself, I experience a sort of terror when, at the moment of setting to work and finding myself before the infinitude of possibilities that present themselves, I have the feeling that everything is permissible to me; if everything is permissible to me, the best and the worst, if nothing offers me any resistance, then any effort is inconceivable, and I cannot use anything as a basis, and consequently every undertaking becomes futile . . . So here we are, whether we like it or not, in the realm of necessity. And yet which of us has ever heard talk of art as other than a realm of freedom? This sort of heresy is uniformly widespread because it is imagined that art is outside the bounds of ordinary activity. Well, in art as in everything else, one can only build upon a resisting foundation . . . My freedom thus consists in my moving about within the narrow frame that I have assigned myself for each one of my undertakings.
>
> I shall go even further: my freedom will be so much the greater and more meaningful the more narrowly I limit my field of action and the more I surround myself with obstacles. Whatever diminishes constraint, diminishes strength. The more constraints one imposes, the more one frees one's self of the chains that shackle the spirit.
>
> . . . From all this we shall conclude the necessity of dogmatizing on pain of missing our goal. If these words annoy and seem harsh, we can abstain from pronouncing them. For all that, they none the less contain the secret of salvation.[19]

No doubt there are others who would give a very different account of creativity, and who would insist that it depends on repudiation of tradition – on doing one's own thing. In the case of religious creativity, at the furthest extreme individuals will emerge who insist that true wisdom, or insight, or salvation, or enlightenment, or whatever is held to be the ultimate goal, *cannot* be attained within or from any system. Thus the *paribbajakas*, before and at the time of the Buddha, were known as *svayambhu,* the 'self-become', who attained enlightenment by their own effort, in independence from each other and everyone else. Furthermore, they refused to teach anyone else, because such teaching would contradict the very way by which they had attained enlightenment. Martin Wiltshire has then applied this to the Buddha's own enlightenment and to his Great Hesitation after it, when he determined not to teach or instruct anybody else:

> The fact that the Buddha hesitated to teach tells us something very important about the nature of Buddhist truth. He was not postulating the existence of a transcendent truth, about which one could formulate certain definite propositions to which one gives credence. He was postulating the existence of *immanent* truth (or, rather, that truth is immanent). This truth had no transcendent reference except *the way (magga)* to its realization. Therefore, there is a very significant sense in which the Buddha found it difficult to teach the *dhamma* because there was no *content* to the enlightenment. That is not the same as saying there was no authentic experience of enlightenment, but simply that it could not be transmitted by set dogma or doctrine.[20]

Yet for all that, the Buddha recognized that cues of information, or of input, may be necessary to initiate the process towards enlightenment (indeed, he received them himself), and that the continuity of the information process, however much it repudiates 'the closed fist of the teacher', requires formalization. Thus the Sangha (the community of Buddhist monks), which is attributed in the canon to the Buddha's initiative and command, is a highly formal religious sub-system.

It may be that we are talking simply of the means that lead towards the end. But however true that may be, the means themselves are not equal; and since, for almost all of us, some means are necessary, and since therefore corporate believing is the condition in which we are bound to be as Christians, it is incumbent upon us to take extreme care in monitoring the nature of the system, or sub-system, in which and from which our lives are enabled – or in other words, to watch carefully that the system is *enabling* and not destructive of life in the Spirit: 'Though for no other cause, yet for this; that posterity may know we have not loosely through silence permitted things to pass away as in a dream, there shall be for men's information extant thus much concerning the present state of the Church of God established amongst us, and their careful endeavour which would have upheld the same.'

So opens the preface to Hooker's *Of the Laws of Ecclesiastical Polity.*[21] Hooker, in dealing with issues of authority, had to find a way between one extreme of systems maintenance and decision-making (in the individual conscience directly inspired, or in *sole scriptura*) and the other extreme (of a papal exercise of authority which was itself unbounded and uncontrolled): 'The disposition of these things resteth not now in the hands of popes, who live in no worldly awe or subjection, but is committed to them whom law may at all times bridle, and superior power control'; but conversely:

> If in so great variety of ways as the wit of man is easily able to find out towards any purpose, and in so great liking as all men especially have unto those inventions whereby some one shall seem to have been more enlightened from above than many thousands, the Church did give every man licence to follow what himself imagineth that 'God's Spirit doth reveal' unto him, or what he supposeth that God is likely to have revealed to some special person whose virtues deserve to be highly esteemed: what other effect could hereupon ensue, but the utter confusion of his Church under pretence of being taught, led and guided by his Spirit?

I doubt if we would wish to establish Hooker's ecclesiastical polity now, as he envisaged it then. But we should nevertheless be profoundly grateful that at least *one* sub-system within Christianity as a whole found, or was guided into, a middle way in the balance between the necessities for the system to mark its boundaries and to continue itself in time, and the freedom of individuals to appropriate what is offered in and through the system in very varied ways. Anglicanism is a constant source of amazed incredulity and unbelievable impossibility, as much to the insider as to the outside observer; and it has its own share of wicked abuse of the necessity for systems to be systems. Yet for all that, the Anglican settlement was a brilliant and extraordinary achievement, in securing a mutually creative balance between the system and the individual. To whom much has been given, much in the way of responsibility accrues.

The balance, then, between the system and the individual can be creative, just as also it can easily be abused. A clearer

185

understanding of the necessities inherent in the process of information through time helps us to monitor more sensitively the nature of that interaction, and the disturbance which individual appropriation *may* cause in the system as a whole. If we know and understand more clearly what is going on, then we are perhaps more likely to retain *within* the system those 'disturbances' – those 'family rows'; and we may, too, gain wiser discrimination and greater courage in allowing them to become a creative enhancement of the system itself – of what the system maintains as the possibility and the purpose of life. Again, if we understand the necessary conditions of a system's continuity (or at least what a particular system identifies as the necessary conditions of its continuity), then we will be in a more independent position to be able to engage the issue of how different systems can be related to each other – different religions, for example, or different parts of the Christian Church.

Perhaps also it will remind us that if systems are necessary (as they are) to make possible the creative freedom of those who derive inspiration, truth and energy from them, we in turn have a *great* responsibility to sustain and nourish those whose work it is to maintain the system – the secretaries, the bishops, the stokers of boilers, the equivalent of the civil servants. Above all, in England, it would be the greatest possible folly if we do not give the highest priority and support to the parish – to the parochial clergy and lay people – where the system and its goals take on a living 'flesh and blood', and on which so much else depends.

Precisely for that reason, this reflection on the nature of religions as systems warns us to be on our guard against institutional imperialism. To allude briefly to an example: the Church in England has moved in recent years to increasing centralization – for perfectly sensible and necessary reasons. But the exercise of that centralized management, in such manifestations as the implementation of the Sheffield Report (in itself a judicious survey), has evoked, from those on the receiving end, impotent cries of frustration and dismay, of which 'brutally stupid' seems to be one of the milder forms. Perhaps those reactions are ill grounded and misinformed. But confidence in a system, which is a decisive part of its efficacy, requires that perceptions (however ill informed) be taken very seriously indeed. It is even harder for the control figures in a system to conceive that they might be wrong (because of the

186

diffusion which occurs in collective responsibility) than it is for individuals.

Finally, it is important to remember how easily and quickly a system can disintegrate if it removes, or allows to lapse, its boundary-markers and its means of maintaining decision, control and communication within the system and its constituent parts. When control becomes oppressive it is not surprising that the protest on behalf of the individual becomes strong – and that *in itself* is a control mechanism, an answer to the question: *Quis custodiet ipsos custodes?* – who keep an eye on Big Brother when Big Brother is keeping an eye (and a heavy foot) on us? Yet still the fact remains that the Church as the recipient and the resource cf grace *cannot* be casual about the organized means through which it offers grace, life and salvation to lives and generations beyond its own. The Spirit indeed 'bloweth where it listeth'; but we cannot deduce from *that* that the Spirit ignores the constraints of information process in a universe of this sort, any more than we can suppose that the incarnation circumvents the constraints of humanity.[22]

The systematic nature of systems is undoubtedly open to abuse and exploitation. All too easily the system becomes the end in itself, instead of the means towards an End which lies beyond itself. The responsibility of all Christians, in any generation, is to transform – or to allow God to transform through them – the dry bones of the system into a living presence which in turn touches, heals, restores, sustains many lives far beyond its own – much as W. F. Stead described it, in miniature, in his poem *Festival in Tuscany*:

> And down the lane a bellman came
> Ringing a warning bell;
> Then pipes were out and heads were bared,
> A grave silence fell . . .
>
> Black-gowned the wives and mothers walked,
> Stark-faced and harrow-lined;
> Under a darkly kerchiefed brow
> Their eyes were wise and kind.
>
> Behind them sons and fathers came,
> With heavy step they trod;
> Earth-stained and dumb with candles lit
> And after them came God.

Christ on the Cross! thorns on His brow!
The spear-wound in His side;
He poured His life into their lives
When He was crucified.

The Priest came bearing the sacred Host
Wherein Christ lives again:
We were but heathen, yet we kneeled
While God went down the lane.

The connection that needs to be carefully monitored is the one that ensures the continuing *availability* of Christian resources without being too dictatorial about the forms of their appropriation. This connection was handled with brilliant and intuitive skill in the Anglican settlement through and after the Reformation. Whether it is being, or can be, handled with the same skill at the present time is one reason why the Doctrine Commission is being asked to attend to the subject of corporate believing.

For as in one body we have many members, and all the members do not have the same function, so we, though many, are one body in Christ, and individually members one of another (Rom. 12. 4–5).

NOTES

1 G. Bannock, *The Juggernauts: The Age of the Big Corporation*. Weidenfeld 1971.

2 M. Frisch, *Andorra* (Methuen 1964), pp. 3, 41.

3 G. MacGregor, 'No Living With or Without God', in G. Johnston and W. Roth, eds., *The Church in the Modern World* (Toronto, Ryerson) p. 15.

4 E. Muir, 'Soliloquy', in *Collected Poems, 1921–1958* (Faber 1960), pp. 194–7.

5 A. Tennyson, 'The Princess, iv', in *The Early Poems* (1900), p. 306.

6 J. Bowker, *The Religious Imagination and the Sense of God* (Oxford University Press 1978), p. 9.

7 In more technical language, religions offer various forms of *constraint*, which, if they are appropriated or internalized, delimit the life of an individual or group, and help to control it into its particular outcomes. The vital point to grasp is that although the notion of constraint sounds negative and restrictive (which initially it is), it is in fact extremely liberating and creative. Without constraints, no life (nor even a universe) is possible, because available energy would, so to speak, flow

randomly in all directions (except, of course, that there could not *be* any direction without constraint!), instead of being organized into planets or people. The paradox is that the more elaborate the constraints are, the greater the freedom there is for possible behaviours; or to put it, as Ashby does, in the context of cybernetics: 'When a constraint exists, advantage can usually be taken of it' (*An Introduction to Cybernetics.* Methuen 1964, p. 130). For a fuller discussion of these points, which are critical in understanding the positive nature of religions as systems, see my own books, *The Sense of God,* pp. 86 ff. and *The Religious Imagination,* pp. 17 ff.

8   New York, Random House, 1979.

9   Jonathan Cape 1979.

10   B. Barnes, *Scientific Knowledge and Sociological Theory* (Routledge & Kegan Paul 1980), pp. 66, 67.

11   On 4 September 1975, the Unification Church applied to the New York State Supreme Court to be admitted to the New York Council of Churches, on the ground that it is 'a Christian Church committed to the ministry of spreading by word and deed, the gospel of the Divine Lord and Saviour Jesus Christ' (see *Occasional Bulletin,* i, 3 (1977), p. 18). However, the National Council of the Churches of Christ in the USA then commissioned a study comparing the official doctrinal text of the Unification Church *(Divine Principle)* with Scripture; and that study concluded: 'The role and authority of Scripture are compromised in the teachings of the Unification Church; revelations are invoked as divine and normative in *Divine Principle* which contradict basic elements of Christian faith; a "new, ultimate, final truth" is presented to complete and supplant all previously recognized religious teachings, including those of Christianity.'

12   H. Rahn *et al.,* 'How Bird Eggs Breathe', *Sci. Am.,* 240 (1979), p. 38.

13   H. R. Bobbitt, *et al., Organizational Behavior: Understanding and Prediction* (New Jersey, Prentice-Hall, 1978), pp. 365 ff.

14   B. Walker, *Hindu World* (Allen & Unwin 1968), p. 520.

15   For an introductory description, see H. von Campenhausen, *Ecclesiastical Authority and Spiritual Power in the Church of the First Three Centuries.* A. & C. Black 1969.

16   J. Phillipson, *Ecological Energetics* (Arnold 1966), p. 34.

17   *Zygon,* 13, (1978), pp. 313–32.

18   I. Stravinsky, *Poetics of Music in the Form of Six Lessons* (Cambridge, Mass., Harvard, 1977), pp. 61 ff.

19   Op. cit., pp. 63–5.

20   Unpublished but forthcoming article.

21   *The Works of that Learned and Judicious Divine, Mr Richard Hooker* (1885), p. 88 (Preface i.1).

22   In *The Religious Imagination,* I have tried to show how these considerations of constraint and creativity can be applied historically to Jesus and how they lead to a thoroughgoing doctrine of incarnation.

The Archbishop's Hat

J Rn.. Srm̲z̲

> Every man who possesses real vitality can be seen as
> the resultant of two forces. He is first the child of a
> particular age, society, convention; of what we may
> call in one word a tradition. He is secondly, in one
> degree or another, a rebel against that tradition. And
> the best traditions make the best rebels.
>
> (Gilbert Murray, *Euripides and his Age*)

Introduction

During the December 1979 meeting of the Doctrine
Commission at Cambridge Professor McManners, Professor
Mitchell and I started to explore the role of black sheep in
corporate believing: the positive contributions made to the
belief of the fold by those who are not of it; not because they
have lacked opportunity but because they have left it. Basil
Mitchell spoke of his experience in the field of ethics. Ex-
Christians often have profoundly Christian moral intuitions
and produce better work there than paid-up Christians who
are too anxious to conform to, or rebel against, traditional
teaching to trust their intuitions. John McManners referred to
the apostate Jean-Jacques Rousseau whose interpretation of
the Bible by the spirit of Jesus instead of by individual texts
taught the French Catholic Church more than it learned from
the aggressive orthodox eloquence of Bishop Bossuet. I
mentioned the instance of George Eliot and the archbishop's
hat which is the theme of this paper. We had a parable in
mind. It can happen in an individual life that the supportive
stalk of corporate orthodoxy dries and withers. But the seeds
may then fall into a new ground, all the more fertile for being
new, and produce a plant with just the nourishing, vigorous,
truthful and graceful religious qualities which orthodox belief
intends. And this can be to the advantage and enrichment of
corporate orthodoxy.

I begin by setting up the particular historical instance in
some detail. It is essential to this paper that it does not deal
with abstract possibilities but with concrete actualities: a way
of tackling the subject which has emerged more and more as a

theme, perhaps *the* theme, of this commission. It could be called a taking seriously of Christianity's often-proclaimed nature as an historical religion. It is very important to realize that people are involved: in this particular instance two people of very different character and biography working hard for goodness, and each, in a different way, in continual engagement with Christian tradition. So sharp historical focus is needed. Having got that, it is obvious that here is an instance of a frequent pattern in the corporate life of Christianity which is a theme for theological as well as historical investigation: that the homeland of corporate Christianity depends for its livelihood on the regions beyond its pale and the individuals who not only visit them but settle in them too, and vice versa. The last part of this paper tries to ease out some of the implications of that two-way traffic and concludes with some defence of the virtues of realistic fiction, as opposed to theorizing or doctrine, as an expression and stimulant of right believing.

The book

Certainly those determined acts of her life were not ideally beautiful. They were the mixed results of young and noble impulse struggling amidst the conditions of an imperfect social state, in which great feeling will often take the aspect of error, and great faith the aspect of illusion. For there is no creature whose inward being is so strong that it is not greatly determined by what lies outside it . . . Her finely touched spirit had still its fine issues, though they were not widely visible. Her full nature . . . spent itself in channels which had no great name on the earth. But the effect of her being on those around her was incalculably diffusive: for the growing good of the world is partly dependent on unhistoric acts; and that things are not so ill with you and me as they might have been, is half owing to the number who lived faithfully a hidden life, and rest in unvisited tombs.

With those words, carefully chosen to witness to a severely modified but tenaciously surviving faith, George Eliot ended her novel *Middlemarch*. A contemporary historian has recently quoted them to describe such Christian value as he, as a believer, finds in his studies.[1] He is far from being alone in this. Numerous readers of *Middlemarch* have testified to the religious comfort and illumination given them by this rigorously realistic book in which, however, 'there is no unredeemed tragedy'. F. W. H. Myers, for whom there was 'no longer any God or any hereafter or anything in particular to aim at', wrote to the author that 'you seem to be the only person who can make life appear interesting without starting from any assumptions . . . one feels that you know the worst, and one thanks you in that you have not despaired'. Other admirers were more fulsome and nearer to traditional Christianity. For the reviewer in *The Daily Telegraph* it was 'almost profane to speak of ordinary novels in the same breath with George Eliot's' (18 June 1872). 'What do I think of *Middlemarch?*' asked the American poet of faith and doubt, Emily Dickinson, 'what do I think of glory?' A West End clergyman, in a sermon on Hosea said: 'Many of you no doubt have read the work which that great teacher George Eliot is now publishing . . . well, that is what I mean by the prophetic spirit.' A Christian critic said that 'nature meant her for a great theologian . . . The saddest of her books have in them a lingering aroma of religion, indeed more than an aroma; for they illustrate many principles which are precise parallels and analogies to some of the fundamental principles of the faith whose historic credibility she had thought well to repudiate.'[2] But perhaps the most interesting instance for a Church of England doctrine commission came to George Eliot via Judge Fitzgerald who reported that 'at the opening of the Dublin Exhibition he was struck with the attention of the Archbishop to the interior of his hat, which at first he took for devout listening to the speeches, but on close examination saw he was reading something, and as this was so intent he was prompted to look into the hat, and found the Archbishop had *Middlemarch* there laid open'.

The archbishop's hat: there is the conjunction. Published material tells of no actual meeting between him and the novelist and, disappointingly, nothing of the archbishop's opinion of the book. His behaviour at the opening of the exhibition is the only available testimony that he was as positively fascinated as anybody. All that we can do, to fill out the glimpse from Dublin before going into its implications, is to say something about each of the two people in this meeting of minds.

The writer

George Eliot was the pen-name of Mary Ann Evans, the daughter of a Warwickshire estate manager. To her father's

stalwart Anglicanism she added evangelical fervour of a pitch
that disapproved of oratorios as 'not consistent with millennial
holiness'. But from this eminence she steadily, from the
ecclesiastical point of view, declined. Sympathy with a 'mildly
Arminian' aunt cast doubt on the doctrine of predestination.
She was struck by the character of an unbelieving doctor in a
novel: he lost his life tending plague victims. She got
acquainted with Caroline Bray, 'the most religious person I
know'. Mrs Bray was a devout Unitarian married to a man
who had abandoned evangelical Christianity for phrenology.
Her husband's freethinking views made her uncomfortable.
Comfort was to hand in her brother Charles Christian
Hennell, the author of *An Inquiry into the Origins of Christianity*
(1838). It was at the same time a pious and a rational book,
incredulous of miracles and revelation yet devoted to
Christianity as 'the purest form yet existing of natural
religion', and to Jesus as the pattern of human virtue. Hennell
spoke of the importance of Jesus in terms which are prophetic
of the realism and moralism of George Eliot's novels.

> To awaken men to the perception of moral beauty is the first
> step towards enabling them to attain it. But the
> contemplation of abstract qualities is difficult, some real or
> fictitious form is involuntarily sought as a substratum for
> the excellence which the moralist holds to view. Whilst no
> human character in the world can be brought to mind,
> which, in proportion as it could be closely examined, did not
> present some defects disqualifying it for being the emblem of
> moral perfection, we can rest with least check, or sense of
> incongruity, on the imperfectly known character of Jesus of
> Nazareth. If a representative be sought of human virtue,
> enough is still seen of his benevolent doctrine, attractive
> character, and elevated designs, to direct our eyes to the
> Prophet and Martyr of Galilee.[3]

Human sympathy and reason were leading her down from
orthodoxy. Compassion, the empathy of being in others,
together with the downward movement from ample theology
to restricted practice: these twin makers of redemptive
goodness were to be the theme and method of *Middlemarch*.

But there was more to come. She learned German and translated two epoch-making books in the story of the criticism of
Christianity. The first was Strauss's *Life of Jesus*. Its insistent
thesis that the gospels were heavy with mythical interpretations

of the Old Testament and light on historical fact has proved its power to trouble orthodox waters in the 1970s. She did not enjoy the job. 'It made her ill dissecting the beautiful story.'[4] She comforted herself by keeping a cast of Thorwaldsen's 'Risen Christ' and an engraving of Delaroche's 'Christ' on her desk. Relentless critical acumen with small nourishment for the spirit, theory floating away from story: these were not her line. But the power and brilliance of Strauss's criticism left its mark. The second translation was much more congenial. It was of Feuerbach's *The Essence of Christianity*.

Here was a critique of the Christian religion which capped Strauss's. It probed more deeply – beyond the Christian text and into the Christian soul. It did this with a sympathetic understanding of the spirituality or inwardness of Christianity much greater than Strauss's: an analysis so cleverly and profoundly done that Feuerbach was able to explain Christianity in entirely humanistic terms without looking, or being, superficial. It was Christianity that he was talking about and not an Aunt Sally. But there was a price for this achievement, a just price which Feuerbach was glad to pay. The external, objective, realistic picture of God must go. This was not only because Christianity could be adequately and positively described without that picture. It was also because that picture was a mistake made by the heart and mind which resulted in moral distortion. For it was a mistake about love, the central thing and not something peripheral. The picture of an external God was very like the idols attacked by Old Testament prophets: a projection of the human self which enslaved and narrowed the human self, a homemade tyrant which rewarded its devotee by giving him a deluded but 'peculiar sense of his own importance' whereby 'the believer finds himself distinguished from other men.'[5] This superior egoism, this higher thinking in the service of the lower selfishness, was the moral symptom which gave away the root of the religious disease. Love had been reified. But not, alas, reified in the way love itself wants, into flesh and blood, but into what sectional interest demanded: a narcissistic ghost, an incubus, which instead of joining humanity separated it. What the real God, love incarnate, had joined, doctrine had put asunder. Incarnation was central for Feuerbach. But it was thorough-going incarnation without the divinity saving clauses of traditional dogma. 'The incarnation is nothing more than the human form of a God, who already in his nature, in the

194

profoundest depths of his soul, is a merciful and therefore a human God.'[6] That 'nothing more' contains the positive and corrective force of Feuerbach's critique. In evading it, Christianity reneged on its own origins, for:

> in relation to the Israelitish religion, the Christian religion is one of criticism and freedom. The Israelite trusted himself to do nothing except as he was commanded by God; he was without will even in external things; the authority of religion extended even to his food. The Christian religion, on the other hand, in all these external things made man dependent on himself, i.e. placed in man what the Israelite placed out of himself in God.[7]

It would be very hard to exaggerate the influence of Feuerbach on George Eliot. The close work of translating him got his ideas into her soul. For her, too, this idea of incarnation became central. It sorted out the morally valuable from the morally pernicious in the religion she had inherited. It was the way of the genuine love, the true human love which impelled sympathy and sacrifice by its descent from the theoretical to the historical and practical.

The closing lines of *Middlemarch* were to conclude just such a pilgrimage from imaginary to real love. The appeal, as ever with her, was untheoretical in another way too. Simultaneously with translating Feuerbach, frequent meetings with G. H. Lewes, a writer with an unfaithful wife, were marking the end of her spinsterhood. She was to spend the rest of his life with him without, such was the near-impossibility of divorce then, ever marrying him. The thinking and feeling personality which in the ensuing years was to bring out the great novels, culminating in *Middlemarch,* was now formed.

When she died there was a question of requesting her burial in Westminster Abbey. The arch-agnostic scientist, T. H. Huxley, was opposed. 'How am I to tell the Dean . . . to do that which, if I were in his place, I should most emphatically refuse to do? One cannot eat one's cake and have it too.' For George Eliot was 'known, not only as a great writer, but as a person whose life and opinions were in notorious antagonism to Christian practice in regard to marriage and Christian theory in regard to dogma'.[8] So she was buried near to Lewes in the unconsecrated part of Highgate cemetery where another learner from Feuerbach, Karl Marx, was to end up later. And Robert Browning, the prince of Victorian religious poets who

had also grappled with the criticisms of Christianity but kept
his orthodox footing, was there at the burial. 'One cannot eat
one's cake and have it too.' Huxley's decisive common sense
hardly does justice to the ambivalence of George Eliot's life
with and against Christianity – or to Browning's attendance.
She had written books which evoked responses which a
clergyman would be glad to hear spoken of the books of holy
Scripture. She had responded to worship (in Bamberg's
Frauenkirche in 1858) in a way which would delight a
clergyman, feeling 'part of one whole, which one loves all
alike, losing the sense of a separate self'. [9] It is not so easy or
obviously right for the faithful Christian to dissociate from her,
apostate as she was, as Huxley thought it should be.

The reader

And there was the archbishop. His name was Richard
Chenevix Trench. [10] When Judge Fitzgerald caught him
reading out of his hat he was sixty-five years old, a sensitive
and dreamy man, battered by the administrative
reorganization and theological controversy which modern
bishops are heirs to. He was in the throes of Gladstone's
disestablishment of the Irish Church (in which his line was to
hang on to as much as possible for as long as possible), and a
storm he had brought upon himself by not condemning an
Anglo-Catholic pamphlet as strongly as the Evangelicals
wished. They called him 'Puseyite Trench'. That was certainly
his ecclesiastical tendency. Liddon and Samuel Wilberforce,
Bishop of Oxford, were his friends. Pusey often wrote him
letters of anxious exhortation. His party allegiance was vague
enough for them to be called for. Lecturing on Baxter, the
puritan divine, he spoke of 'a positive duty, that we heartily
thank God for all which he has wrought in any of his saints and
servants, for the likeness of Christ which he has formed in
them'. He was a man of wide and generous culture who
thought that clergymen should share in 'whatever is best and
highest in the general culture of their age'. That kind of
liberalism was not what Liddon and Pusey most liked to hear.
Still less was his diffident remark, 'I hope it is not unlawful to
say so, but to me there is something *Biblical* about Plutarch.'

Trench was no tearaway. He had read Strauss when he was
in his first living. His reaction was typically Anglican and
fitting for a future archbishop in its mixture of justice and
alarm.

196

Life is so short that one cannot read a tenth of the positive constructive books one desires. I am therefore very unwilling to consume two or three months on a negative and merely destructive one . . . I have examined it in a few places . . . the idea of the book is not, I think, in the main to overthrow Christianity, though could he make out his points it would be equivalent to an overthrow, but to turn it from an historical religion in which the facts are and contain the doctrine into a philosophy which shall be equally valuable whether the facts in which it has hitherto been implicitly involved but which now he asserts cannot stand the test of close examination, be true or not . . . The mischief which it could do in England is, I fear, considerable.[11]

His own New Testament work began with his famous books *Notes on the Parables of Our Lord* and *Notes on the Miracles of Our Lord* (1842 and 1846). They are from the point of view of the critical cataclysm that Strauss unleashed, antediluvian: rich in symbol, allegory and reference to the fathers of the Church, muffled and minimal in critical discipline, averse to anything negative. An otherwise sympathetic modern biographer sees in them 'the substitution of scholarship for thought' and invokes G. M. Young's judgement that 'there are times when the reader of Victorian apologetic, whether the theme be miracles or the authorship of the gospels, is nauseated by the taint of sophistry and false scholarship, and feels as the better intelligence of the time did feel, that if men could force their intellect to think like that it cannot matter much what they thought'. As with the disestablishment of the Irish Church, so with the criticism of the Bible. He hung on to as much as possible for as long as possible. The archbishop lacked the novelist's zest for the steep and rugged pathways of free inquiry, her capacity for choice and the big sacrifice.

He had, in fact, trodden those pathways in his youth, but after much argument 'about it and about' had made his choice – for the Church of England and its doctrine.

But he never became the total, dogmatic, Anglican churchman in Pusey's and Liddon's mould. His roots were not in the doctrinal orthodoxy of their tractarian Oxford. Nor were they in the stalwart country Anglicanism of George Eliot's never-forgotten childhood. He was a member of the Cambridge Apostles' Club. This was a discussion group, centred on Trinity College and still flourishing, founded on 'a belief that we *can* learn, and a determination that we will learn, from people of the most opposite opinions'.[12] Its members included F. D. Maurice and Alfred Tennyson, but Trench was by no means dwarfed in such company. Gladstone called him 'a spiritual splendour'[13] and one of the Apostles wrote of him to another:

> You and I have seen and known many men very far and indeed above the vulgar, but none among them comes near to Trench – He blends the deepest earnestness of purpose with the most solicitous kindness and regard for the feelings of others that is possible: the best of men, he distrusts his own goodness and the most completely disinterested he half suspects himself of selfishness – I know of no one who so completely realizes Shelley's words 'to fear himself and love all human kind'.[14]

Into such a character the Apostles' commitment to 'a process of painfully honest self-scrutiny'[15] bit dangerously deep. He longed for a cause to which he could commit himself and so be delivered from self-doubt and doubt in general. So when, in 1830, some of his fellow Apostles contrived a quixotic expedition to liberate Spain, he threw himself into it. 'It is action, action, action that we want, and I would willingly go did I only find in the enterprise a pledge of my own earnestness.'[16] But what he found was a Graham Greene world of espionage, incompetence and innocent idealism betrayed in corruption. It ended up with one of the Apostles, Boyd, being shot with forty-eight other men on the beach at Málaga by a firing squad – at the second attempt. But by then Trench had come home. Even the violent stimulus of the expedition had failed to break 'the dead, stirless pool my mind is at present'.[17] The basic need was still there, unfulfilled, for 'some steady and constant occupation which shall be the aim of his being'.[18] His friends thought that literature would fit the bill, that he was at least as good a poet as Tennyson. He did not, but, looking elsewhere, wrote to F. D. Maurice for advice about theological reading and wrote to another friend: 'Literature will not do for me . . . There is always the central hollowness, the cold black speck at the heart, which is spreading and darkening, and which must be met by other arms than those which letters supply.'[19] This gloomy agitation was not only an expression of his troubled soul. It was also a reaction to the critical and alarming state of the country on the eve of the first Reform Bill. Arson at Coton had got Trinity undergraduates acting as firemen, and others patrolled the streets as vigilantes. It was against such a background that Trench began his life commitment to religion, so it is not surprising that he went for a hot and strong form: the Irvingites with their speaking in tongues and expectation of the approaching personal coming of Christ.

Two years later he had cooled enough to be ordained and so set his feet on the road that led to Dublin. He had had more than enough of doubt and of adventure and his choice was made. But his wide literary sympathies never left him, as we have seen. He kept up with his old Cambridge friends. He belonged to the Sterling Club, a dining club where high and liberal churchmen met with doubters such as Carlyle and John Stuart Mill; which got its name from a clergyman and Apostle who had notoriously lost his faith under the impact of German criticism, and of which the evangelical *Record* said: 'We almost wonder that it is not called the Strauss Club'.[20] He was at King's College, London in 1853 when Maurice was sacked from his Chair for doubting the doctrine of eternal punishment. He was in judiciously qualified sympathy with Maurice but thought that Maurice's doubts could detract from the moral earnestness of feeling that within the narrow limits of historical life we make great decisions in which 'everything must be gained or everything must be lost'.[21]

Contrast and likeness

There is plenty of contrast between Richard Trench and George Eliot. He had become aptly cautious and conservative for the job of standing guard over a traditional religious institution in troubled times of criticism. She had become aptly bold for the job of blazing a new religious trail for people who felt the troubles more deeply. He was the doubter turned corporate, ecclesiastical believer; she the Evangelical turned individual believer outside the walls. He was all for hanging on to what he had painfully won. She kept the nerve for bigger choices with the bigger losses and gains entailed. He was happy among the rich furniture of ancient symbols and allegories. She went for realism and the present – or the immediate past. But there was common ground as well. If she (as Huxley noticed) had stood critically against the dogmatic spirit in Christianity, he (as Pusey noticed) was not entirely happy or foursquare about it. They both had other loves and other homes than this. Trench was a poet and a philologist in an exact and a general sense: an expert in, and a lover of, words. He had hesitations about the Revised Version of the Bible because of the hallowed associations of the words of the King James Version in untutored minds. He warned his clergyman son against 'a fatal facility in writing and talking which some clergymen possess from the outset of their career'.

That 'fatal facility' is the besetting sin of the complacent dogmatist, the bugbear of those who use words in the patient exploration of elusive fundamentals. The times Trench and Eliot lived in were marked by strenuous criticism of dogma and equally strenuous assertion of it. A thunderous battle of 'isms' was in progress which made it the easiest thing in the world for a person to be 'viewy'. One could espouse an 'ism' and become a corporate believer. Or one might take the path of working out one's own salvation in fear and trembling and become an individual believer with a vengeance. The corporate believer found his reward in belonging to a distinct group. The individual believer found his reward in belonging to humanity at large. So the corporate believer got his nourishment from the dogma of his group. And the individual who wanted to be a believer in his own way could get his nourishment from the serious novel of personal pilgrimage set in human society at large: the *Bildungsroman* or novel of personal development of which *Middlemarch* is the crowning English example.

The distinctions are overdrawn, of course, and it is integral to our story that both its protagonists had a foot in the other camp. But the differences were there, they had to be confronted, and the quality of the confrontation and decision was decisive for character. Both Trench and Eliot were valued by their contemporaries for their integrity, and that was largely achieved by the loyalty each of them kept towards the place each had left: doubt for Trench, faith for Eliot. Where a person comes *from* is integral to character, and the quality of relation to the *from* is integral to integrity. In the stormy setting of dogma criticized and dogma revived it was hard to achieve – by no means a bygone theme.

The roots of the revival of dogma in Victorian Christianity are multiple and hard to uncover. Oxford in the 1830s, the time of the Oxford Movement, was certainly a major root. 'First was the principle of dogma,' said John Henry Newman in his *Apologia*. 'My battle was with liberalism; by liberalism I

meant the anti-dogmatic principle and its developments.' For
the preceding generation or two, dogma had not been an issue.
It was there, but the focal interest of Christianity was in social
duty and good works. To this cool kind of discipleship the
Evangelicalism of the turn of the centuries added warmth and
individual drama. Newman, like George Eliot, owed much to
it – his soul, he said. But it was not intellectually tough enough to
stand against the continued onslaught of liberalism and
criticism. Newman thought it played into their hands. For that
a bigger and stronger citadel was needed: corporate dogma.
An Oxford don of the 1830s had a lot of time on his hands. If
his heart had been excited by Evangelicalism along with a
romantic nostalgia for the remoter past, if he had been shaken
by the growing critique of Christianity (by politicians as well as
foreigners and intellectuals), if he had a consistently logical
mind to put at the service of transcendent mystery, then the
door was wide open for the return of dogma.

So Evangelicalism provided a positive religious stimulus for
those who revived dogma and for those who hated its revival.
The subsequent difference was made by one's attitude to
human nature in particular and society at large; was
belonging in it the point of departure or the goal, the city
of destruction to flee from or the Jerusalem to build in
England's green and pleasant land? Your answer to that question
was a major part of your answer to the question of
ecclesiastical dogma (or, corporate believing) and still is.

George Eliot gave her answer, loud and clear, in her essay
'Evangelical Teaching – Dr Cumming'. It is so hostile that it is
hard and important to remember that she is attacking a
distorted projection of something dear and integral to her.
And corporate dogmatism is in her view precisely the distorting
factor. 'Fatally powerful as religious systems have been,
human nature is stronger and wider than religious systems,
and though dogmas may hamper, they cannot absolutely
repress its growth.' She hated Cumming's view that goodness
was not good unless done in a consciously Christian way to
'make the name of God better known'. Goodness, demoted by
dogma, became instrumental at best – and even suspect.
Direct compassion would not do for Dr Cumming. But for her,
'only in proportion as it is compassion that speaks through the
eyes when we soothe, and moves the arm when we succour, is
a deed strictly benevolent. If the soothing or the succour be
given because another wishes or approves it, the deed ceases to

be one of benevolence and becomes one of deference, of obedience, of self-interest or vanity.' True Christianity is 'an extension and multiplication of the effects produced by human sympathy. And it has been intensified for the better spirits who have been under the influence of orthodox Christianity by the contemplation of Jesus as "God manifest in the flesh".'

It is impossible to ignore that final reference to the doctrine of incarnation. But what should we make of it, coming from her? She is using it polemically as a dogmatic stick to beat the dogmatist. There is no evidence for her being enthusiastic about it *as a dogma or a theory*. But just that is characteristic of her whole drive away from theory and into practice, the drive of *Middlemarch*. 'There is no general doctrine which is not capable of eating out our morality if unchecked by the deep-seated habit of direct fellow-feeling with individual fellow men' (ch. 61). And if we catch a note of genuine reverence in her reference to it along with the note of polemical triumph, it is because this doctrine is *the* doctrine that points down and away from the ideal fortified heights of corporate theory, into the 'hidden life' of being good 'amidst the conditions of an imperfect social state'. As modern theologians of liberation insist, incarnation commands a primacy of spirituality and action over theology.

General

When Judge Fitzgerald peered into Archbishop Trench's hat and saw '*Middlemarch* there laid open', he relished the secret meeting of apparently incongruous minds that it betrayed. Corporate orthodoxy and individual apostasy have trysts that neither of them like to advertise, but which have obvious importance in nourishing the lives of each. Orthodoxy has liked to see itself as a tradition tightly sealed within the sacred, 'the faith once delivered to the saints' uncontaminated by worldly influences. Two centuries of scientific criticism have broken that seclusion decisively. If Christianity is not to defy the historian it has to submit to his finding that noble, even divine, impulse is always 'struggling amidst the conditions of an imperfect social state'. To use its own more radical doctrinal language, such impulse is always unreservedly incarnate in an imperfect social state, can only work out salvation with the materials it provides. In practice, of course, it has not liked to take its own tendency so far. Some element of the special, of miracle or the unconditioned absolute, has been

202

posited at some such point as Scripture or the events behind it, in order to check its self-emptying career. George Eliot, following Feuerbach, would not allow that. She went the whole hog and it carried her beyond the fold of corporate Christian belief. But she had a problem of consistency too. She never got clear enough of Christianity to attain the purity of the thoroughgoing secularist. Nietzsche damned her for this very thing in the paragraph devoted to her in *Twilight of the Idols*.[22] 'They have got rid of the Christian God, and now feel obliged to cling all the more firmly to Christian morality: that is English consistency, let us not blame it on little blue-stockings *à la* Eliot.' He based his dismissal on the questionable premise that 'Christianity is a system, a consistently thought-out and complete view of things', which had to be decided for or against as such. But with sounder judgement he noticed Eliot's Christian debt, even allegiance. 'If they think they no longer have need of Christianity as a guarantee of morality, that is merely (!) the *consequence* of the ascendancy of Christian evaluation and an expression of the *strength* and *depth* of this ascendancy' (his italics). She lived deeply off reserves of Christian capital just as much as Christianity lives deeply off reserves of secular capital. This bothered many of her agnostic contemporaries more than it bothered her because of her decided distrust of all theory, her marked preference for the human reality. What sort of a problem is this worry about consistency? It is felt most acutely by those concerned with the conservation of 'a system, a consistently thought-out and complete view of things'. They are, as this commission has appreciated, doing an essential job. But when they look at the historical genesis of their system, and when they recall that the system is for people's good and salvation, they confront the other essential job of maintenance: that nurturing of healthy human development which depends on the Cambridge Apostles' 'belief that we *can* learn, and determination that we will learn, from people of the most opposite opinions'. It is as necessary as the more conservative kind of maintenance to a living and life-giving system.

For George Eliot those 'opposite opinions' were religious. They belonged to something she had left (but not entirely), still wrestled with though they hardly suited her system or immediate environment, and would return to in her last novel, *Daniel Deronda*. There is no doubt that they mattered to her, deeply and inconveniently. By the same token Trench had left the Apostles' world of literature pursued in terms of questioning self-development. Yet again, he had not entirely left it. It remained with him as an enrichment and an embarrassment. For each of them the loss of the opposite opinions for which the other stood would have been a loss of integrity.

A sharp and probing problem is posed by the one who walks out of the family circle, the black sheep. Not the one who leaves home for good, taking nothing away with him and sending nothing back, let alone returning himself, for he is no problem but rather a blank. He wanted something completely different and, presumably, got it. He is scarcely a black sheep at all. That title is reserved for the one who lives elsewhere and differently but keeps up the family connection in some form. He got something out of home which, precisely because he had got it so strongly – from the point of view of the delicately poised family *ethos* so exaggeratedly and lopsidedly – that he wanted to exploit and explore it elsewhere and without the constraints of other aspects of the family life which he was eccentric in not valuing much or at all. The very depth of his receiving enabled and impelled his departure and his subsequent ambiguous relation to home. There is a thread of attachment between him and the folks back home which is infrangible so long as no one breaks it out of doctrinaire pique. Letters from him are, perhaps, as welcome as parcels from freedom to prisoners of war. It could be of him that grandfather speaks as he dies. But the thread is always in tension. To the stay-at-homes he is always 'our own and not our own'. To get the pitch of the tension, that phrase should be said in tones of embarrassment and wonder alternately. To get its resonance, it should be remembered that 'our own and not our own' is just what the Christian believer wants to say about God and neighbour as an expression of the love of both which is his central duty and being.

Believing and fiction

It is not a coincidence that this exploration of the scope and mode of corporate belief has revolved around the writer and the reader of a novel. As a contribution to the commission's discussions of the function of stories in corporate belief it may be worth adding a note about realistic fiction in this context.

The head and front of the offence of Strauss's *Life of Jesus* was the damage it did to the credibility of the gospels.

'Dissecting the beautiful story' made George Eliot ill. Trench smelt 'mischief' in it. But Strauss himself was relatively complacent. He thought that it would be possible to reunite on speculative grounds what he had broken up by criticism: in his own words, 'to re-establish dogmatically that which has been destroyed critically'. The contrast is a measure of the difference between English and German culture in the nineteenth century. The great age of philosophers in Germany was the great age of novelists in England. Doctrine was the chief moral and spiritual instructor in one, story in the other. But that cultural balance has not been reflected in theology where the philosopher has until very recently been honoured with much more serious attention than the novelist. This, we are beginning to realize, is a misfortune. Realistic narrative, with fiction closely related to the disciplines of history, has roots in our Bible which contains examples of it (the Joseph story, the succession narrative of 2 Samuel 9–1 Kings 2.46) which have scarcely been equalled or excelled since. To lose track of it, to fail to identify it positively, was to lose an ally and a discipline of immense popular appeal. Far more people can get their minds and hearts round stories than can get them round philosophical discourse. Above all, the growth of realistic fiction was tied in to the criticism of Christianity and offered a solution to the problem of 'how, then, to be religious?' which it posed.

Nowhere is this clearer than with George Eliot. She knew the methods and force of biblical criticism as well as anybody in England at the time. It had a strong thrust against the miraculous. Earlier critics had tried to explain biblical miracles in terms of the reigning naturalistic/scientific outlook. Jesus was not walking on the water but on a shallowly submerged spit of land, did not multiply the loaves but got everyone to share, and so on. But to the great nineteenth-century critics this was an explaining away rather than an explanation and failed on two grounds. One was seriously religious. Such interpretations were empty of religious meaning. The other was seriously historical. They did no justice to the different outlook of a different age and place. They were beside the point to the succeeding generation with its much more acute sense of 'the pastness of the past', its much more positive appreciation of the 'oriental', the 'primitive' and the 'antique'. For all his brutality, Strauss wanted to say that the gospel writers were saying things of religious importance in their miraculous tales

205

and were not just the victims of laughable misunderstandings.

Miracle was out. That was the agreed ground of biblical criticism and remained so in the sense that the defence of miracle could not get away from the taint of special pleading and the rearguard action. On the evangelistic level, it lost its persuasive appeal. How, then, was one to persuade people of the truth of Christianity? One way was to abandon the stories which had come to pieces on the critic's desk, to catch the vital fluids which had spilled out of them in theoretical containers, in the pots of ideas and spirituality. That was Strauss's way and it was at the heart of Bultmann's demythologizing too. But will it do? Are ideas a good swap for stories, good enough to do justice to the heart of Christianity, good enough to convert people to it? Edwin Muir thought not. 'The word made flesh here is made word again.'[23] And there he touched on the Christian symbol or doctrine which was George Eliot's touchstone too – incarnation as the symbol which points commandingly down to the actual, the theory which insists on the story. But now it could not be the same story. The miracle-packed tale just would not serve the same serious religious purpose which it had once. The times really had changed. But the supernatural was far from being the only ingredient of biblical narratives. In Jesus's parables, arguments and aphorisms, in the story of his fate, there was a realistic religious humanism which could be transposed into the popular Lives of Jesus which flooded from the presses. Or into the realistic novel like *Middlemarch*.

The judgement of literary history is that the latter has won the day. *Middlemarch* is better nourishment for the believing soul than Dean Farrar's *Life of Christ,* or Strauss's *Life of Jesus.* This is not just because George Eliot was a better writer than either of them. It is because she chose a more far-reaching and penetrating path. Impelled by an incarnational 'no' to mere theory and an incarnational 'yes' to down-to-earth goodness working itself out in unmiraculous conditions, she struck gold which too many of the theologians of the orthodox camp missed. She got there by a more circuitous and unpromising route than theirs, through a far country in their view – though it lay at their doorsteps and was, indeed, a large part of their home ground.

Conclusion

But Trench at least was no stranger to it. When Judge

Fitzgerald saw him, his attention and interest were there rather than with the opening speeches. *Middlemarch* was home ground for him. Here was the painful progress from the incandescent vision (Spain, the Irvingites) to the round of duty. And within that transition there was the finding, through self-doubt, of something worth a life's commitment. Here was the moral rigour which he had always felt essential to true living combined with the compassion which his friends saw in him, the realization of how other people feel. Perhaps the greatest triumph of that in the novel is the tender handling of Mr Bulstrode's ruin, for Bulstrode embodied all that Feuerbach and George Eliot most hated in religion – yet was still entitled to a gentle understanding. For Trench, always under fire from prospering Bulstrodes, such understanding was a wearing and official duty. His life, in fact, was an extraordinarily exact embodiment of the muted virtues celebrated in the last paragraph of *Middlemarch,* the 'noble impulse struggling amidst the conditions of an imperfect social state', the misunderstanding, the 'finely touched spirit' that 'had still its fine issues', the 'incalculably diffusive' influence for good – and the relative obscurity into which he has sunk compared with noisier and more partisan or fortunate clerical contemporaries. What the judge saw was not something accidental, nor as incongruous as it looked at first sight. It was a glimpse of the subterranean springs which supply believing in the corporate individual.

NOTES

1   Maurice Keen, 'Beginning with Abel', in *Theology,* November 1979.
2   T. G. Selby, *The Theology of Modern Fiction* (1896), p. 8. All the other views of *Middlemarch* quoted in this paragraph may be found in G. S. Haight, *George Eliot – A Biography.* (OUP 1968).
3   *Inquiry,* 2nd edn., p. 451.
4   *Letters of George Eliot,* 1.206, ed. H. Haight (OUP 1954).
5   Feuerbach, *The Essence of Christianity,* tr. G. Eliot, p. 249.
6   Feuerbach, p. 51.
7   Feuerbach, p. 32. Readers who are put off by his German rhetoric will find many of his leading ideas explored more clearly and coolly by Don Cupitt in *Taking Leave of God.* (SCM Press 1980).
8   T. H. Huxley, *Life and Letters,* ed. L. Huxley, 2.19.

9 Haight, op. cit., p. 256, quoting George Eliot's journal.

10 My sources are J. Bromley, *The Man of Ten Talents*, (SPCK 1959); and Peter Allen, *The Cambridge Apostles: The Early Years*, (Cambridge University Press 1978). Trench still awaits a thorough biographer.

11 J. Bromley, pp. 65 ff. No date given.

12 Sidgwick, quoted in Peter Allen, op. cit., p. 4.

13 ibid., p. 86.

14 Blakesley to Milnes, quoted by Allen, p. 94.

15 F. D. Maurice, quoted by Allen, p. 70.

16 Trench, letter to Donne, quoted by Allen, p. 104.

17 Trench, letter to Donne, quoted by Allen, p. 112.

18 Donne, letter to Blakesley, quoted by Allen, p. 113.

19 Trench, letter to Donne, quoted by Allen, pp. 125 ff.

20 Quoted in O. Chadwick, *The Victorian Church* (Black 1971) 1, p. 542.

21 Sermon, 'Christ the Judge of All Men', in *Sermons preached before the University of Cambridge* (1863).

22 1889, tr. R. J. Hollingdale (Penguin Books 1968), p. 69.

23 'The Incarnate One', in *Collected Poems* (Faber 1960), p. 228.

8

The Individual in the Church of England

J. McManners.

Commitment

What do I mean when I say 'I believe'?[1] If I say 'I believe that
Bismarck distrusted German patriotism', it means that the
evidence points this way, though as an historian I reserve the
right to change my mind if new evidence comes along. If, like
the American in the joke, in reply to the question 'Do you
believe in baptism by immersion?' I say 'Sure, I've seen it
done', the implication is that the improbable fact is admitted to
be true, but I dissociate myself from it. A similar realistic
admission is made by the devils in the Epistle of St James, who
'believe and tremble' – they admit the fact, it has a powerful
effect on them, but not the right one. When a Christian
prefaces the creed with 'I believe' or 'We believe', he means
more than these examples convey. He is not just saying
(though he is saying) that such evidence as he has seen is
congruous with the belief. Nor is he attesting the facts in a
neutral spirit; on the contrary, he is reacting to the facts, and
reacting rightly. He is obeying the purpose behind the facts he
is rehearsing. To him, belief implies commitment.

All this is included in the content of 'I believe'. But an
inventory of content falls short of an explanation, and we
would have to venture far into the realms of psychology and
spirituality to understand better the process by which desire is
born, trust is established and choice is made. In the last resort,
generalization will break down, and the only explanation that
remains will be my own dimly understood individual spiritual
autobiography. It is difficult to know oneself, yet at the very
least I have an obligation to know something about how and
why I got to my position of commitment – if only because men
who give themselves to a cause without reservations are
dangerous if they never ask these questions. It will not do to
say that I am here because some external authority has
vouched for the propositions in which I believe, for·if so, I must

209

have accepted that authority, and the tacitly understood first proposition of my creed is 'I believe in the authority of . . .' whether it be Church, Bible, pope, etc. How did I get to the position of commitment to this authority as well as to the propositions I am accepting under its shadow?

One thing is certain: I do not come to believe as a lonely individual. There is no isolated man according to Nature: there is no solitary religion. What comes to me is always, in some sense, an inheritance – 'What hast thou that thou didst not receive?' 'We all start life', writes Father D'Arcy,[2]

> with beliefs which we have learnt from others, and we all need a discipline to mould our character and our thought. Nor does this cease at some adult stage. We never cease to rely on community life and to lean on good friends, to give of the one talent which may be ours and to gain by the gifts and talents of others which we do not possess ourselves. We stand on the shoulders of the past and learn to the end of our lives from the accumulated experience of mankind.

When I say 'I believe' it is as the heir to a tradition, as a member of a community. 'I believe' is always 'We believe'. What sort of comfort, and what sort of constraint (for both are involved) does this 'we' imply?

We can only begin to answer the question when we recognize that the word 'authority' is ambiguous, and that the word 'belief' does not stand alone. 'Authority' – exercised for what end? – for what desired result? In the Church, there must obviously rest a regulatory authority, as in a golf club, making decisions about common procedures, eligibility for membership, etc. This sort of controlling force may, on occasion, resemble the activities of 'the kings of the Gentiles', though one would hope that it would not be so among us. But a regulatory authority cannot settle my position in the eyes of God, and cannot tell me to say 'I believe'. If it does so tell me, and I obey only for obedience's sake, what content is left in the word 'believe'? My response must have real worth. In matters of personal belief, the authority of the Church can only be evocative and inspirational, and the end and aim of its exercise should be to bring me to a deeper faith and trust in God (with all the implications that follow concerning my conduct towards men).

The Church talks to me of 'belief' only because I have faith, and the Church's duty towards me is to deepen that faith.

Some of the questions of authority that concern us are answered if we return to the word 'faith' rather than to the word 'belief'. Faith involves risk, loyalty and total commitment; and belief is, as it were, a regulator for faith. Throughout the history of the Church, Christians have lived and died for Christ, putting their trust in his love, forgiveness, example and victory. The Church is, in the first place, the community of faith, rather than of belief. The commitment, the free self-giving, comes first – just as Christ gave himself for us freely, before anyone could know who he was. It will take us, it will take the Church, all eternity to find out what to believe – but the commitment of faith is total now. It is in the community of those who live by faith – faith as an inheritance and faith as a personal possession – that we say 'I believe'.

But the problem of defining the comfort and the constraint involved in saying 'we believe' remains. The Church, by its regulatory authority, prescribes forms of words concerning belief – this is inevitable if questions concerning membership and office-holding are to be settled, and if liturgical observances are to proceed with decent unanimity. The Church is telling me to say 'we believe' by its regulatory authority, but by the exercise of a different authority, persuasive, evocative and inspirational, it is encouraging me to make this into 'I believe', through my life, through my prayers and in my complete allegiance. In this sense, 'we believe' and 'I believe' are different things, though they are inseparable even so. When I say 'we believe', I do not mean that there are some propositions that I personally accept while hoping that the remaining ones will be accepted by other people to make up a complete creed; on the contrary, I am striving to appropriate them all in a more intense and inward fashion. When I say 'I believe', I do not mean that I have independently and in isolation assessed the propositions coming to me from the community and found them logical and satisfying. What it does mean is that I am committed by faith to Christ and that I find him within a tradition and within a community. Loyalty to that tradition and membership of that community impose restraints on will and intellect. These I must interpret for myself; this is my continuing and lifelong Christian responsibility.

The simplicity and mystery of the gospel

W. G. Ward once said that he would wish to find a papal bull published every morning in the newspapers, to read while he was having his breakfast. He rejoiced in the interventions of 'infallibility'. His *boutade* may serve to remind us, not only that it is frivolous to find delight in the exercise of authority, but also that it is dangerous to take pride in our devoted singularity, or to congratulate ourselves on our complacent unanimity in the face of our fellow Christians of other persuasions. The assertion of marginal doctrines as an act of internal solidarity or external defiance should not become entangled with the proclamation of the gospel. If the trumpet ought to speak with no uncertain sound, this should be to proclaim our hope and trust in the love of God, and to rehearse our social and moral duties. Doctrinal assertions derived from the original redemptive intervention of God in history come to be shored up with logical inferences, doctrines, as it were, of the second rank. Too much logic allied to too great an insistence on structural completeness, and we may find that we (I mean each of us individually) are playing a sort of intellectual game, a giving and taking in 'Monopoly' money rather than real currency. The Pauline exhortation to forswear things legitimate in themselves rather than cause a brother to stumble, does not apply solely to meats offered to idols, or to other manifestations of external conduct. Our personal doctrinal baggage may contain items repugnant to our fellow pilgrims, embarrassing if produced as a badge of privilege or praised with disproportionate fervour.

There should be a fundamental simplicity about the proclamation of the love of God manifested in Jesus. There is a 'story' to be told, a message of salvation to be given. Doctrines exist to guide the preacher's inspiration in telling that story, in transmitting that message. They are not propositions to be proclaimed in their own right. Their role should always be subordinate. They are markers (not fences) on the far boundaries of the paths that lead to Christ – indicating, not the point where a man must draw back, but simply warning that those before have glimpsed some danger there. They are signposts affording guidance in the rich complex world of the Scriptures – not mandatory warnings, but encouragements to exploration. Doctrines should look forward to the time, nearer than we think for each of us, when they will have no further meaning. Few Christians have been as zealous for the strictest niceties of doctrine than the Jansenists at the end of the seventeenth century, yet it was Quesnel who advised his pious readers, when they approached the end of their lives, to turn their thoughts solely to meditation on the final vision of God – the vision before which theology, St Paul and the gospels themselves become irrelevant, lamps burning in the darkness, and due to be extinguished at the dawning of the day.[3]

Christians do certain things as their bounden duty, and proclaiming the truth that is in them is one of these obligations. Inevitably, as they do so, they invent or – more likely – repeat, propositions summing up their belief, drawn or adapted from the Scriptures, the Fathers, articles, liturgies, creeds, the writings of theologians, and so on. But the definition of doctrine by an act of 'authority' for the whole of the Church concerned should be an event so rare as to be almost unthinkable. Definitions of this kind should take place only in a time of desperate crisis, at a time, indeed, when to remain silent would in itself constitute a definition on one side of the argument. To define draws a line around part of the Christian community, giving confidence, maybe, to those inside the newly drawn circle, releasing them from their doubts and perplexities. But however much this sort of mental consolation, sometimes called 'certainty', is yearned for, is it really calculated to help us to progress in our Christian living and Christian thinking? And we must not forget that the drawing of that consoling boundary must, by definition, leave other people outside it, people who would have wished to remain within. There are evangelical provisions for mounting a search for lost sheep, but not, so far as I know, for barring the gates of the fold against them. More than this, the drawing of a doctrinal line is likely to sharpen the boundaries of disagreement which separate Christians of different persuasions. It is true that the schisms which separate us from each other are not unrelieved tragedies – for they are the inevitable and inspirational outcome of the exercise of Christian liberty and the determination to preach the gospel in season and out of season. Even so, while we rejoice in the unique insights which our own branch of the Church has given us, we have a duty not to add to the tragic effects of disunity. We must ask ourselves seriously what right the members of a particular church have to add definitions to the historic documents which have so far accumulated: documents coming from the Church undivided, and also documents which are evidence of the bitter discussions in which our peculiar allegiance has been forged. New propositional statements, it

213

may be argued, should in future only be made in an ecumenical context (the recent Roman Catholic and Anglican discussions, for example, are a case where the dominating motivation of the scholars concerned was to talk of what unites us). A Church that speaks alone, speaks necessarily in schism.

But the decisive reason why doctrinal definition of the formal kind should take place only in extreme and desperate circumstances is because the natural state of the Christian individual ought to be freedom. He serves a God 'whose service is perfect freedom'. Christianity is a life, and life must be spontaneous; Christianity is love, and love must be freely given; Christianity is union with Christ, and the riches of his nature are unsearchable, beyond all human language. St Augustine's 'Have love and do what you will' may be amended to apply to doctrinal issues: 'Have love and believe what you will.'

Just as the antinomian recklessness of the original phrase may seem dangerous to morals,[4] so 'Have love and believe what you will' may seem precariously libertarian so far as doctrine is concerned; indeed, there are qualifications of a practical nature to be made to it. But it is now being set out as the ideal – so far as possible in this evil, contentious world, a church ought to be trying to say this to its individual members. (Note that the argument is limited to what happens inside the redeemed community, and to how the 'authority' of the Church should be viewed from within. The constraints on will and intellect which life within a community engender are assumed as existing, to the highest degree, in 'love'. Inheriting the Scriptures, living within the tradition, turning ever to Christ in faith, I am free; and whatever guidance it may offer me in propositions, the Church is saying to me 'Have love, and believe what you will'.) As an ideal, the phrase has the advantage, first of all, that it recognizes the way in which Christian allegiance begins, endures and intensifies. The early Christians offered to each other a mutual aid which the crowded cities of imperial Rome had never known. They cared for widows, the aged, the orphans; they regarded marriage as sacred and honoured women. To their intense life of fellowship they admitted all classes and all conditions; the pagan Celsus complained that they made fools and sinners welcome. E. R. Dodds writes, 'Christians were in more than a formal sense, "members one of another". I think that was a major cause, perhaps the strongest single cause, of the spread of

Christianity.'[5] Men and women were converted, not to a doctrine, but to a way of life. It was the way of Jesus, and in the eucharistic observances which stemmed from him, recalling the tragedy and triumph of his passion, they came to an instinctive knowledge of who he must have been, who he continually was, and how they would be welcomed by him at the end of the world. The proclamation of the *love of God in Jesus Christ* is and was the *raison d'être* and inspiration of the Christian community. But the pattern of developing allegiance of the first Christians seems to have been: the 'story' preached and the message of salvation given; the way of life accepted; the liturgy conveying the full force and practical obligations of the story – then he that had willed to do of the will came to know of the doctrine.

Generalizations of this kind are, of course, guesses about how the confusions of the past should be interpreted. When he has access to comprehensive information, the sociologist will find many a complexity of motivation in conversion to a 'sect' – the consolation of 'belonging', the desire to escape from the feeling of 'relative deprivation', the rejoicing in formulae which seem to make sense of existence (this latter, according to Bryan Wilson, being particularly powerful in the case of Jehovah's Witnesses).[6] By contrast there is another kind of sociological investigation – the work of the school of Gabriel Le Bras in France, which studies the continuing force of motivation within the long-established Christian Church. The surprising endurance of patterns of religious practice and contrasting irreligious attitudes in various areas of France is evidence of the importance of family and folkway in maintaining traditional religious allegiance. From this evidence, one is tempted to say that Christianity is not taught, not caught, but inherited. But there can be a general conclusion: intellectual adhesion to doctrinal propositions is normally secondary in bringing an individual into the Christian community and in keeping him there.

The ideal, 'Have love and believe what you will' also recognizes that God is mysterious, known to us only in his acts of self-revealing love. Beyond these acts, there is 'natural religion', but no sure understanding. Definitions are marginal to the story of what God has done for man, and the worship which man is obliged to offer to God. We have a doctrine of the Trinity because the process of revelation and redemption, freely initiated and entirely completed by God, seems to

215

demand this sort of formula when we talk about the divine nature. The original events of revelation from which our faith flows must always be mysterious.

There is mystery at the beginning of God's revelation – and caught up in that revelation and its eternal consequences, we are carried on into mystery. Michael Ramsey expresses the forward-looking inspiration of the Church memorably – an inspiration in which hope is sweeping on beyond the bounds of all possible knowledge.

> The Church can never be said to have apprehended the truth. Rather is the truth the divine action which apprehends the Church. Dimly it understands what it teaches. For the more the Church learns of God, the more it is aware of the incomprehensible mystery of His Being, in creation and in transcendence and on the Cross. Christ 'has made God known as Father, Creator, Saviour, and has made possible a new access for man in worship to God', yet the more God is known as Father, Creator, Saviour, the more 'other' He is found to be from all that man can express or imagine of a Father, a Creator, a Saviour. 'If any man thinketh that he knoweth anything, he knoweth not yet as he ought to know; but if any man loveth God, the same is known of him' (1 Cor. 8.2–3). The more the Church knows, the more it is aware that a great unknown lies ahead . . . The Church's perilous office of teaching is inseparable from the Church's worship of the mystery whereby it exists.[7]

Thus, Ramsey goes on, 'Creeds are dangerous documents.' As St Hilary, one of Athanasius' supporters, wrote: 'We are compelled to attempt what is unattainable, to climb where we cannot reach, to speak what we cannot utter. Instead of the bare adoration of faith we are compelled to entrust the deep things of religion to the perils of human expression.'

Thus, God is at the beginning and at the end of the Church, and God is directly available through Christ to every Christian believer in prayer and sacrament. How can this possibly be so? We do not have an explanation; we simply describe the events of love in history, and use them as pointers, backwards and forwards, to the mysterious heart of the universe. The first reaction to the Christian message must be wonder. Speculation without wonder is a soul-destroying thing, and a doctrine is deadly if the sense of mystery is not woven into it.

216

The very God! think, Abib; dost thou think?
So, the All-Great, were the All-Loving too –
So, through the thunder comes a human voice
Saying, 'Oh heart I made, a heart beats here!
Face, My hands fashioned, see it in Myself.
Thou hast no power, nor may'st conceive of Mine,
But love I gave thee, with Myself to love,
And thou must love Me who have died for thee!
The madman saith He said so: it is strange!'

(from *An Epistle, containing the strange medical experience of Karshish, the Arab Physician* (1855) by Robert Browning.)

Christians have a lesson of reverence to learn from unbelievers. It ought not to be easy to believe that the All-Great is the All-Loving. 'It is strange!' And since it is strange, we must wonder, and because we wonder, we must worship.

The Holy Spirit and Church history

The late Professor Butterfield taught us to beware of the 'Whig interpretation of history'. Revolutions, wars and social destruction always turn out to be 'for the best' – some ideal of freedom is enunciated or realized, for example, some new and achieving class arises. But things only turn out for the best because men make the best of their tragedies, make a virtue out of necessity. The potentialities for good in the order that has been destroyed are forgotten. We are preoccupied with making the best of the world which we inherit – it is all we have.

There is a danger that Christians may adopt a 'Whig interpretation' of doctrinal development, taking the working of the Holy Spirit, the directing power of Providence and the promise that the Church will be led into all truth, to mean that everything that happens is for the best, and that doctrine develops in a linear and cumulative process. One extreme way of putting this view would be to say that at any point in time the doctrine of the Church is found to be 'right', given the circumstances and needs and understanding of the day. Another would be to say there is a pattern of ebb and flow, but that each time the waves of challenge and strife recede, the solid bulk of orthodoxy is revealed, a lighthouse intact on its unshakable rock, and furnished with new safeguards against the recurrence of the recently averted dangers. In either case, it was necessary for the good of the Church and, maybe, of the world, that the Arians should have been routed, that Augustine should have defeated Pelagians and Donatists. Even on this view of doctrinal development, we should be more respectful than we usually are to heretics, for orthodoxy was defined and fortified because of their challenge – it was the evolutionary product of the pressures and insistencies of heresy. But, in fact, is the story of the victory of 'orthodoxy' the only possible one for providence to have sponsored? The universal society, inspired, at least in theory by Christian principles, built on a solid foundation of doctrines identical everywhere, and everywhere accepted, the Christendom of the Middle Ages, is one of the splendours of human history, a monument of culture and civilization which men will always admire and to which they may yet look back with hopeless nostalgia. Even so, it is not just the thinkers of the Enlightenment who are entitled to have reservations. What would have happened both to religion and to material and social development if there had been no Christendom? Instead, there might have been a vast diversity of Christian and quasi-Christian religious concepts fragmented over a more diversified social order, and such a richly varied pattern of Christian traditions might have shaped the culture of a more heterogeneous European civilization. Then (we may imagine) by our own day it would have been slowly coming towards federation and a doctrinal consensus might have been emerging. Would all this have been better, one wonders, than what actually did happen – the story of a splendid monolithic Christendom shattered eventually by the Reformation and the rise of national states, and now trying to find its new role in an alien world unified by technology but divided by ideologies and inequalities?

Because religion has played such an enormous part in history as the bearer of culture, there have been times when doctrinal decisions have involved the whole structure of the human future. At the end of the seventeenth and the beginning of the eighteenth century a few courageous Jesuits in Pekin were attempting to accommodate the Chinese religion to Christianity. They were disowned by Rome. A loyal churchman may, perhaps, take pleasure in the official intervention which guaranteed the purity of the faith. But the historian is bound to ask, what might have happened, what enormous consequences for good might have ensued if the syncretistic ingenuities of the Jesuits had been allowed to

218

proceed and bear their fruit? Nowadays, we are conscious how faiths other than our own have much to contribute to our Christian heritage. Was this almost forgotten incident in doctrinal prohibition the greatest of missed opportunities? And secularly speaking, what would the West not be willing to give now to be able to rewrite from the beginning the story of its relations with the ancient civilization of China? These speculations on what might have been sound alarming, but all they imply is the obvious fact that we do not regard the Church as infallible, but simply as indefectible, and that we do not know how God's providence works to ensure indefectibility, nor the time scale on which it operates. Christians believe that the Church is indwelt by the Holy Spirit, the Spirit of Christ working among his people. But this does not mean that men are no longer free agents, that the shaping of the destiny of the Church is taken out of their hands. Still less does it mean that any particular form of church government is sacrosanct as the exclusive vehicle of the Spirit's guidance. Nor does it mean that at any given moment all the doctrines Christians are propagating are guaranteed to be veracious or, even, salutary and useful. The wind bloweth where it listeth; if we must attempt to describe more precisely the working of the Spirit in the Church, we should look in the first place at the Pauline list of the fruits of the Spirit, and at the multitude of Christian biographies over the past 2000 years, stories of courage and sanctity. These lives, in all sorts of ways and with all sorts of heretical, confused and mistaken ideas about the person of Christ and his will in matters concerning his Church, proclaimed his leadership and affirmed their loyalty. The Spirit gives illumination enough to live by – not light to make clear every detail of the landscape and to enable a treatise on its geography to be written, but light to show the next step further on the way – 'one step enough for me'.

For Christian history in the connected, institutional sense, we should – I imagine – consider the Spirit working, not only as a guide on a pathway seen to be good, leading us into truth, but also as inspiring us in choosing between alternative paths each with its own particular good, as giving us courage to rectify the disorders springing from our free and frequent mistaken choices. Under the Spirit, we learn from our mistakes, and do collective penitence for them. There is no predestinate future (short of the final hope of glory) for either mankind or for the Church. We are free. The guidance we are to expect is not that God will show us the road he has chosen for us – the only single road; it is rather that God is helping us to choose our own road to serve him. If, subsequently, we find that we have chosen wrongly, God is still with us. He is a God who is present in the joyful consensus of the faithful when they go forward confidently; he is there equally in the shadow of despair. There is a light of hope ahead, but not just a single way towards it; Christ is there, not only at the goal, but with us on our journey. He is with us, for his habit was, as we know, to consort with sinners. Among the many enheartening consequences that flow from the continual presence of Christ and his Spirit there is one of a different kind that churches collectively seem to find harder to accept than individuals. We must always, whether in ethics, church order, ecclesiastical politics – or doctrine – in Cromwell's words, 'think it possible that we may be mistaken'.

Authority and consensus: Roman and Orthodox views

What has so far been argued is, I hope, compatible with a reverence for the Scriptures. They tell of Jesus Christ and of the mystery of the divine origin of his Church, and of the sacramental observances going back to the magic years when, scattered abroad among the cities of the Roman Empire, there were those who had walked and talked with the Master. But this view of the working of the Holy Spirit is indeed incompatible with any view of doctrinal pronouncements in the post-apostolic Church as being infallible, either individually or cumulatively.

Properly understood, the claim to infallibility, even in the Roman Church, has never been quite so extreme as it sounds, and it is certainly no longer what it once was. [8] To be infallible, the pope or a general council under the headship of the pope, must be speaking *ex cathedra,* on a matter of faith and morals, in a declaration clearly recognizable as a dogmatic decision, and addressed to the whole Church. The Second Vatican Council has integrated the ruling of the First Vatican Council into the concept that the episcopate collegially united with and under the pope, has infallible doctrinal authority. Catholic thought today does not make concessions about the past (the pope can act as the head of the episcopate without necessarily asking previous assent, and the *magisterium* is guided by the Holy Spirit when it decides the boundaries of its own right to pronounce). Even so, it is conceded that the language of any past definition is conditioned by its time. Infallible dogmas are not regarded as 'ultimates', but as 'milestones in the development of Church doctrine'. And the Second Vatican Council is essentially appealing to the consensus of all the people of God, dioceses being considered as represented in their bishops when chief pastors meet collegially under the pope. 'Infallibility', says a recent Catholic commentator, 'does in fact aim at the *consensus ecclesiae,* and lives by it.'[9]

There is a lesson here for Anglicans. While, to an Anglican, the individual conscience is supreme, the ideal of 'consensus' stands as a corrective to excessive individuality. Those who value conscience so highly must pay equal regard to the consciences of others. And consensus includes the past generations. Tradition and consensus go together, and together they are to be revered. Through them alone can a church remain a unity in the service of Christ, and the divided churches be brought into communion.

For the Orthodox Church,[10] the decrees of the seven ecumenical councils are taken as infallible. These decrees, together with the Bible and the Nicene Creed, are unique witnesses to the truth, and they are supported by the Fathers, the liturgy (the essential source for some doctrines not fully proclaimed in the formal way, e.g. concerning the Mother of God, the saints and the departed), Canon Law and the holy icons. In strict theory, the 'doctrine of the Lord' is being preserved as it was delivered. But, says Kallistos Ware, loyalty to the tradition requires a 'creative fidelity' – the list of the Fathers is not closed; another ecumenical council could meet, so the possibility of change exists. What, then, is the argument to defend the absolute status of an ecumenical council? Ware says that the number of bishops and the comprehensive nature of their geographical incidence is not the final test: the test is, the decisions of a particular council have to be accepted by the whole Church, not juridically, not by a plebiscite, but by an assent that is lived. The role of 'guardian' of the truth belongs to the whole people of God – bishops, clergy and laity in organic unity: 'The people possess the truth, but it is the bishops' particular office to proclaim it.'[11] The worshipping Church is also the Church that lives the creed, and it is in praying and living that the doctrines are validated. Indeed, in the end, the doctrines only have meaning because they are being lived right through in the name and in the Spirit of Jesus. Thus, in the Byzantine liturgy, the creed is introduced by the words: 'Let us love one another, that with one mind we may confess Father, Son and Holy Spirit, Trinity one in essence and undivided.'[12]

If one accepts this explanation of why the seven ecumenical councils are infallible, and follows it right through in all its consequences, 'infallibility' is redefined, and is seen to be something needing continual renewal – the *continuing* assent of the people of God, which is not to be presumed to have been 'frozen' at any particular moment and irretrievably given. However this may be, the Orthodox view of the final authority in the Church in matters of doctrine seems to be near the heart of what we are concerned with in 'corporate believing'. The whole people of God appropriate the credal formulae and make them a living reality by worship and by sacrificial living. And if we look at the New Testament records concerning our origins, is it not clear that this is where the credal formulae came from in the first place – from a vortex of intense worship and deeply sacrificial living, which swirled around the infinitely attractive and eternally inscrutable figure of the man who walked the hills of Galilee in perfect love and died on a cross outside Jerusalem? Worship and sacrificial living and the sense of the redeemed community inform the credal statements which emerge from the New Testament age in a way in which later and more formal creeds could not reproduce.

> This then is the message which we have heard of him, and declare unto you, that God is light, and in him is no darkness at all. If we say that we have fellowship with him, and walk in darkness, we lie, and do not the truth: but if we walk in the light, as he is in the light, we have fellowship one with another, and the blood of Jesus Christ his Son cleanseth us from all sin. (1 John 1.5–7 AV)

The Anglican appeal to tradition and consensus

The idea of an 'alternative' history put forward above can be used as a criticism of what exists, as a warning against complacency. This does not mean, however, that Christians are drifting at the mercy of every wind of doctrinal speculation. To say that the pattern of history, including doctrinal development, could have been different, is not to say that, *sub specie aeternitatis,* it could have been radically different. The overwhelming impact of Jesus on his friends, the astonishing honesty of his teaching, his complete openness towards God, his demand for total allegiance, the brooding mystery of salvation bound up with his cruel death – this remains, and whatever inadequate formula men devise to describe it, it is an eternal heritage. The Holy Spirit works continually within the Church, and in the heart of every Christian; that we may be mistaken or limited in a particular formula we follow to describe Christian truth, does not deprive us of that continual presence. The Spirit, we might say rather recklessly, does not guarantee the veracity of a particular doctrinal formula, but does guarantee that those who seek Christ honestly, right formula or wrong formula, will find him. We belong to the Christian community, and while we must always in the end follow our individual conscience, we are aided continually by the consensus, by the accompanying faith of our fellow Christians. The vast procession of the past generations which have loved Jesus (whether in heresy or orthodoxy) is our inheritance, and in our worship we reach out to Jesus as they reached out to him. Their quest is our quest; whatever they discovered is ours. We live within a consensus and within a tradition.

The Church of England above all others lives by consensus and appeals to tradition. But it does not thereby accept an infallible authority vested in men or in the works of men. General councils are not infallible (cf. Article 21). True, there is a reverence towards conciliar decisions. 'The Church of England', says Jeremy Taylor, 'receives the four first Generals [i.e. general councils] as of high regard, not that they are infallible, but that they have determined wisely and holily.'[13] This is the test – did they make resolutions in a wise and holy spirit? The question follows, who adjudicates what was wise and holy in the context? Similarly to the Anglican, Scripture contains all that is necessary for salvation, but the interpretation of Scripture is guided by what the preface to the Prayer Book calls 'the godly and decent order of the ancient Fathers'. But there are difficulties about this 'tradition'.[14] What are the chronological limits of the appeal to primitive antiquity? Who says which writer is one of the Fathers? It is easy to see the authority resting in the generation which knew Jesus – but what of the generation which knew the first generation, and the successive generations after that? No doubt the Anglican appeal to antiquity was a weapon against Rome – an appeal to the tradition before the Church was divided. This is, indeed, the force of the Prayer Book's reference to 'the godly and decent order of the ancient

Fathers'; it is a question of reading the Bible, instead of the 'multitude of responds, verses, vain repetitions, commemorations and synodals'. But tradition has not been simply a weapon of controversy for Anglicans. First, since Scripture is the essential source of all we believe, the nearer we can get to the primitive testimony enshrined in Scripture, the better tradition is likely to be. Thus, in Simon Patrick's counterblast against Bellarmine (*The Second Note of the Church Examined,* 1687), we find: 'And who dare say that this is a new Religion, which is as old as Christ and His Apostles? With whom whosoever agree, they are truly ancient Churches, though of no longer standing than yesterday; as they that disagree with them are new, though they can run up their pedigree to the very Apostles'.[15] Second, since Scripture is our essential source, we must give special reverence to the earlier generations which defined the canon. This no doubt is why the first four centuries are a convincing length of time to constitute primitive antiquity: a reverence for this formative period is logically required of those who make Scripture their sole guide.

I suppose that there must be many theological works about the meaning of 'tradition'. Not knowing them, I venture the idea that, with the exception of the tradition of the actual knowledge of the historical life of Jesus, we must consider each Christian generation as equidistant from eternity. Each generation is bound up with those that go before, learns from them by both attraction and repulsion – yet in the last resort, the access to God is direct, instantaneous and self-sufficient. We do not reverence tradition by wrapping it in a napkin and burying it in our garden, reflecting that in due course we will be able to produce it intact again. We reverence tradition by using it. Locke's theory of property applies in intellectual matters – a man must 'mix his labour' with the land he claims to possess, a believer must examine, reshuffle, reorder, reflect upon his creed before it becomes part of him and he can be said truly to possess it. Maurice Wiles, properly rejecting any idea of a radical discontinuity in doctrine, argues that we are mistaken if we define reverence for tradition as retaining as much of the old as possible. What we ought to mean is maintaining the continuity of Christian objective. We do not need to use the same distinctions as the Fathers concerning the nature of Christ – the New Testament is concerned 'with the functions of Christ, not with his nature'. 'I believe', says Maurice Wiles, 'that we are more likely to prove loyal to the past, in the important sense of the word "loyal", if we think not so much in terms of the translation of old formulae into new sets of words, as in terms of the continuation of the same tasks of interpreting the Church's Scriptures, her worship, and her experience of salvation.'[16]

But who decides what is a genuine 'continuation'? The answer can only be, the individual conscience – but with a very important proviso: the individual conscience operating within the Christian community and as part of the Christian witness to Jesus. Christianity is not a set of beliefs, but a 'way', the following of Jesus, a life of discipleship within the community of the faithful. The fashion in which the individual Christian reacts to, follows or challenges corporate beliefs can best be understood on the analogy of how corporate beliefs operate within an ordinary family. The analogy is only partly helpful, for in no family can one find the demand for total overriding allegiance to a person, as the Christian is required to give his allegiance to Jesus. Nor do families have the vast background of a shared tradition which the Church possesses. But, accepting that the analogy goes only part of the way, we can notice that a happy family has its conventions of speech, its established beliefs, its standard of what is acceptable as an observation about the family and its affairs. There are recognized forms of phrase that make life in common easier. To take a comic example, Uncle was a 'turf accountant and an hotelier', not a 'bookie and a pub-keeper'. More seriously, there are magic days in the family history which we look back on as times of innocence, unity, inspiration – 'the fun we had in the tree house', 'staying with Aunty Margaret', 'at Doris's wedding'. Or there are our traditions – 'we weren't lacking when our country wanted volunteers', 'we always vote Labour'. Respected figures from the past are defined in a way we can agree on. Certain traits of their character and appearance have become proverbial; we express love this way. We have a family language – jokes, taboos, memories, loyalties enshrined in it. It is a language about our common past, about our inspiration. It is a language which we use when we confront the world outside, telling it what we stand for. In a pale and limited fashion, the intimate language of the family reflects what church doctrine is. It is something we have agreed on by consensus, direct or tacit, as a basis for common discussion, exchange of spiritual insights, reflections on our past and common propaganda to the world outside, constituting

225

a base from which the individual can operate, a sign of our unity in love, a recalling of the overwhelming allegiance which dominates our horizon and unites us, a conscious self-defence against the uncomprehending world.

If we see doctrines thus, as the consensus language of the family, the 'in talk' of a group bound together by love, at least we can then understand why it is that we can accept other churches' views of authority as legitimate, even if we regard them as mistaken. Strictly speaking, Church of England men ought to regard the Roman claim to 'infallible' authority as both sinister and irrational. Yet we regard it in practice with friendly complacency. Why? Because while we regard the 'infallibility' claim as intellectually indefensible and morally unsatisfactory, we also see it as part of the Roman Church's consensus language. Roman Catholics have organized their family cadre of discourse and living by accepting the existence of a superior authority. Within its dictates they are content to conduct their intellectual debates, sometimes with great discomfort. But essentially, it is a cadre within which the Roman Catholic Church's religious experience, worship and sacrificial living roll on, to the glory of our common Master – and as a lesson to all of us. Anglicans rely on family affection and respect for past generations to provide us with our cadre of discourse and living. These emotions and loyalties do not push us into the acceptance of absolute authority, but, we hope, will give us a due respect for constitutional and persuasive authority, and keep us on the path of loyalty, communal friendship and co-operation.

In the Church of England, the statement of the supreme responsibility of the individual conscience has always to be tied to the question of loyalty to tradition, affection for the community of the faithful and the desire to work within the family conventions. For example, Hugh Montefiore's excellent statement of the status of dogma needs to be so qualified.[17] Dogmas, he says, can be reinterpreted, but never repudiated or refuted.

> That does not mean that I must necessarily assert them *ex animo*. They are a stimulus to my renewed attempts to interpret my belief in a way that is intellectually rigorous, personally satisfying and pastorally relevant. Dogmas are profoundly important as guidelines to the Church's thinking, and as safeguards against heresy and error.

True, but by what authority is it that dogmas cannot be repudiated or refuted? The answer is, all reinterpretation takes place within the Christian community, for the benefit of the right understanding or amelioration of the consensus language of the family.

The guidance of the Holy Spirit should not be considered as justifying the existence of some infallible source of authority in the Church; nor should it be taken as conferring infallibility upon the rulings of a particular Council, whether by assumed presence among the assembled prelates, or by the manifestation of assent in the lives of the faithful. Indeed, the idea 'of the guidance of the Holy Spirit should not be considered in isolation as guidance towards doctrinal truth, for doctrine is a subsidiary matter. The Holy Spirit is working in the Church over the entire field of its mission – in its worship, its sacrificial living, its unity in love. The Spirit binds us together in a service that is perfect freedom. And one of the agents of the Spirit's working is our love of the past, of our fellows, of our tradition and our community. The final decision always rests on the individual conscience, but it is a conscience restrained, informed and inspired by participation in a corporate discipleship.

Authority and the individual conscience in Anglicanism

In another chapter, the many sources in which the doctrine of the Church of England can be found are listed. There is a presumption that Scripture is pre-eminent, yet as the Bible is given to us by the Church and needs the Church to give guidance in its interpretation, we are driven back to a consideration of the sources which may be said to be regulative of Scripture – creeds, articles, pronouncements, etc. The fact is, while some sources of doctrine have a manifest primacy of honour, all are interdependent. In theory, it might seem logical for a church to have some creed or confession in propositional form as its charter, the Scriptures as the quarry of evidence and argument from which the propositions can be 'proved', and a mass of 'pronouncements' by preachers, theologians, artists, liturgiologists and propagandists to explain, expand and clarify the propositions to the faithful within and to the unbelievers outside. In practice, we have not got this logical structure operating, and it would be unfortunate if we had, though we sometimes talk loosely as if this was, indeed, our case.

The basic documents which define (or should we say, describe?) the doctrine of the Church of England have been legally prescribed. Canon A5 of the Revised Code states: 'The doctrine of the Church of England is grounded in the Holy Scriptures, and in such teachings of the ancient Fathers and Councils of the Church as are agreeable to the sacred Scriptures. In particular such doctrine is to be found in the Thirty-nine Articles of Religion, the Book of Common Prayer and the Ordinal.'[18] These documents would, no doubt, be examined in the courts if a case arose involving the 'trust deeds' under which the Church of England (like other churches and charitable associations) holds its property, or if the new Court of Ecclesiastical Causes were to be invoked under the Ecclesiastical Jurisdiction Measure of 1963 against a clergyman accused of departure from the forms of worship or doctrines of the Established Church. But the most obvious and everyday instance of tension between individual and corporate belief comes, of course, at the point where these documents are used when a candidate for the ministry is tested. The problem of the Church is that it must find pastors who will not only repel wolves from the fold, but will also lead the flock to new pastures – ministers who are at once conservative and revolutionary. *The Report of the Archbishops' Commission on Subscription and Assent to the Thirty-nine Articles* (1968) said that subscription should be forward-looking as well as backward-looking. 'The developing consensus of Anglican thought' was not to be hindered; 'the possibility of fresh understanding of Christian truth must be explicitly left open.'[19] Many would hold that the Articles are, today, unsatisfactory. (Scripture is 'God's word written'; the work of salvation is described in Augustinian categories; justification and predestination, faith and works overweight the emphasis; the character and teaching of Christ hardly appear.) David Edwards' desire to have 'one last heave'[20] to get their status changed arouses sympathy. But it would be difficult to change the Articles without reopening forgotten controversies and threatening the unity of the Church of England. The problem thus created, and the solution which at present obtains, are set out in Tom Wright's section of Chapter 5.

In my view, the new form of Assent[21] (following the report of 1968) does no more than make rather clearer the entirely satisfactory casuistical position as it had been from 1865. A clergyman from then onwards, as he is doing now, was

228

essentially making an act of allegiance to the Anglican Church, to its continuing tradition of worship and to its overruling loyalty to Scripture, to its long and glorious history and to the civilized compromises to which it has resorted to avert religious strife and civil war. This consideration, indeed, brings us to a vital point concerning the belief of the individual within his corporate allegiance. The individual is bound, in a sense, by the tradition as a limiting factor: but from the tradition he also receives his liberty to think freely. The past, so often thought of as a 'dead hand' is, in fact, when properly used, a liberating factor and a reconciling agency. There may be – there always are – difficulties about the intellectual point where we are now. We know that belief is evolving and will evolve, and we can make guesses – divisive ones – at the nature of future consensus. But by addressing our allegiance to the documents of the past, we can at least show an understanding of how we came to be here. We do not stand in an ideal position, nor is where we are an ideal starting-point to go on further, but we came to be here by a process that had its logic, by responses elicited from good men by overwhelming pressures. We understand our position not in the abstract, but historically, and historical documents of belief must be reviewed against the background and assumptions of the age in which they were written. This may be disappointing to those who want instant guidance here and now. But there is a safety factor in their use. These documents, the fruits of bitter controversies in the past, unchurch no one today. They unite us because they represent a great tradition which we all love and which has moulded us. Our resort to them declares our continuity with all who have gone before.

Reformers anxious to change 'out-of-date' creeds, liturgies and formularies should beware. Tradition and the freedom of the individual are more interdependent than they suppose. This indeed is one of the attractive paradoxes about the Church of England – *because* it is formal and traditional in its worship and so many aspects of its life, it *preserves* the freedom of the individual. A left-wing dissenter observed: 'It is easier to be heretical inside the English Church than outside it. So long as the forms are observed, the thought may be free . . . It is as true now as it was in the times of Elizabeth or James that Anglican thought may wander widely, while a Dissenter may not look over the hedge.'[22]

Though subject to differing interpretations, the documents

229

of the past are fixed. By contrast, some sources of doctrinal information necessarily reflect change. A sermon is not, in essence, an enunciation of sound doctrine adorned with frills to attract the hearer's interest. A sermon expresses the faith of the preacher himself, and everyone's faith has peculiarities. Also, the preacher is attempting to recognize the point at which his hearers stand, and to lead on from there to some chosen inspiration to thought or action. Almost every member of a given congregation will have some sort of heretical twist to his understanding (concerning the nature of Christ, for example), and it is not the preacher's task to qualify everything he says to provide correctives ('Ah!' said the university don to the rustic congregation, 'I know what you are saying to yourselves now – Sabellianism!').

Like preachers – and more so – the theologians do much more than enunciate and illustrate doctrine: they are not just engaged in hauling away fallen rocks that prevent the smooth passage of the doctrinal convoy. Their duty is to adventure out on all the frontiers of knowledge, trying new hypotheses, testing speculations, bringing the new knowledge of their age (e.g. scientific, psychological, historical or inspirational) to bear on all the problems of Christian believing. Nor are they working merely to edify the faithful. What they say may strike a blow somewhere among the heedless, who long ago had rejected the propositional doctrines to which they believed the Church was committed. The Church needs its foursquare 'orthodox' theologians, just as an army entrenched in fortifications needs staff officers to arrange the transport of the rations; but it also needs snipers outside the main trenches, free from all responsibilities except loyalty to the cause, and picking off the enemy at their own discretion. Scholarly progress works, normally, by the forensic method, by the clash of opposing views pushed to their extreme, and human nature and professional pride being what they are, the extreme may be uncompromising indeed. It is unsettling to some Christians to find 'dangerous' theories aired and, what is worse, greeted with suspect enthusiasm by unbelievers. Yet living dangerously is, after all, the only way of living intensely. The truth that makes us free is found only by the exercise of freedom. As Christians, we have to get used to being totally committed to a faith which can only be provisionally stated.

The Church of England has a peculiar privilege and responsibility here. It is true that we sometimes find ourselves envying the monolithic certainties of the Roman Catholic and the changeless serenity of the Orthodox Church. It is true that we gain comfort from their – at least apparent – stability. Anglicanism has something different to offer to the common treasury. We have as part of our way of life two virtues which these great churches have sacrificed in the pursuit of other, and noble, ends. Toleration and compromise are built into the fabric of Anglicanism; similarly, we cherish the spirit of adventure and the right of intellectual freedom. These two sets of virtues are complementary – the one making the other possible, the one justifying the other. A society that is tolerant grants intellectual freedom; a society that lives by compromise has a place for adventurers. To say this justifies the snipers and *francs tireurs*. But tolerance and compromise must work both ways: there is equally a place in Anglicanism for the solid conservatives. In a sense, these have always been the unsung heroes of the Anglican tradition – the difficult immovable men who have acted like a sea anchor in the gales, holding the head of the ship towards the wind – or, to return to the army metaphor, the static infantry who bog down so many adventurous strategic plans, but who can be relied on to stay put come what may, 'last man, last round'. The more mobile and reckless troops should pay tribute to their role and pay more attention to their susceptibilities. Theologians tempted to doctrinal 'brinkmanship' are free, in the Anglican Church, to go to extremes, but they have a duty to the whole community and to all the different emphases of belief and understanding within it. They have a duty too to the tradition, and all the generations which have gone before. It is no easy thing to combine progress by controversy and experiment with charity and fraternity, to allow men to be free yet trust them to be moderate. The Anglican Church more than any other has made this possible.

The Church of England does not indulge in ringing, authoritative, doctrinal formulations. There are plenty of people within it, in official positions or otherwise, who do make formulations, and sometimes in more than ringing tones. But none of them is entitled to speak with final authority – or at least, there is no authority which cannot be answered back. On doctrinal matters, the authority which would be generally recognized would, one imagines, be the one which was relevant to the particular issue. On formal questions of liturgical worship and clerical subscription, the parliamentary system of the Church of England, through the General Synod, would pronounce, with the ultimate authority of Parliament proper in the background. (Doctrinal motions are not accepted in the General Synod unless proposed by the House of Bishops.) If it is a question of defining our belief in discussions with other churches, the most formal way of doing so would be in the meetings of all the bishops of the Anglican Communion assembled at Lambeth.[23] If it is a question of starting a discussion on the topicality of doctrines, the report of the Doctrine Commission seems to be the appropriate point to begin – but only to begin – for no one seems to expect such a report to settle anything. The consideration of 'the nature and grounds of Christian doctrine with a view to demonstrating the extent of existing agreement within the Church of England and with a view to investigating how far it is possible to remove or to diminish existing differences' (1938) was a subject tailormade to encourage everyone to declare these differences enthusiastically. A. G. Hebert and the Church Union described the report as erecting 'an excellent superstructure of soteriology on an inadequate doctrine of Revelation . . . It has the air of belonging to the past generation rather than to this.' The Fellowship of Evangelical Churchmen, alarmed by what was said of the Scriptures, entitled their manifesto *The Failure of a Commission*.[24] If, however, simply and uncontroversially, a Christian layman wanted to tell an inquiring friend 'what the Church of England believes', he would look for some judicious book by someone who had the art of seizing on the 'consensus' of opinion among theologians and, to some extent, devising a solution to current problems of debate, of seeing the relevance of the best modern interpretations of Scripture, and of the tradition viewed in historical perspective (to identify such a book one would look to the consensus of informed opinion in the first place).[25]

On some issues, various potential 'authorities' are concerned. The problem of the ordination of women is a case where every possible authority which has a right to make a pronouncement is involved, from the individual diocesan bishop to the Lambeth Conference, from the General Synod to the Crown in Parliament. Almost certainly, the conclusion of this matter will be that individual branches of the Anglican Communion (possibly even, individual dioceses) will follow their own consciences with the blessing of the others, and the federated Anglican Churches will have to make tricky adjustments to cover anomalies and avoid confusions. Purists concerned about an 'honest' Christian pronouncement on the status of women, and purists on the other side concerned about a particular doctrine of priesthood, will find such a muddled outcome unsatisfactory, constituting a censure of the libertarian attitude of Anglicans to ecclesiastical authority. Yet, if we believe in the necessity of doctrine being accepted by the people of God in their worship and in their living, what better outcome could there be? A Christian must follow his conscience as far as it leads him, and the Church ought to give the individual the fullest opportunity for doing so.

The doctrine of the Church as the Body of Christ is central to every Christian community, and the Body is, by definition, an organic unity. But the Pauline texts emphasize the manifold diversity of the members – all knit together in the service of Christ, but all different and performing different functions; Paul also emphasizes the deplorable results that follow if one part censures another, or claims a priority of honour. The Church is indwelt by the Spirit, and the Spirit is a unifying influence. But, by definition, the Spirit is recklessly creative, inventive, unpredictable; and a community in which the wind of the Spirit blows should welcome and use originality, diversity, eccentricity even. The Spirit creates unity, but not uniformity. The fragmentation of Christian practice within the Anglican Communion concerning the ordination of women is no disaster; it is a convincing example of the 'diversity of operations' of the one and the self-same Spirit.

It is probable that the zeal for liturgical revision of the present generation of Anglican clergy will lead to a similar fragmentation of practice; the Book of Common Prayer and the Alternative Service Book will both be legal tender. If this happens, we must freely recognize that we are not only ending liturgical uniformity in our church: we are also loosening, and to some extent, in different ways, tightening, the bonds of doctrinal constraint, since liturgical revision inevitably leads to changes of colour and emphasis in the presentation of our heritage of belief. We make 'allowances' for the Book of Common Prayer as an historical document. We have to make different sorts of allowances for the alternative services. But why not? If ever churchmen should be generous to each other's prejudices, it ought to be when worship in common is involved. I would venture to guess that in future years there will be many innovators who will learn from 1662, and many conservatives who will gain new insights from the pedestrian prose of the modern revision. Besides, what other solution is there that would recognize both individual freedom and corporate responsibility?

Michael Ramsey has spoken of the 'three ways' in which the Church must be 'faithful to the biblical meaning of truth'. These are:

1 By reverencing the works of God everywhere and the Spirit of God manifested in the endeavours of men's minds;

2 By keeping before itself and before men the Scandal of the Cross;

3 By remembering that orthodoxy means not only correct propositions about God, but the life of the One Body of Christ in the due working of all its members.[26]

On the second and third points the great churches all agree – and without at least attempting, sacrificially, to follow these two precepts, a church becomes a mere club and Christianity becomes dust and ashes. It is in their attitude to the fulfilment of the first point that the churches differ, and it is at this point that Anglicanism makes its unique contribution by believing supremely in the duty of 'reverencing . . . the Spirit of God manifested in the endeavours of men's minds'. The Anglican Church has a genius, not so much for compromise, as is generally said – but for forbearance, for sensing when it is God's will that we all agree to differ. The cement that binds our church together is not a supreme ecclesiastical authority, not an established confession of faith, not an unshakable reverence for the decisions of certain councils. It is something difficult to define – a state of mind and an attitude to our religion instilled into us by history. Compromise, tolerance and agreement to differ all play their part in it – and a respect for the individual conscience, a love of freedom, a distrust of authority, a sense of humour, a reluctance to be piously demonstrative, a love of understatement, a hesitation to take ourselves too seriously on the stage of the world, a reticence, a scepticism, a reverence for mystery. This is not a description of an ideal religious temperament but it is a temperament which we believe God accepts, and one that is being used and refined by the work of the Spirit of Christ.

234

NOTES

1 See John Henry Collins, *Basis and Belief.* Epworth 1964. A work which has been useful throughout this section. Proposing to act as if 'I believe' is a proposition that deserves more consideration than it normally gets. 'It is my prerogative to decide to act decisively, it is not within my prerogative to decide to believe unreservedly,' writes Professor Baelz – hence the role within the Christian circle of half-belief – 'experiment with life in love' (P. Baelz, *The Forgotten Dream* (Mowbray 1975), p. 142).

2 D'Arcy, *The Nature of Belief* (Epworth 1931), p. 207.

3 H. Bremond, *Histoire littéraire du sentiment religieux en France,* ix, 1932, p. 375.

4 C. H. Dodd distrusted it. *Gospel and Law* (C.U.P. 1950), p. 72.

5 E. R. Dodds, *Pagan and Christian in an Age of Anxiety* (C.U.P.1963), p.138.

6 Bryan R. Wilson, 'Becoming a Sectarian: motivation and commitment', in *Religious Motivation,* Studies in Church History, xv, ed. D. Baker (1978), pp. 504–5. See p. 501 for Wilson's discussion of the theory of 'relative deprivation' of Cy Glock, B. B. Ringer and E. R. Babbie, *To Comfort and to Challenge.* University of California Press 1967.

7 A. M. Ramsey, *The Gospel and the Catholic Church* (Longman 1936), pp. 126–7.

8 What follows is from K. Rahner, C. Ernst and K. Smyth, eds., *Sacramentum Mundi* 3 (1969), articles 'Magisterium', pp. 351–8 and 'Infallibility', pp. 132-7.

9 ibid., p. 135.

10 T. Ware, *The Orthodox Church* (Penguin 1963), pp. 253–8 for what follows.

11 Cf. Afanassief's view of the organic unity of the Church as manifested essentially 'eucharistically'. The local church, led by its bishop, is 'the Church of God in all its fullness', because Christ is fully present with the people in the breaking of bread. N. Afanassief, 'The Church which presides in love', in *The Primacy of Peter,* ed. J. Meyendorff (St Vladimir's Seminary Press 1963), p. 73. Cf. pp. 138-9.

12 Ware, op. cit., p. 215.

13 'A Dissuasive from Popery' in P. E. More and F. L. Cross, *Anglicanism* (SPCK 1935), p. 162.

14 See G. W. H. Lampe in *Authority and the Church,* ed. R. R. Williams, being conversations with the German Evangelical Church (Wellham 1965), pp. 8–19.

15 In More and Cross, *Anglicanism,* p. 141.

16 M. Wiles, *The Making of Christian Doctrine* (C.U.P. 1967), p. 181.

17 H. Montefiore in *Christian Believing: Doctrine Commission of the Church of England* (1976), p. 154.

18 On the status of canons see *Synodical Government: Opinions of the Legal Board,* 5th edn. (1975), p. 1/5: 'The Convocations have had power from time immemorial to pass Canons, and this power is now transferred to the General Synod to the exclusion of the Convocations. The Queen's

Assent and Licence is required to the Making . . . etc. . . . of Canons, but they are not laid before Parliament and while they are binding on the Clergy they do not of their own force bind the laity. Canons cannot have effect if they are 'contrary or repugnant to the Royal prerogative or the customs, laws and statutes of this realm'. It is, therefore, sometimes necessary for a measure or in certain circumstances an Act of Parliament to be passed to enable a Canon to go forward . . . Subject to recent additions, including the Canons set out in this work, the Canon Law is contained in the Canons of the Church of England.' For what follows, see *Church and State: Report of the Archbishops' Commission* (1970). I am grateful to Professor Owen Chadwick and to Dr D. M. Carey for their advice on these matters.

19 *Report of the Archbishops' Commission on Christian Doctrine: Subscription and Assent to the 39 Articles* (SPCK 1968), p. 72.

20 In *The Modern Churchman,* January 1967 (cited in *Report,* as above), p. 29.

21 p. 74.

22 H. Gow, *The Unitarians* (1928), cited A. R. Vidler, 'Religion and the National Church', in *Soundings: Essays concerning Christian Understanding* (Longman 1962), p. 258.

23 Cf. the Lambeth Appeal evoking the Baptist counter-definition of faith centring around 'the principle of the freedom of the individual Church under Christ', 4 May 1926, in E. A. Payne, *The Fellowship of Believers: Baptist Thought and Practice* (1952 edn.), pp. 142–7.

24 A. G. Hebert, *Memorandum on the Report of the Archbishops' Commission on Christian Doctrine* (1939); *The Failure of a Commission; a Reply to the Report . . . by members of the fellowship of Evangelical Churchmen* (1939).

25 And would finish up with, say, John Macquarrie, *Principles of Christian Theology,* 2nd edn. (1966).

26 Ramsey, op. cit., p. 126.

9

Why This Story?

W.H Vanstone.

Why this story for the Church?

In earlier chapters of this report writers have pointed out how much of the common or corporate activity of the Church of England consists in 'attending together to the story'. On the occasions when the Church most obviously 'comes together', the telling of the story, both through scriptural readings in office and liturgy and through certain forms of liturgical enactment, is either prescribed by rubric or hallowed by custom as a major element in that which must be done: and the building in which the Church comes together will normally be one which, through its works of art and adornment, also 'tells the story' in the language of the eye. It would be arguable that the common activity which the Church of England ordains most clearly and in the largest measure for its people is not 'praise' or 'fellowship' or even 'prayer': it is 'attention to the story'.

The story as the focus

Attention is more than attendance. At the points in the office and the liturgy where we are exposed most directly to the story – that is, in the reading of Scripture – it is laid down in familiar rubrics of the Prayer Book that, through the precise identification by the reader of the passage to be read, the hearers shall be left in no doubt that it *is* Scripture; and, furthermore, that the Scripture shall be read 'distinctly with an audible voice . . . he that readeth so standing and turning himself as he may best be heard of all such as are present'. We are not to 'attend the telling of the story' merely as a mark of deference and respect – as the mayor might attend the induction of a new vicar: nor are we to treat the telling of the story as a kind of 'verbal wallpaper', helpful in creating a recognizably Christian atmosphere. We are to hear the story 'distinctly read': there is to be at least the possibility that we shall 'mark,

237

learn and inwardly digest it': the story is to be the focus of our attention.

Now there are certain fairly obvious reasons why the ordinary Christian of today may find it difficult, or even think it improper, to pay to the Christian story the close and constant attention which the Church prescribes.

A blurred focus?

The first reason is that the man of today finds in the story difficulties which were far less evident to his forebears – difficulties about the historical veracity of at least certain parts of it; about the moral propriety of some of the incidents which it recounts; about the acceptability of some of the pre-suppositions which it contains; and about the relevance to the modern world of a story set in the pastoral and peasant society of a pre-scientific age. It would require volumes to catalogue these difficulties in detail, but some at least of them are so generally familiar that no reasonably informed person can attend to the Christian story without being aware of them.

In general the Church no longer attributes these difficulties to lack of faith, or condemns the 'doubt' or 'unbelief' of the person who feels and raises them. The Church recognizes many of them as real difficulties, and devotes a great deal of its study, preaching and apologetic to the attempt to meet and overcome them. That the attempt is made implies, on the one hand, that the difficulties exist, but also, on the other hand, that they are not necessarily insuperable. The continuing commitment of the Church to biblical study and elucidation is, in effect, an assertion that, despite the difficulties which we find today in the Christian story, our attention to it is still appropriate and still, indeed, of the greatest importance.

So a Christian of today may be persuaded by the preaching and apologetic of the Church that the difficulties which he encounters in the Christian story need not preclude his attention to it. But there are further reasons why he may be reluctant to give to it that close and even exclusive attention which the Church prescribes: he may be disposed to argue that the consequences of such attention are likely to be socially divisive and spiritually restrictive.

A divisive focus?

Let us consider how such an argument might proceed. The majority of Christians today deplore the evil and divisive consequences of that 'racism' which, while not advertising itself as such, is constantly drawing attention to the differences between the races rather than to their common humanity. It is probable that more overt and aggressive forms of racism are nourished and sustained by this attitude, and a Christian may reasonably fear lest, if he constantly gives his attention, and draws that of others, to the points of difference between his own religion and the religion of other groups in the community, he may be nourishing, however unwittingly, the growth of a divisive and even aggressive form of 'religionism' or 'religious triumphalism'. Now the stories told in different religious traditions are obvious and obtrusive points of difference between them, for the stories mention different names, are set in different locations and belong to different periods of history or prehistory. So a Christian of today may reasonably be anxious lest the constant attention which he gives – or is asked to give – to his own story may become a source of divisiveness and alienation in a society or neighbourhood which now contains people of many different religions. The Christian headmaster of a local school whose children come from several different religious traditions may well hesitate to 'make much' in the school of such occasions as Christmas and Easter which 'tell the Christian story', and may prefer to emphasize, as the major religious occasion of the year, some form of Harvest Thanksgiving or Commemoration Day which contains no explicit or 'obtrusive' reference to the Christian story.

A restrictive focus?

A Christian of today may think it not only divisive but also restrictive to pay to the Christian story the exclusive attention which the Church ordains. Of course the Church does not forbid him to 'inquire into' or 'learn about' the stories told in other religious traditions, but it does seem to forbid – or at least to discourage – his 'attention' to them. Certainly it excludes such stories from the attention of its people when they come together as the Church. We would not suggest, of course, that a large number of Christians feel this exclusion as a restriction and would prefer an office or liturgy which presented or drew upon the stories of Islam and Buddhism as well as that of Christianity. But we observe that in academic circles and other areas of society where there is a good deal of social and intellectual contact between people of different religious

239

traditions, a certain number of Christians are demanding, claiming or assuming the freedom to develop the kind of religious contact which would imply that each religious tradition, including Christianity, has something to learn from the others as well as something to give to the others. Hopes of 'cross-fertilization' between religious traditions would imply that a Christian whose attention is monopolized by the story told in his own tradition is necessarily restricted and in some sense impoverished.

The argument for openness

We must recognize, then, that a certain number of our fellow Christians have reservations about paying to the Christian story the close and exclusive attention which the Church prescribes. They believe that the Church's prescription is divisive or restrictive or both. Now they would no doubt admit that a degree of division or restriction is sometimes the necessary and inevitable cost of adhering to the truth; if one believes in vegetarianism as a principle one is necessarily divided from those who do not, and necessarily restricted from sharing certain dishes. But those of our fellow Christians whom we have in mind would probably go on to say that, over the matter of attention to the Christian story, the Church's prescription and practice is *gratuitously* divisive and *unnecessarily* restrictive.

They would argue that the importance of the Christian story lies in the truth which it contains, communicates or discloses; that of this truth the story itself is simply the medium or container; and that, however valuable our story may be as the medium or container of truth, it is unnecessary and even presumptuous to regard it as the only possible medium or container. Truth, they would say, is truth whatever the medium through which it is expressed or the container in which it is received; and it is at least possible that the very same truth which Christendom has received through the Christian story may have been received by people of other cultural traditions through *their* traditional story. If this is the case, then we should recognize that, just as the western world has been culturally and aesthetically enriched by the contributions of other societies, so Christianity may be enriched by attention to the stories told in other religious traditions. For if the same truth is contained in these alternative media, then – to put the case no higher – the very unfamiliarity of these media to

240

Christian ears may make them the more effective in conveying the truth.

The argument we are considering is an argument that Christianity should be more 'open' – open to the possibility that the truth which Christianity believes and teaches may also be expressed and received through other stories or media. It does not imply that other media do in fact contain the same truth. It simply implies that they may. It implies that the possibility should not be ruled out *a priori*; that the Church should at least countenance the attentive exploration by its people of other religious traditions; and, possibly, that the Church should go so far as to expose its people to alternative media of truth in the context of its own corporate worship. This argument for greater 'openness' on the part of the Church largely coincides in its practical implications with the often-heard popular argument that all religions, or at least all the major religions, 'mean the same', 'come down to the same thing' or 'are saying the same thing'. The popular argument is rarely based on investigation or experience, and usually smacks more of indifference than of breadth of sympathy and understanding. It assumes as fact what the more sophisticated argument for openness only envisages as possibility. But the two arguments coincide in questioning or deprecating the exclusive attention which the Church, when it comes together, pays and prescribes to its own story.

Medium and message

We find such arguments unconvincing for two reasons, and, in the present state of Christian opinion, it seems to us important that these reasons should be set out as clearly as possible. Virtually all the rest of this chapter will be devoted to them.

Our first objection to the kind of argument mentioned above is that it presupposes a sharp distinction between the truth contained in the Christian story and the story itself; or, in more general terms, between meaning and the expression of meaning, between message and medium, between *what* is said and *the manner in which* it is said. Against this presupposition we must set the important element of truth contained in the familiar maxim, 'the medium is the message'. In this maxim, as in most, there is some exaggeration, but it can hardly be denied that the medium often *affects* the message, and that *what* is said is often dependent upon, and inseparable from, *the manner in which* it is said.

241

This is evident in the most commonplace incidents of life. Two brothers whose mother is in hospital may express their affectionate care – the one by sending a card, the other by travelling 200 miles to her bedside. The card and the visit are both expressions of filial care, but from the different 'expressions' of filial care the mother would undoubtedly receive different degrees or qualities of filial care. What each man 'says' to his mother, the 'truth' which he conveys to her, depends upon, and is inseparable from, his manner of conveying it. A child who has misbehaved during the day may have a reluctant 'I'm sorry' wrung from him at bedtime; or he may come to his mother of his own accord and cling to her and sob 'I'm sorry'. When the father comes home, the mother will have one of two stories to tell to him. The truth that 'John is sorry' is conveyed in both stories, but which story the father hears will not be a matter of indifference to him. What John's 'sorrow' really amounts to 'comes through' very differently in the two stories of what actually took place.

In such commonplace incidents 'medium' and 'message', 'container' and 'content', 'story' and 'meaning' are interdependent and inseparable. What is said cannot be received in isolation from the form and manner in which it is said. A person who disregards the manner in which other people communicate with him will miss a great deal of what they are saying to him.

The meaning of a poem

The same is true at a more elevated cultural level. It would be absurd to say that a poem such as *The Waste Land* or *The Ancient Mariner* 'has no meaning', but it would be equally absurd to attempt to abstract or isolate the meaning from the actual form and words in which the poet has expressed it. One may receive the meaning only in and through attention to the poem itself. It is true, of course, that, in order to assess and evaluate a pupil's attention, a teacher might ask him to 'put into his own words' the meaning of a poem, or of a part of it. But, however good the pupil's précis or explanation might be, no teacher would regard it as a substitute for the poet's own words. No teacher would put it before the class instead of the poem itself, or suggest that, now that the class knew 'what the poem meant', it would be a waste of their time and attention actually to read it. 'What the poem means' can be received only through attention to the poem itself.

It is also true that a teacher might guide the attention of a pupil – or a critic the attention of a reader – by offering some hint of, or pointer to, the meaning of a poem. A teacher might suggest that *The Waste Land* is 'about life' rather than 'about London', or that *The Ancient Mariner* 'means' that man should respect nature rather than that a seafarer should be prepared for anything. But the hint, however useful, is no more than a hint. It is certainly not a distillate containing all that is valuable and memorable in the meaning of the poem. As a matter of fact, since schoolchildren tend to notice first the concrete detail which lies on the surface of a poem, there are many poems of which a teacher may need to say that they are 'about life' – rather than 'about London' or 'about seafaring' or 'about a village called Stoke Poges'. The teacher may use the same phrase – 'about life' – to hint at, or point to, the meaning of several different poems, but we do not deduce from this that all the poems in question are 'saying the same thing', or that they all 'contain the same truth', or that, through all these different media, one will 'receive the same message'.

The popular belief that 'all religions are saying the same thing' probably has its basis in the fact that the exponents of different religions are likely to use, for the guidance of their adherents, some of the same hints or pointers to the meaning of the stories they tell. Presumably the adherents of many different religious systems must be guided to see that the story which they hear is relevant to them, that response to it is always a possibility, and that the actual response which they make is a matter of ultimate importance. So the exponents of these different systems are likely to make use, as hints or pointers, of similar or even identical phrases – phrases such as 'God is *your* God', 'God is approachable', 'God is sovereign'. Very similar pointers may be used to the meaning of different stories. But this by no means implies that the meaning of these stories is identical or very similar. That similar phrases – or even phrases which are verbally identical – may be used in different religious systems to point to the meaning of the stories which they tell by no means indicates that the stories themselves are identical in meaning or that they 'contain the same truth'. It is of no more significance than the fact that a schoolteacher may say, both of *The Waste Land* and of Gray's *Elegy*, that 'the poet is not describing life in a particular place; he is reflecting on life in general'. The meaning of a story, as of a poem, is not to be received from any such hint or pointer. It is to be received only in and through attention to the story itself.

For this reason we are sceptical about the popular dictum that 'all religions are saying the same thing'; and we are even sceptical about the possibility that they *may* be saying the same thing. We are therefore sceptical about the propriety of the Church becoming more 'open' to receive, through the novel and therefore compelling media of other stories, the truth which it detects in its own story. Truth is not easily abstracted from its container.

Different functions of language

We turn now to a second reason, more complex but even more decisive, why we believe that the Church must continue to give its close and even exclusive attention to its own story. This reason is rooted in the distinction which may properly be drawn between the informative and the performative functions of language – or of any means of communication.

If I say, 'The door is open', the obvious function of my words is to inform – to tell another person what the situation is. My words *may* also alter the total situation in that, if the other person believes me and does not already know that the door is open, he has a new piece of information. But my words do not necessarily and directly alter the situation. The speaking of them does not in itself create a changed situation. If, on the other hand, I say, 'Open the door', the immediate function of my words is to perform. The very speaking of them creates a situation which did not exist before. For by speaking the words I immediately put the other person in a situation where he must obey or disobey; and I put myself in a situation in which I must be obeyed or disobeyed. Language as informative may or may not alter the situation in which it is used. Language as performative necessarily does so.

In the instance we have used, the informative group of words is a statement in the indicative mood, whereas the performative group is a command in the imperative mood. But the distinction between the informative and the performative functions of language does not correspond neatly with the distinction between the indicative and the imperative mood, or indeed with any formal or syntactical distinction. A group of words which has the syntactical structure of a command – 'Remember that Mr Reagan is nearly seventy' – may serve primarily to inform; and, more importantly, a group of words which has the syntactical structure of a statement may have a strongly performative function. The words 'I promise to come' are identical in syntax with the words 'I intend to come' but they have a stronger performative function. If I say, 'I intend to come', I simply give information; but by speaking the words 'I promise to come', I thereby give another person the right to expect me, and I myself incur the duty of coming. The performance-effect of such 'statements' as 'I promise . . .', 'I order . . .', 'I forbid . . .', 'I forgive . . .' is very obvious – so obvious that one sometimes hesitates to make them. For one knows that, by the very act of making them, one is 'creating a confrontation' or 'exposing oneself' or 'giving up one's rights'.

The importance of 'telling'

The performative function of language may be detected not only in the limited class of 'statements' which we have just mentioned but, on occasion, in almost any kind of statement. On many occasions *what* is said may be less important than *the fact that it is said*. What is said may be trivial or may be already known: it may provide no information of any consequence. Nevertheless, the fact that it is said may be extremely important. A man may know that an attractive girl is already married, but the fact that at a particular moment she tells him so may constitute a sharp and painful rebuff. A woman may actually see the boy next door hit a cricket ball through her window, but the fact that he 'comes and tells her' will probably make a good deal of difference to the situation between herself and the boy. To take an actual and rather poignant instance: a friend of mine went into hospital, and when I visited him we exchanged the familiar banter of old friends – 'Have you nothing to do but lie in bed?', 'I know you've only come to eat my grapes'. After some weeks I was told by the doctor that he had an inoperable cancer, that he was unlikely to live long and that he himself was aware of his condition. On my next visit the patient began the usual banter, and I felt it right, though I did not find it very easy, to respond in the same vein. But a few days later he fell suddenly silent; and then said, 'I know how things stand. I've got cancer and they can't operate. I don't think I'll be here long.' What my old friend told me was all too well known to me, but the fact that he told me was extremely important. It invited or challenged me to speak with him in a different way and at a deeper level; it conveyed his trust in

245

me; it imposed on me a certain responsibility; it altered my situation. It altered the patient's situation also, for it exposed him to the possibility that, through the embarrassment or insensitivity of my response, he might be disappointed in, or let down by, one of his oldest friends. By telling me what I already knew, the patient radically changed the situations in which both he and I were placed.

The receiving of performance

A statement may be important for the information which it conveys or for the performance which it effects – or, of course, for both reasons. Now the information contained in a statement is often – as in all the three instances mentioned above – available from some other source: it may be received from one's own observation, or from what someone else has told, or by some kind of deduction. *But the performance effected by a statement cannot be received from any other source.* If I ask someone to a party, I may learn or deduce from various sources that he intends to come – from seeing him put the date in his diary, from his remark that he always enjoys parties, from my knowledge of his sociable habits. I can know that he intends to come even if he does not actually say, 'I intend to come'. But I cannot receive his promise to come from any other source than his actual words 'I promise to be there' or similar performative words. If my elderly neighbour tells me where she hides the spare key of her front door, the information which she gives may already be available to me: I may have noticed her hiding the key, or another neighbour may have told me. But the compliment of trust and confidence which she conveys by telling me cannot possibly be deduced or received from any other source. It is available to me and received by me only when she actually tells me.

It is worth noting that there are familiar occasions when, being reluctant to 'perform' in what we say, we *pretend* that performance may be learned or deduced from some other source. So, if I am asked for forgiveness but cannot bring myself to forgive, or if I am asked for a promise which I do not wish to make, I use such phrases as 'You know that I don't bear malice', 'You know I'm not easily offended', 'I've told you my intentions already', 'How many more times do I have to tell you what I am going to do?'. We pretend that the performance for which we are asked is deducible from information which is already available: but we know, and the person to whom we are speaking knows, that this is pretence. What performance effects becomes available and can be received through nothing except performance.

Before we apply these considerations to our attention to the Christian story, there are two more points to be made. The first is to emphasize again that the performance-function of language, or of any means of communication, is not limited to those phrases or expressions which are always and obviously performative. Almost any group of words may be used performatively. We have noticed that a promise is not performed by 'I intend', but it may well be performed by such words as 'Shake on it' or 'You can depend on me'. Forgiveness is not performed by the prim statement, 'I do not harbour resentment', but it may well be performed by 'How nice of you to come and see me' or, even more effectively, by 'Will you do me a favour?' In our ordinary social intercourse we are able, with occasional exceptions, to recognize and receive the performance-effect of many things that are said to us as statements of fact, as questions, as interjections or jokes, or in almost any form. The person who lacks this ability is blamed for his insensitivity or pitied for his *gaucherie*.

Performance through report

The second point to be made is that although the effect of performance cannot be directly received from any source other than performance itself, it can sometimes be mediated by report of performance. Let us once again illustrate the point from ordinary life. An employer who is giving a party may convey the invitations through his secretary. The secretary will not convey the invitation to, let us say, the foreman by giving him the information that the boss is very hospitable, that he thinks well of the foreman and that the party will be very good. This information does not constitute an invitation. The secretary must say to the foreman, 'You are invited to the boss's party', and if the foreman, being normally at logger-heads with the boss, finds this hard to believe, the secretary must go on to tell him exactly what happened – how the boss came in with a list of names, how he particularly mentioned that the foreman's name was on it, and so on. By reporting what the boss said or did to 'perform' the invitation, and only by so doing, the secretary can, so to speak, mediate the employer's invitation to the foreman. The only information which can in this way mediate performance is *report of performance*. The only way in which performance can be received indirectly is through report of that performance – through the story of something which actually happened and which constituted a performance. In this way, and in this way only, invitations and promises, commands, prohibitions and other verbal performances can be conveyed and received beyond the range of those who are in direct contact with the speaker.

The Christian story

Now let us return to the consideration of the Christian story. A story is a report, true or false, accurate or inaccurate, of things that happened, things that were done and said. If we are satisfied that the Christian story contains, despite its difficulties, some element of truth, then certain of the things which it reports did in fact happen, were in fact done and said. The attention which the Church prescribes to the story implies that these things are important. But – and here is the crux of the matter – if we are asked, as Christians, *why* they are important, our answer often tends to suggest that they are important as sources of *information*. For, although we may refer to the events reported as 'saving' events, we tend to explain their capacity to save in terms of the 'information' about the purpose and forgiveness and love of God which is contained in them or disclosed through them; and although we may speak of what God has 'done' for mankind in those events, we tend to explain this 'doing' in terms of 'informing' mankind about the faithfulness of his purpose and the depths of his forgiveness and love. A great many of the familiar terms of Christian exposition – 'the truth which we see in Christ', 'what God reveals to us in Christ', 'what we learn of God through Jesus', 'what Jesus shows us of God' – carry the suggestion that the importance of those events which our story reports lies in what they tell us, in what they reveal to us, in the information which they convey to us.

Now, as we have suggested earlier, the information-content of anything that is said or otherwise communicated can be received, in principle, from other sources. So if we were really satisfied that the importance of the events of the Christian story lay entirely in their information-content, we should have no reasonable grounds for confining the attention of the Church to those events; for we should have to admit the logical possibility that the same information might be available through, and received from, other sources. We should have to admit the logical possibility that all that is important in our story might be received from the story of some other religion or even deduced from the speculations of a philosopher or natural theologian. But in fact we are not so satisfied. We recognize that the events of our story have an information content, and that this is important. But we are also aware, however vaguely, of a further reason for the importance of those events, of something beyond information which is available from or through them and which is not available, even in principle, from any other source.

The function of the Christian story

We suggest that the 'further reason', the 'something beyond information', may be described as the 'performance-effect' of those events; and that the story to which we attend may be described as 'report of performance' through which performance itself may be mediated and received. The terms are extremely inelegant: but they have the merit of being clarified by reflection on ordinary and familiar human experience. We are suggesting that the events in question have not only an information-content which might be received from some other source, but also a performance-effect which could not, even in principle, be received from any other source, and that the performance-effect, considered simply from the point of view of logic, is the kind of effect which comes about when someone whose intentions I already know makes a promise; when a wronged friend whose generous nature I already know actually says 'I forgive you'; when a dying patient whom I know to be aware of his condition actually tells me that he knows he is dying.

Reflection on such incidents helps us to see the logical grounds for the exclusive attention which the Church pays to its own story: it understands that story as report of performance – through which alone performance itself can be mediated or conveyed. The nature of the 'performance' mediated through the Christian story is a much larger question, and much beyond the scope of this chapter. We commonly describe it in terms such as 'redemption', 'the salvation of mankind', 'the reconciling of the world to God through Christ', but it is important to recognize that, just as the meaning of a poem in terms of information-content, of 'what the poet is saying to us', is unique to that particular

249

poem, so the meaning of an event in terms of performance-effect may be unique to that particular event. The meaning in terms of performance of the events reported in the Christian story is not to be received in isolation from the story. It is not capable of being distilled into and encapsulated in a word or phrase. The meaning of the performance is to be received only through the report of the performance, and words such as 'redemption' and 'reconciliation' should be understood rather as pointers to that meaning than as its comprehensive description or distillation. To put flesh upon the phrase 'the performance-effect mediated by the Christian story', it is necessary neither to resort to a familiar theological phrase nor to invent a new one, but to attend to the Christian story.

The effect of performance

Phrases such as 'I promise' and 'I forgive', and any words which have a performance function, actually change the situation. When they are spoken, the speaker may incur, for instance, risks and responsibilities which were not there before, and the person to whom they are spoken may come to have new rights and duties. The situation is *objectively* changed: it may even be changed in ways that are not willed or intended by one or both of the parties concerned. When Jephthah makes his vow, he does not intend to put himself under an obligation to sacrifice his daughter, but, having made it, he finds himself under this obligation. If I give money to a friend in need, I may have no wish that he should repay it, but if he says, 'I promise to pay it back', I receive, even against my will, the right to repayment. The situation may even be changed in ways which are unknown to the participants. An exchange of letters which is thought to be no more than innocent co-operation may constitute, in the eyes of the law, the offer and acceptance of a bribe. The situation may be changed objectively even when it is not known to be changed.

But response to the change which performance effects cannot be appropriate unless that effect or change is received and understood. If an invitation to a party is sent to me but is lost in the post, then, although I have in fact been invited, my attendance at the party is still inappropriate: I am still a gate-crasher. If I do not know myself invited, then I cannot attend in the manner and frame of mind appropriate to one who has been invited, for my confidence in entering through the door becomes brashness and my thanks to my host can be no more than an affectation. If my needy friend promises to repay and if I do not hear his promise, then although I have a right to repayment, I cannot exercise that right appropriately. If I have not heard the promise, then my expectation of the money's return becomes presumptuous, and my request for its return offensive. Behaviour which would be appropriate if I knew of my friend's promise becomes inappropriate if I do not. Relying on my friend's promise I may properly approach him in a certain way, but if I approach him in the same way without reliance on his promise my approach becomes improper. The situation is changed by his promise, but it is logically impossible for me to behave appropriately to the changed situation except through attention to, and understanding of, the promise which has changed it.

The necessity of appropriation

Christians want to say that the situation between God and man is changed objectively by those events which our story reports, but they also want to say that the changed situation cannot be 'appropriated' except through attention to, and understanding of, those events, or the report of them. In the Christian view all men 'are placed' by the events of our story in a new relationship to God; but any man who infers this relationship from anything other than the events by which it is created is logically incapable of behaving appropriately to his 'place'. He is logically incapable of behaving appropriately to the new relationship. His failure – or, rather, his inability – to respond appropriately is not to be regarded as sin which deserves, or will attract, punishment. It is to be regarded as 'loss' rather than 'sin'. To compare great things with small, his loss is analogous to the loss of a person who, having been invited to a party but not knowing of his invitation, deduces from his host's well-known courtesy that he will not be turned away; and so he gate-crashes the party. Although he receives all that the party has to offer in food and drink, his 'loss' is that he does not receive the 'gift' of the host's respect and affection which was offered and expressed in the invitation. From this he is necessarily and logically excluded by his failure to 'know about' and receive the invitation.

The double tragedy

We notice in this simple illustration that the 'guest's' loss is the host's loss also. The host 'performed' the invitation in order that an intended guest might receive the particular compliment of being invited; and when the 'guest' received only food and drink and not the intended compliment, then, to that extent, the host's generous aspiration 'came to nothing'. For both guest and host the incident ends in 'loss', or even, if one may use the word of a small social mishap, in 'tragedy'. It is the host's tragedy as well as the guest's. One may mention an actual and very poignant instance of this kind of 'double tragedy'. The matron of a children's hospital took under her care an infant boy, the pathetic victim of severe spina bifida, who, for whatever reason, had been deserted by his parents. The matron was wonderful with all her patients, but for this particular child she cared with a devotion, a wisdom and a tenderness which seemed more than compensation for the failure of his mother's love. Through her care the boy lived quite a full life up to the age of seventeen; but at that age he died. And he died sighing, 'If only somebody had loved me'. To see the matron's ravaged face as she told of how he died was to realize that the tragedy – the tragedy of the 'performance' of love not recognized or understood – was her tragedy no less than his.

Zeal and urgency on the part of the Church in missionary and evangelistic work – in 'telling the story' to those who have not heard it or, having heard, have failed to attend to or appropriate it – must clearly depend on the conviction that such failure *matters*: that it is real 'loss' or 'tragedy'. The note of urgency is heard within the story itself. The performance which the story reports is urgent, and the reporting of it must not mute or obscure its urgency. Missionary and evangelistic work seems to have been undertaken in some cases primarily 'for the sake of the heathen' – in order that they may be saved or rescued from 'loss'; and in other cases primarily 'for His sake' – in order that, as the *Dies Irae* puts it, 'so great labour may not be in vain'. Psychologically the two motives may be distinguished, but their logical basis seems to be the same – namely, that the effect of performance is to 'raise the stakes', to heighten the intensity, in the relationship between the two parties concerned. Performance does not 'leave things as they were'. It cannot be treated as if it had not happened. There *must* follow the 'gain' or 'triumph' of the appropriate response or the 'loss' or 'tragedy' of the inappropriate. One may understand this without finding it possible to identify the precise nature or degree of the gain or loss or, so to speak, to estimate the distribution of gain or loss between the two parties concerned. Our desire to heal a rift in the marriage between two of our friends does not depend on our estimate of the consequences for each if the rift continues and deepens. The rift itself is a tragedy and remains a tragedy even if the two 'get along very nicely' on their separate paths. Similarly, the urgent desire of Christians that all men should appropriate that which God has performed towards all men does not depend on an estimate of the consequences for those who fail to do so, nor, if the expression may be allowed, of the 'consequences' of their failure for God himself.

The Church as steward

It is far beyond the scope of this chapter to discuss the proper relationship between Christians and those who, as adherents of other religious systems – or of none – decline to attend to the Christian story. Our concern is simply with *the logical basis* of that close and exclusive attention which the Church pays to its story. As we see it, the Church is not thereby claiming 'a monopoly of truth'. Truth is a quality of information; and this quality depends in principle on the correspondence of information with facts and not on the source from which the information is derived or the person or persons by whom it is announced. That of which the Church claims to be 'steward' or 'guardian' or 'witness' or 'ambassador' is not information but performance; and performance can continue to be appropriated only through report of performance and through attention to that report. A situation created by performance can be known to exist only by knowledge of the performance; and one cannot, in principle, respond appropriately to that situation except by attending, directly or through report, to the performance. Nothing other than report of performance can create the possibility of response appropriate to the performance: and it is for the maintaining and actualizing of this possibility that the Church believes itself responsible.

The Church as inheritor

Let us return to the beginning of this chapter. 'Attention' is more than 'knowledge that something is the case'. If someone has promised to come, and if I know of his promise, it is inappropriate that I should consider and discuss the likelihood that he will come on grounds other than his promise. I ought not to say, 'I think he will come: the weather is good' or 'He will probably come: he has nothing else to do on Thursdays.' I owe it to his promise to attend to *that* rather than to the state of the weather or his known social habits. To do him justice, to behave appropriately, I must not only *know* that he has promised: I must also give my *attention* to his promise rather than to any other feature of the situation. I must base my confidence on his promise, and, if my confidence should flag, it is to his promise, and to that alone, that I should return. To attend to his promise – whether given directly or reported to me – is, one might say, to go on receiving his promise. It is to hold myself within the situation created by his promise. It is, it seems, in some such sense as this that the Church is obliged to go on attending to its story. For the Church is not only 'steward' or 'guardian' of that story, with the responsibility of preserving it for the future and telling it throughout the world, it is also – or at least it aspires to be – the 'place' or the 'body' of ever renewed and recreated response to the story. By attention to its story, the Church aspires to become and remain 'inheritor' as well as 'steward' of that which is performed in the events reported in the story. It aspires to be a body of people who, by responding appropriately to the performance which the Christian story reports, actually enter the inheritance which is offered by that performance to all mankind.

Why this story for all mankind?

Other households of faith

In the previous section of this chapter we have attempted to answer the question: 'Why should the Church give its attention to this story rather than to any other?' In this section we raise questions consequent upon the recognition of other households of faith, who have been formed in different historical circumstances and who pay attention to other stories.

If excessive individualism leads to a relativizing of belief – each person taking what is appropriate for him or herself –

then the recovery of the corporate dimension might be thought to lead to an absolutizing of belief, a recovery of the sense of objective truth standing over against the individual. However, the belief of a community is not the same as objective truth. Although each community may claim that its corporate knowing in some way contains or reflects absolute truth, the fact that a number of communities make this claim encourages the reflection that each of them may be wrong.

Differing teachings

What is clear is that they cannot all be right in making such claims. A study of the differing teaching of various households of faith suggests that such households look to differing moments of history or personal experience for their indication of where truth is to be found, that they express such truth in teachings which are not only diverse but also at times contradictory. They tell different stories.

Each household of faith has its own way of pointing to the mysteriousness of life, of weaving the events of personal life and social history into a web of belief, so that the individual is able to make sense of his own existence and to give to it some meaning and purpose in relation to the whole. Each household claims that the web it weaves corresponds in some manner to the way things actually are.

It is possible that all such claims are wrong, that each household is mistaken in attributing any kind of absolute truth to its own teachings over against other and different teachings. It is also possible that one such claim is right. The difficulty in justifying such a claim is that the criteria for doing so are often drawn from within the framework of thought and belief which supports such a claim. The argument is circular. Arguments based upon the notion of 'healthy religion' have at their heart assumptions about what is healthy and what is unhealthy which are found within a particular outlook. Arguments based upon the notion of 'doing justice to the whole of experience' assume that it is the whole of experience which derives from God, and this in turn is dependent upon a particular view of God, who or what he is and what is his relationship with such experience. The commitment expressed by membership of a household of faith remains primarily a matter of faith. A significant element in the present dialogue between members of different households is the search for criteria which may be held in common.

Tension in other households

The question 'Why this story?' acknowledges that there are other stories, told within other households of faith, which also purport to tell of the ways of God with men, or to tell of the pathway of salvation which all may tread. Within these other households the tension explored in some of the preceding papers between individual and corporate belief exists also. The reality of 'corporate believing' is not confined to the Christian community. The theme is explored by Wilfred Cantwell Smith in his work *The Meaning and End of Religion*. He uses the term 'cumulative tradition' to refer to the entire mass of overt data which constitute the historical deposit: buildings, Scriptures, theological systems, dance patterns, legal and social institutions, conventions, moral codes, stories, and so on. He uses the term 'faith' to refer to the individual's belief, commitment, attitudes. This is personal; men's faith is their own. Each man's faith is determined by the particular form of the cumulative tradition at that point. In turn the tradition is enriched by the faith and activity of the individual within it.

Cantwell Smith may be criticized for a lack of emphasis upon the tension between the individual belief and the objectivity of the tradition. We do not just take from the tradition what is meaningful for us, but we feel with our indebtedness a sense of obligation. The tradition is not there for us to do just as we like with it. We choose to stand within it, to associate ourselves with it and to become, humanly speaking, responsible for it. That responsibility may be exercised in differing ways, for instance by stressing fidelity to a particular form of the tradition or by stressing the need to express it in conformity with knowledge from other sources. The responsibility cannot be relinquished without a sense of placing oneself at a distance from the tradition.

Nevertheless, Cantwell Smith is right in drawing attention to these concepts within a number of households of faith. Tradition and individual apprehension are to be found in other corporate religious groups. Within them there are conservatives, liberals, radicals. There are the outrunners, those who push on ahead in an endeavour to reach new and creative ways of expressing the truth contained in the tradition, and there are the defenders, those who guard the deposit. There are difficulties about boundaries; there are difficulties about defining the essential core of the tradition; there are changes of interpretation in which a teaching or a passage from the Scriptures is brought out and given a new emphasis in new circumstances.

Theological account of other faiths

The existence of a number of corporate religious bodies, each having features in common, and each laying claim to some kind of consonance between its own teachings and absolute truth, lays upon each the obligation to give some kind of account of the others. It may be a negative account, reckoning them as in error or of the devil or based upon illusory concepts and events. It may be a positive account, discovering within them elements which reinforce and strengthen its own teachings. It may be in part positive and in part negative. Such obligation to give an account of other faiths within the purpose of God is laid upon a Christian community such as the Church of England.

In doing so, we must not lose sight of the fact that religious traditions are not self-contained and isolated from one another. They exist alongside one another and influence one another. At some times their relationship is supportive and creative. At others it is hostile and deeply destructive.

It is in part this mutual interaction which necessitates a reappraisal of the theological account we give of other faiths.

Three examples may be cited. The first is drawn from Asia. After several centuries of Christian mission in Asia, the Church remains a minority, in some countries a tiny minority, of the population. The great Christian educational movement in India was intended to bring India's finest minds and spirits within the Christian fold. Instead it sent them back into their own Hindu traditions to discover afresh and to interpret anew the treasures they found there. In what sense can the supremacy of Christian truth or the centrality of the Church in the purpose of God be maintained in the face of this historical revival? Does not the survival and apparent permanence of the great Asian religions indicate the necessity to reconsider whether they are to disappear before an all-conquering Church? When Dr Ambedkar was looking for a religion into which to take the Indian untouchables whom he led and to whom he wished to give identity and significance, it was not to the Christian Church but to the Buddhist community that he looked.

A second example is drawn from the one continent where success may be claimed for the expansion of the Christian

Church, the continent of Africa. This is the success of Islam alongside the Christian Church. It is apparent that large areas of the continent of Africa are looking to Islam for a religion which will give them a sense of world brotherhood in an African context. Is this simply lack of zeal on the part of the Christian Church? Or ignorance and prejudice in the African mind and spirit? Or is Islam to continue to play a significant role in world history?

A third example, perhaps the most acute, is drawn from the complex interaction between Judaism and the Christian Church. Constraint of space forbids discussion of this tangled relationship in which affection and fury are mingled. But the 'holocaust' of the 1940s must not be ignored in any such discussion.

Such historical considerations should drive the Christian Church to reconsider its relationship to other households of faith. It is not possible in this chapter to give an account of such a reconsidered relationship. Perhaps this ought to be the task of a future doctrine commission. Rather, its intention is to indicate some of the questions which are raised and possible answers which might be given. These questions will be grouped under the Christian concepts of revelation, salvation and mission.

Revelation

Christian teaching claims that knowledge about God is given through the Scriptures, or through reflection upon the Scriptures embodied in the Church's tradition, or through those events and experiences of which Scripture is a record. It claims that the will and purpose, and therefore in part the nature, of God is understood by revelation; the uncovering by God, at certain moments, of his eternal glory and unchanging being. What then is his relation to other events, and in particular to those events and moments which are determinative for other households of faith? What is his relation to the histories of which other scriptures are a record? What is his relation to the teachers of the Upanisads, to the moment of the Buddha's enlightenment, to the writings of the Quran? Is this a similar relationship to that which he bears to the prophets of Israel? It is possible to approach this question in an individualistic way. It may be said that the Spirit of God enlightens all men, or that their consciences are touched by him. But if the question is asked in relation to their corporate belief, an individualistic answer will not do. What is his relation to their histories and their articulations of belief? It is possible to claim that he is active in their histories although they are unaware of it. Second Isaiah makes such a claim for the history of Cyrus and his armies; the prophet Amos for the history of the Philistines brought from Crete and the Syrians from Kir. If such an answer is given, then the further question must be asked about his purposes within these histories. Is he giving to those outside the Judaeo-Christian tradition some glimpse of his glory, some foretaste of his purpose which they will understand fully in the light of determinative revelation, determinative in the sense that all other intimations of God will find their proper place in relation to it? Some within the Christian tradition would wish to give a more radical answer. They would claim that within the corporate belief systems of other faiths there are truths about God which required those histories in order to be uncovered. In the phrase of John Robinson's book, 'truth is two-eyed' or perhaps multi-eyed.

However, historical events must be distinguished from the doctrine drawn from within them. It is one matter to claim that God is active within a particular historical tradition. It is a different matter to claim that doctrines fashioned within that tradition are true. This consideration sparks another question. Do such systems of belief make available to those within them an encounter with God? Or do they hinder such an encounter? Some systems springing from the Indian tradition make use of the concept of *karma,* the teaching that every action performed by an individual has a result in his or her own life. Does this teaching, with its emphasis upon the individualistic path of rebirth to be trodden by every creature, enable an encounter with the God who redeems and liberates those who place their faith in Christ, and know the grace of God? Or does it render such an encounter more difficult?

Salvation

A second cluster of questions may be grouped around the concept of salvation. Recent emphasis in the continuing Christian tradition has placed the weight of meaning in the concept of salvation upon a present experience. There has been a move away from the emphasis upon salvation as the final declaration by God of the believer's standing in the Last Day. Much contemporary Christian teaching draws attention to the possibility of a present experience of joy, love and celebration of the Kingdom. This experience is distinct from the experience of salvation within other households. The goal described by them is a different goal. The path to be followed in order to reach it is a path which leads in a direction different from the Christian way. What then will believers of other households discover when they stand before the God of mercy and judgement? Will they understand their goal to be fully realized in him? Will they stand rejected because they had no faith in Christ and were not incorporated by baptism into Christ? Some contemporary Christian thinking shrinks from such a conclusion, bearing in mind the high correlation between the household into which one is born and the commitment which one makes. Is place of birth to be a factor of such importance at the final judgement? Agnosticism at this point is a proper Christian attitude.

Mission

This leads to a third cluster of questions around the concept of mission. Mission describes those tasks entrusted to the Church by its Lord as it shares in his mission. Among those tasks is evangelism, the proclaiming of good news. In the nineteenth century this task was interpreted by many missionaries (and still by some in the twentieth century) as the rescuing from final damnation of those souls who, unless they believed in Christ, would be lost for ever. If this, for some, is no longer the motive for evangelism, then what is to replace it? Is it the intention of the Christian mission that all should in due course become Christian (or all alive at a certain moment in history) so that other households of faith wither and die? Or are other households part of that creation which will be set free to share in the glorious freedom of the children of God? Is the purpose of proclamation the setting forth of that goal for the whole of creation, corporate bodies of religious knowing included? This is not the same question as the one frequently asked about the relation of proclamation to dialogue. Dialogue is both a means to effective proclamation and also a way of proclaiming. The question is rather about the relation of proclamation and dialogue on the one hand and conversion and incorporation by baptism into Christ on the other. Is the sole purpose of proclamation to lead others to faith in Christ and to baptism, or is it to point to the God in whom all will find their ultimate freedom?

Practical questions

To these three clusters of questions may be added two more which have to do with practical questions now facing the Church of England among other Christian bodies in this country. The first question concerns the right of those who belong to other households of faith to belong to their tradition and practise their faith. Are there limits to this right and to the recognition which the churches should give to other religious traditions? Should they be regarded as guests in a household which is offering them hospitality? It is often said that we are now a religiously plural society. But the implication of this phrase is that all households stand on an equal footing. Is this the case or does the host stand in a relation to guests which is not that of equality? Furthermore, are there those who are not welcome as guests? There is considerable concern about the activities of certain religious organizations. If there are to be limits, by what criteria are these limits set? Is it possible to claim that there are some groups, whose activities are so destructive of human life and relationship, as understood in the Christian tradition, that they should not be welcomed?

The second question concerns the practice of inter-faith worship. It is one thing to acknowledge the right of others to belong to another religious tradition, to attend as a guest in their household and to invite them to attend in our own household. It is quite another thing to share in activity such as inter-faith worship which apparently sets out to embrace different households within one structure. What are the implications of such activity, and if this is undertaken, how are the dangers of confusion and misunderstanding to be overcome?

These questions are far-ranging, and although the present commission has touched on them, it has not felt competent to deal with them adequately. However, we thought it wise to indicate that we were aware of them and of their significance, if only to encourage others to take up with greater competence the task of answering them. Our discussion of the Christian Church as a body of corporate knowledge has helped us to understand the nature of other households. We suggest that it may be a fruitful dimension for future discussion of these questions.

261

10

'Carried about by Every Wind?':
The Development of Doctrine

*J. Austin
Baker.*

'Doctrine' has a peculiarly sensitive and significant place in any discussion of corporate believing. Though covering a far wider field than creeds, articles, confessions and suchlike formularies, it does have a representative character. To call some piece of writing 'Christian doctrine' implies that a majority of Christian people, of whatever church or tradition, would acknowledge what it says as in substance something to which they could give their assent. To speak of Lutheran, Catholic or Anglican doctrine is to refer to the Christian beliefs of those traditions put in ways that distinguish them from those of other Christians.

Doctrine is not the same thing as 'theology'. One can quite naturally talk of Calvin's or Paul Tillich's 'theology' of creation, for example; it would feel slightly odd to say 'their doctrine of creation' – or, if one did, it would normally imply something they shared with others, something derived from the Christian community. All the more, therefore, doctrine is a different animal from 'speculative theology'. What scouts, skirmishers, explorers, of whom we have heard a good deal in this report, feel it proper to write is not doctrine; and it is a very good thing for everyone that it is not. The community ought not to be committed to what they write, for its own sake and for theirs. That would disastrously restrict their freedom with fatal results both for their integrity and for the eventual enrichment the community might receive from their voyages of discovery.

What do we mean by doctrine?

Broadly speaking, doctrine is whatever Christians say when they speak or write about beliefs with a sense of doing so on behalf of the body to which they belong. Doctrine is expressed under other constraints as well as that of one's individual perception of truth. The latter is fundamental and must never be violated. But to propound anything that can correctly be called doctrine, this perception must be in harmony with the deliverances of a kind of obedience, a willing service to the corporate mind of the group. One would look for doctrine, therefore, in a wide variety of places – encyclicals, official reports approved by the highest authority in a church, in catechetical literature, in sermons of accredited teachers, in publications commissioned for teaching purposes, in individual writings which had won a place in the authoritative traditions of the particular church, and so forth.

Doctrine is not merely the bald statement of heads of belief. It includes an apologetic element, reasons generally accepted within the community for holding such beliefs. It naturally tends also to be systematic. The relation of one area of belief to another is set out; the whole body of belief is given coherent form. Moreover, because it is written at particular times and within particular cultures, it will use the assumptions of this or that philosophy or view of history or understanding of the natural universe.

For all these reasons doctrine is continually, if slowly, changing. It changes continually because certain new ideas, new slants are widely adopted, new individual works are admitted to the authoritative stock, new knowledge in other spheres modifies the way beliefs are understood and expressed. It changes slowly because any changes have to be absorbed into the system as a whole. As Jung was fond of pointing out, in any age there are some who are happy with the climate of thought as it is, some who are baffled by it because they see the world spontaneously in the terms of generations or even centuries earlier, some who are ill at ease because their minds have already glimpsed insights which will not be generally accepted for a long time to come, and for which the necessary framework of knowledge does not yet exist. Given this characteristic of human society, changes in the 'received wisdom', whether religious or any other kind, are bound to be slow and to seem to many too little and too late, while to others they seem dangerous and unnecessary – whence the pressures that build up to outbursts of revolutionary change.

To these natural processes of all corporate conviction, however, we have, in the case of 'revealed religion', to add another. Wherever we find at the heart of a religion loyalty to a founder with a distinctive message and achievement, we also very naturally find resistance to change or to the admixture of beliefs from other sources. This is not to say that these things do not happen. But when they do, there is a profound need to show that the changes are not changes of substance and that the new ingredients are essentially in harmony with the old. Greek philosophy was eased into the early Church by the thinking which saw Socrates as a foreshadowing of Christ and Plato as a Gentile Moses. Likewise, revolutionaries either believe themselves to be or intuitively present themselves as those who seek to return to the pure teaching of the founder or the first disciples. The Reformation is the classic instance.

How does doctrine develop?

These features are reflected in the ways in which doctrine is developed, for develop it does. In general, we may discern three patterns of development.

The first is that of logical elaboration. Additional beliefs are inferred from existing ones, stated in propositional form. For example, in Roman Catholicism the doctrine of the Immaculate Conception seemed to be demanded by the way in which the doctrine of the incarnation had been worked out in particular categories over the centuries. Adjustments or corrections may be made to one statement in the light of other conclusions. Thus, in scholastic theology, more precise definition and classification of sin led to reappraisal of the state of unbaptized infants. Traditionally they were held to be guilty of original sin by their descent from Adam and Eve, but clearly this 'sin' was not one they themselves had voluntarily committed. The degree of guilt attaching to it was therefore minimal, assessed by St Thomas Aquinas as less than that of ordinary mortal sins, by Suarez as less than that of venial sin. This adjustment went in step with the change from the early view, that infants dying unbaptized endured the torments of hell, to the current Catholic orthodoxy, that their eternal state is one of perfect natural happiness but without the perfect supernatural joy of the vision of God.

It is in doctrinal systems like that of Roman Catholicism, which are wide-ranging and impressive intellectual structures, that this pattern of development is most easily seen. It will always have an important role, so long as Christians are prepared to put their names to propositional statements of belief. If we make such statements seriously, we can also be held to believe what those statements logically entail. It is therefore necessary to make these entailments explicit, and to check on inconsistencies. Nevertheless, there are serious defects in this approach to doctrine. First, mistakes can easily be made in the starting-points – for example, by using as propositions hallowed traditional language which is really poetic, analogical or symbolic. Second, as step after step is added to the argumentation, the consequences of these initial errors become more and more disastrous; and one may end with pronouncements *de fide* which are very hard to reconcile with some fundamental tenets of the faith. Third, the community becomes trapped in its own logical building. Since everything is assumed to follow from something else, there are no grounds for treating one belief as more secure or more necessary than another. A 'hierarchy of truths', as suggested by the Second Vatican Council, is possible in the sense that there may be some root beliefs from which all others in the system derive, but it is quite impossible in any sense of some truths being more crucial than others. As the generations go by, therefore, change in the deposit of faith becomes more and more marginal, and the inherited burden of things to believe irreducibly heavy.

This account of development in terms of logical elaboration is in any case too limited, too rationalistically precise to cover what actually happens. Many changes in doctrine are more subtle. The end-results feel like a natural progression from what has gone before, but it is not possible to trace that progression in terms of deductive argument. Hence a second account which uses the model of organic growth. The later chapters of the history of doctrine record the unfolding not of what was logically implicit in the origins but of what was embryonically present. Certainly some more open and creative model of this kind is needed to contain within the bounds of legitimate development the ministry, for example, of bishops, priests and deacons, or the varied understandings of the atonement. Yet for all its advantages this model, too, leaves us with serious unanswerable questions. Not all natural, spontaneous development is desirable. May there not be mutations in doctrine as in plants and animals, which are undesirable, even in the long run non-viable and destructive of the organism? May not the environment inhibit certain functions, as when, for example, certain trees never produce mature fruit in colder latitudes? The picture of the faith developing itself in response to innate potentials is an inadequate one because in essence it is sub-human. It is a mark of the human race that, however imperfectly, it has some conscious, reflective control over it own becoming. Any model of doctrinal development must incorporate this distinctively human quality. We cannot accept that whatever doctrines emerge are true. We have to do justice to the power of criticism and of rational self-correction.

In *An Essay on the Development of Christian Doctrine,* which appeared in 1845, Newman laid the foundations for all modern discussion of this subject by treating development objectively as a complex historical process and as the result of human interaction within the community under the impact of events. If the Church was entrusted with the stewardship of revelation, and guided by the Spirit of God, nevertheless these factors worked themselves out in ways not untypical of the development of ideas in general, both moral and political. The vast expansion of Newman studies in this century has given his thought a wide and merited influence for which earlier the time was not ripe.

Newman tackled the key issue: how do we tell a true development from a false one? He proposed seven tests: a development must preserve the essential ideas of the faith; it must allow for continuity of those principles on which the life of the Christian community is conducted; it must unite organically with what has gone before; there will be hints and growth-points in earlier tradition which can be seen to have foreshadowed it; there will be logical sequence, the later evolution revealing characteristics in the original deposit which had been overlooked; a true development will help to conserve what has gone before; and finally, it will prove to be enduring.

In short, doctrinal development may be described as the community working out a fuller understanding of its inheritance of faith and submitting this to the test of time, that is, of the life and thought of the Christian people in future generations. Newman's account does, however, raise certain questions. He himself draws attention to the difficulty of deciding what are the essential ideas of the faith; and in the last few years we have seen the truth of this in the debate over the doctrine of the incarnation, with theologians disagreeing whether this is essential to Christianity, and if so, in what range of formulations. The test of conservation needs careful scrutiny. Are we seeking to conserve what has gone before in its original detail and as understood in the context of that period, or in its essential insight which we are free to reset and reinterpret? More radically, are we bound to conserve *all* previous doctrine, provided it has hitherto passed the tests described? Clearly this is impossible where we belong to a church which has parted from other churches over a doctrinal issue. Does conservation apply only to our own tradition? If so, where is there room for repentance and amendment of life in respect of past errors? Is not one of the main sources of vitality in the Church the constant sifting of our accumulated stores of belief and practice, and a return to older simplicities, even if expressed in contemporary forms? All of which simply emphasizes that the crucial, and yet most ambiguous, test is the last, that of duration. Is there in fact any point at which it can be said that a development has lasted long enough to be beyond criticism? Would it not be a sentence of death for Christianity if this were so? In what sense, anyway, can we hold that a development has endured when it is itself subject to constant change, as are all living things?

One preliminary conclusion perhaps ought to be that our description of development may be sound, but that from the very description itself we realize there can be no infallible guarantees that any particular development is of permanent validity. We have to live with our provisionality, and stand boldly to the truth of matters on which we may, now or later, be considered mistaken.

There is one particular feature of doctrinal development which can be illuminated by a specifically twentieth-century analogy. A scientific hypothesis is a pattern, arrived at by insight and verified by experiment, which enables us to explain and predict the course of phenomena. The more evidence that can be covered by the hypothesis, the better it will be. But no hypothesis is absolute and eternal. Bit by bit new knowledge strains it, calls for modifications and qualifications and eventually breaks it down altogether. But the fact that a hypothesis is never final does not make it irrational or useless. On the contrary, so far as it goes it is true, it 'works'; and even after the limits of its validity have been discovered, it still works perfectly well within those limits, and remains true for

267

many purposes. The axioms of Euclidean geometry, or the 'laws' of Newtonian physics, are sound and truthful tools for most people's ordinary living. The parallels with theology are obvious. The intellectual side of religion is, so to speak, the working out of a super-hypothesis, arrived at by the insight of informed faith. Using the idea of God, theology attempts to embrace in its hypothesis all the evidence there is, not only physical but spiritual, not only in the world but in the tradition. Theological systems or doctrines both can and must be checked against the facts of experience, including those mediated by Scripture. From time to time a reigning hypothesis will break down catastrophically under the avalanche of events. At other times there will be a constant process of modification and qualification. Either may eventually lead to a new framework, which will involve a redrawing of the picture of God, often in what may seem drastic ways. But the old pieties will still be sound within certain limits, and will continue to work for many people. In some contexts they are still true; and their truth is organically related to the newer and more comprehensive truth into which we have been led.

Having looked at some general theories of doctrinal development, it may now be helpful to describe some of the particular concrete factors which operate within these general frameworks. Can we detect any recurring patterns in the ways in which the Christian community develops its official teaching? In the following sections an attempt has been made to give some examples of such patterns, choosing a fairly wide range of topics as illustrations; but in such limited space anything that is said can be no more than a starting-point for discussion.

The limiting of options

In one sense the possibilities for Christians when reflecting on the Eucharist, their distinctive act of worship, were in the beginning wide open. Clearly they were obeying Christ's command, 'Do this' – but what was implicit in the doing? There is no need to enter into the debate about the nature of the Eucharist in the New Testament. The very fact that it is so hard, for example, to draw a firm line between a fellowship meal of the disciples and some kind of ritual act by which they 'remembered' Jesus and his death, or to be sure what for them 'remembering' meant, warns us that here we have to do with a whole gamut of only vaguely defined possibilities.

The range begins to narrow as a result of a number of changes in the Christian situation. Congregations grow, and depend more on the large weekly gathering. Not only can this no longer be held easily in a house, but more and more converts come in as individuals, not in whole families. In some places many are slaves, with no home of their own, whose time is almost all at the command of others. The heart of Christian corporate experience perforce becomes what we would call 'going to church'. 'The Way' has to be more like other religions; and in fact this proves rather reassuring. Christians, as the true holy people, possessors of the true knowledge, the true law, the true worship, have everything that others have but in the form God really intended: the true cult, the true mysteries, the true synagogue, the true teachers. The Lord's Supper, as their own distinctive action, becomes their equivalent of the forms of worship of other people, both Greek and Jew.

Vis-à-vis the Jews, the Christian position is defined by Malachi 1.11. The Eucharist is the 'pure offering' which the prophet foretold would be offered 'in every place' and 'among the nations'. But this offering is still understood in a variety of senses: the self-offering of the believers (the *Didache*); the thank-offering for redemption (Justin). What sharpens the focus is the thought that, on the authority of Jesus's own words, the gifts offered, the bread and wine, are the Body and Blood of Jesus himself, made so by 'the words of the prayer that comes from him'. Now, 'Body and Blood' cry out to be thought of as a sacrifice. Already in the New Testament Jesus is described in various ways as a sacrifice. Indeed, his own words on Maundy Thursday evening imply this in some sense. Paul, John, Hebrews, all classify the sacrifice as expiatory or propitiatory. It was hardly surprising that the eucharistic 'Body and Blood' should be linked to this classification, and the eucharistic action become the Christian 'sacrifice', superseding the animal sacrifices offered to the same end by Jews and pagans alike. For Origen (185-254) and Hippolytus (170-236) the Eucharist is itself propitiatory. Cyril of Jerusalem (315-86) teaches that it can be offered to plead for the dead (cf. 2 Macc. 12.42-5). For Tertullian (160-220) the minister who offers the Eucharist is *sacerdos*, a sacrificing priest.

This view of the Eucharist was not at first the only one. Gregory Nazianzen (329-89), following the tradition of

269

Ignatius (died 107), expounds it as medicinal, as the food of salvation, the means by which we are deified. Augustine has a rich and many-sided account of it. But more and more the attention of theologians is given to working out this model of sacrifice, in particular the two component questions: in what sense are the bread and wine the Body and Blood of Christ? What is the relation of the Eucharist to the one sacrifice of Calvary by which we were saved? John Chrysostom (347-407), for example, is already putting forward a view still repeated sixteen centuries later: 'It is not another sacrifice but the same – or rather, we make a memorial of the sacrifice.'

This problem became almost an obsession in the West, in the eucharistic controversies of the ninth century (Paschasius Radbert, Rabanus Maurus, Ratramnus) and the eleventh (Berengarius, Lanfranc). Lanfranc's ideas eventually won the day; and, when accepted as the official orthodoxy of the Roman Church from the Fourth Lateran Council (1215) onwards, marked out one narrow arena for eucharistic doctrine for almost 700 years.

Even the Reformers, radically different though their answers were, could not escape from the tyranny of these particular questions. The view that 'is' in 'This is my Body' means 'signifies' or 'represents'; the insistence that the elements are 'bare symbols'; the Receptionist doctrine, by which Christ dwells spiritually in the heart by faith, and the elements are occasions not means of this indwelling; these and many other variants served merely to concentrate attention on this one topic, and to ensure that the Eucharist would breed and perpetuate divisions.

Modern historical study of the Bible, and the normative value attached to Christian origins by some theologians in recent times, seemed to promise a possible breakout. But the habit of centuries dies hard; and for all that the 1971 report of the Anglican–Roman Catholic International Commission, for example, presented the Eucharist in a wide variety of aspects and in a vocabulary that, so far as possible, avoided the polemical associations of the past, it was significantly on this narrow front that misgivings arose, and criticisms, often passionate, were voiced from both sides of the ecclesiastical divide.

The interplay of doctrines

The various individual topics of Christian belief are related to one another at so many levels and in such a number of ways that the task of describing these relationships is a would-be systematist's dream or nightmare according to his degree of of conceit or realism. Three examples only must serve here.

First, there is interplay resulting from shared terminology. The Eucharist and the Church are subjects that could hardly not be linked in some way. Augustine seizes upon the New Testament image of the Church as the 'Body of Christ' as one obvious starting point for exploring this link. The Church is one with Christ: as the Body of which he is the Head, it forms one entity with him. When, therefore, the Body of Christ is offered on the altar, it is the Church which is offered in union with him. Symbolized by the loaf, it is consecrated to be Christ's own sacrifice. To communicate and to offer thus become two aspects of one and the same act; and the Eucharist in which we give thanks for Christ's sacrifice on behalf of the Church is simultaneously the sacrificial oblation of ourselves, made possible by our identity with him. 'Be what you see, and receive what you are.' The vertiginous paradoxes are devotionally exciting, at least to those who respond to them; and response may lead us to assume that here a doctrine is developing in a valuable way as a result of cross-fertilization from another doctrine. But is there really any solid development? Is not all that has happened merely this: that two different metaphorical or symbolic uses of the same word, 'Body', have been equated by treating both as literal, and that from this quite inadmissible misuse of a word all sorts of seemingly logical inferences have been drawn?

Second, there is the attempt to find common philosophical structures for different doctrines. This has happened more than once with the Eucharist and Christology. Thus, John Damascene (675-749) believed that he could 'explain' and so fortify the Eastern Church's view of the bread and wine as truly converted into Christ's Body and Blood by making use of ideas from the Chalcedonian account of Christ himself as both God and Man. He argued that the bread and wine became the Body and Blood while remaining apparently unchanged, but that this did not mean that two separate entities coexisted in the sacrament. Just as Christ himself was one individual being, one *hypostasis*, but with two natures, humanity and divinity, so the consecrated elements were each one entity but with two natures – bread or wine, and divinity. This was, in fact, an alarming doctrinal gaffe, because in Orthodox belief

271

Christ's Body and Blood are themselves already a hypostatic union of humanity and divinity, and so the eucharistic elements ought to be a union of three natures, not two – bread or wine, humanity and divinity. Much later, in 1520, Luther also tried a christological move in order to escape from Thomist transubstantiation philosophy in giving an account of the Eucharist. The bread and wine, he argued, remained entire and unchanged, but the Body and Blood of Christ were given with them, just as fire is given in red-hot iron, and Christ's divinity in his humanity. Here inadequate science was coupled with equally erratic doctrine. For though Luther certainly believed he was conforming to orthodox Chalcedonian teaching on the Person of Christ, his analogy was in truth Nestorian. The moral would seem to be that philosophical patterns which serve to make one doctrine accessible to the reasoning imagination may be merely confusing to another. In so far as one form of doctrinal development is the search for common patterns running through many areas of belief, and demonstrating their coherence, this may be a more arduous quest than has sometimes been thought.

A third aspect of the interplay of doctrines is that of the effect developments in one area have on another. This can be well illustrated from the doctrines of the Eucharist and the ordained ministry. The increasing emphasis on the Eucharist as sacrifice naturally reinforced the use of the term 'priest' to denote those ordained to celebrate it. The threefold ministry of bishop, priest and deacon was presented as the Christian fulfilment of the Old Testament high priest, priest and Levite (Cyprian, died 258). The growing importance of the Eucharist as the heart of Christian devotion helped to reduce the diaconate to a mere stage on the way to priesthood, and even, in Catholic theology, to blur the distinctiveness of the episcopal order. At the Reformation, therefore, not surprisingly the question whether to keep or reject the title of 'priest' was a key issue of conscience. A church which, like the Church of England, retained the term seemed to many to have jibbed at complete scriptural reform, however carefully it redefined its eucharistic teaching. Seventeenth-century Anglican piety (Herbert, Taylor, Ken) went far to give fresh content of a pastoral kind to the idea of priesthood, in keeping with the 'reasonable, holy and lively sacrifice' of 'ourselves, our souls and bodies'. But the eucharistic altar and priestly sacrifice were still there in the general Christian background, and with the Tractarian Movement revived within the Church of England a conception of priesthood whose exponents soon came perforce to look to Roman Catholicism in various forms for authoritative guidance.

This divergence within the Church of England, primarily eucharistic in origin, has now created an impasse in the doctrine of ministry on two key matters which could make it impossible for that church to move as a united body into closer relations with any other. First, the conviction that the ministries of the Free Churches are not 'priestly' in intention, in the sense we have described, means that for a substantial minority of Church of England members some gesture implying supplementary ordination of Free Church ministers is indispensable before there can be mutual recognition of ministries. For others any such ingredient would be as totally unacceptable as it would be for the Free Church ministers themselves. The position of the former group is reinforced by another consideration: any other attitude to Free Church ministries could be held to undermine the point they feel it vital to make in discussions with the Roman Catholic Church, that Church of England ministerial order is truly priestly in a Catholic sense, and that therefore there is no need for the Church of Rome to insist on any kind of reordination in the case of Anglicans.

The second matter is that of the ordination of women. The opposition to this within the Church of England has numerous strands, but only one need concern us here. This is the stress on the ordained ministry as a 'priesthood'. The question, 'Can women be priests?' is the preferred battleground, and the use of the word 'priests' here is very far from a neutral denotation of the second degree of holy orders. Women ordained in the Free Churches, it is argued, though they preside at the Lord's Supper, are not ordained to the priesthood, because the Eucharist for them is not a sacrifice. Hence, too, the polemical use of the term, 'priestesses', differentiating in the light of the history of cults between the pagan religions, which allowed women to serve the altars, and the Jewish, which did not. A study of the controversial literature shows clearly that the conviction that women priests would be an impermissible development of doctrine is in part, at any rate, a manifestation in other guise of the unresolved Anglican argument about the Eucharist, carrying one side of this back to very early Christian

273

speculations about the Eucharist as a replacement for the sacrificial cultus of the old Israel. Another related aspect, peculiarly significant for some Anglicans, is the so-called 'iconic' theory of the priesthood. The celebrant at the Eucharist is an 'icon' of Christ, the true High Priest, as he presided at the Last Supper. This is, in part, the logical conclusion of the western theory of the Eucharist, which sees the consecration of the elements as accomplished by the words of institution: Christ, present in his risen power, brings about what he first gave at the table in the upper room. Naturally, from this a line of argument follows that the one who represents Christ should be an image of him, not female but male. We do not here pass any judgement on the theological quality of this mental picture of the Eucharist; the purpose of mentioning it is simply to show how assumptions about the Eucharist exert the very strongest effect on discussion about the ministry. It is perhaps worth pointing out, however, the various factors which converge to give force to this approach. The prayer of consecration in the 1662 book means something very different when used in the spirit of a Catholic ethos of the priest as sacrificer from its sense and feel in the framework of Cranmer's theology. In the former case the prominence and critical importance of the institution narrative do indeed favour an understanding of the priest as acting the part of Christ. The recent widespread adoption of the westward position for the celebrant has intensified this interpretation, where it exists, because the priest visually and tellingly occupies the place of Christ in the traditional artistic representations of the Last Supper. When approaching such a tangled subject as the debate over the ordination of women, it is as well to bear in mind that some of the most important issues are not specifically about the role of women at all, but about the Eucharist. If we are asked to assess, for instance, whether the ordination of women is a legitimate development of Christian doctrine, we need to be clear *which* doctrines we are in truth talking about.

The influence of secular culture

In H. G. Wells's novel, *The Faith of a Bishop,* the hero as a young clergyman is talking to an elderly prelate and complaining that the Church never adapts or develops its teaching. From this the older man firmly dissents. When pressed to give an example, he asks, 'Where is the doctrine of hell now?' It has, he agrees, never been formally disowned, but 'we have repressed it below the level of consciousness'.

The example is well taken, and the points made perceptive. Little time is given to hell in most Church of England pulpits nowadays. To many the New Testament imagery, some of it in the mouth of our Lord, is embarrassing. Reinterpretation, often entirely in terms of this-worldly history, is common. But for the most part the subject is left severely alone. Much the same could be said of teaching in other denominations. What, then, of official guidance on the subject? Two examples, from widely differing traditions, may be quoted. The first comes from *A Declaration of Faith*, accepted by the Congregational Church in England and Wales in 1967 as a representative statement of faith:

In faith we expect God to complete his purpose for all mankind and for each individual person by endowing men beyond their death with new resources for being alive unto God in fellowship with Jesus Christ. In the powers already granted through the gift of the Holy Spirit, Christians have a foretaste of this new being. It has, for its indispensable grounds, the judgement of God through which men will know at last the whole truth about themselves, and the saving love of God which removes all condemnation from those joined in manhood with his obedient Son their Saviour Jesus Christ. For those who trust the grace of the Lord Jesus Christ the judgement of God's holy love is the gateway to his everlasting mercy.

Whether every human being will be able to endure so searching a judgement and thankfully to take back his life from the judge's hands, we do not know. Those who do, will live henceforth transfigured in the glory of God's perfected creation. That God should discard from this creation any creature precious to him is inconceivable. Yet we are sure that God will for ever respect human freedom and will not impose salvation upon any who may be everlastingly recalcitrant. Human beings are warned not to harden themselves in opposition to God or seek to defeat his gracious purpose. To be banished from the presence of the Lord and from the glory of his power is a prospect to be envisaged by the rebellious with appropriate fear. Yet, in affirming this, we know Christ as the Good Shepherd who seeks until he finds, and we disclaim any right to speak of

275

limits beyond which the patience and compassion of God are exhausted.

The second is from *The Thyateira Confession* (1975), an official handbook of faith and prayer for teachers in Orthodox churches and schools in Great Britain:

> His judgement will be based upon our love and on the extent of our forgiveness of others and our sacrifices for the benefit of others. The more the people love and help others and forgive others the more easily they will be able to approach and reach Christ. The less we love and help, the less willingly we sacrifice, the more difficult it will be for us to reach the glory of God and be near those people, that is, the saints who have loved, who have helped, who have forgiven willingly and joyfully other people.
>
> The nearness or distance of men from God is the measure and the reason of their virtue and their moral and spiritual excellence. We will see God from afar or from near according to the measure of our love and moral and spiritual preparation. This measure for those who will be far away from God is called punishment or damnation and the measure of being near God is called justification and paradise.

It is true that debate on this question within the Christian churches goes back at least to the writings of Origen in the third century. Nevertheless, it is only in modern times, subsequent to the savage and contemptuous denunciation of the doctrine of eternal punishment by secular moralists, that the kind of changes illustrated in the above quotations have made real headway. (*Christian* moral sensitivity was not sufficient to protect F. D. Maurice from being hounded out of his professorship at King's College, London, in 1853 for questioning not even divine punishment but only its everlastingness.) Is this kind of change properly called 'development in doctrine'? Is it not perhaps an amputation or discontinuous change, in response to external pressure, simple subservience to the 'spirit of the age'? In the instance just considered we can resist so harsh a judgement. We may properly distinguish between the source of an insight and its compatibility with Christian teaching. Here the main impulse to change may have come from a secular critique, yet the gospel itself does contain materials for the same reappraisal.

Moreover, in this case we are talking about a judgement that morally good and sensitive men and women felt forced to pass on traditional beliefs; and Christian doctrine has in almost all periods been sympathetic to the view that God's voice and spirit are to be discerned in every genuine expression of human goodness.

A similar discovery of ideas present but only embryonic in Christian tradition, under the stimulus of independent secular developments and consequent criticism of Christian attitudes, has resulted from the growing human concern over our global environment and resources. Work in many quarters on the doctrine of creation, and on human stewardship of this planet and responsibility for the welfare of other species, has been the effect not the cause of anxiety and agitation outside the churches. Nevertheless, there is no need to twist and strain passages from the Bible and the Fathers to ally Christian thinking with the best of the secular world in this matter, nor to read alien ideas into them. The sympathy is there and authentic, and is being rapidly acknowledged by the common mind of the faithful. Such support, however, is less unambiguously forthcoming for the modifications in marriage discipline proposed by two successive theological commissions (and now contemplated by General Synod) or for the official shift in traditional attitudes to abortion. Where the impetus for change comes from society there will always be severe problems in deciding with integrity whether particular developments are indeed in harmony with Christian faith. This is perhaps especially so, when we remember the argument of Anthony Thiselton's chapter, in cases of that behaviour to which faith commits us, and which has hitherto been a mark of identity for the community within which alone our faith has its full meaning.

The influence of science and philosophy

This has from an early stage been a major factor in the development of doctrine, and with good reason. If people are to believe with any vigour or peace of mind, then heart and head need to be on reasonably friendly terms. At least our scientific picture of the universe and our general habits of thought, the ideas we are prepared to find meaningful, must be such that 'God' does not become a nonsensical term, totally alien to everything else in our mental furniture. In fact, at various periods in Christian history, the prevailing

277

cosmologies and philosophies have been congenial to faith. The Ptolemaic universe, for instance, was a great improvement, for educated Gentile Christians, on the crude, early Semitic cosmos of the Old Testament. The concepts of Middle Platonism lent themselves well, at least in some respects, to the working out of the doctrines of the Trinity and incarnation, well enough anyway for certain fatal difficulties to be ignored and for some of the Fathers to regard the whole Platonist system as of divine inspiration.

In modern times scientific and philosophic thought has become less hospitable to religious belief. For many people the evolutionary chain from inorganic matter to intelligent life seems to leave little room for God as Creator in any worthwhile sense. Some believers became excited when 'Big Bang' theories of the origin of the universe were thought to be winning over 'Continuous Creation' views; but now some scientists are offering an endless series of universes, each Big Bang start being prepared by the collapse and implosion of the previous cosmos – a nice return to the ancient cyclic theory of the Great Years, and one at odds with the linear, eschatological outlook of the Bible.

Anthropology and psychology have thrown doubt on revelation and religious experience. Philosophy has mounted some considerable challenges against the meaningfulness of religious language in general and the coherence of the concept of God in particular. The notion that basic reality is material, and that all mental and spiritual facts are parasitic on this, has become the unexamined assumption underlying the world-view of most educated western people, and has been through them diffused into popular culture.

Small wonder that these developments have had their impact on theologians. The general evolutionary ethos, by way of Bergson, emerged in the 'process theology' of Whitehead, whose wholly immanent view of God has been modified by Hartshorne to make God partly the force of love urging creation forward from within, and partly the perfection of love above and beyond creation, drawing all things to itself. More radically there has been the theme of 'Christian atheism', to the spiritual seriousness of which a variety of writers have borne witness: Bonhoeffer in the 1930s and 1940s with his emphasis on living 'as though' there were no God; the 'Death of God' school in the 1960s; some Liberation theologians in the 1960s and 1970s; and most recently in England, Don Cupitt.

Within the traditional systems of faith there have been other effects. Critique of the philosophical concepts underlying the creeds has led some theologians to argue that doctrines such as those of the Trinity and incarnation must be replaced or reinterpreted because they were no part of the original faith, but arose simply by the inner logic of that particular philosophical approach, and cannot make coherent sense in any other. This line has been reinforced by studies stressing the pluralism of the New Testament, in which, it is argued, no one view of the person and work of Christ is found; and by the work of church historians who see early Christianity in terms not of one mainstream orthodoxy attacked by various heresies but of equally authoritative theologies locked in a competition from which the familiar version of Christianity emerged the winner.

All these upheavals have very understandably given rise to a good deal of wide-ranging theological speculation in the cause of intellectual integrity. These speculations have, however, not yet led to any substantive changes in *doctrine*. To change doctrine, the official corporate formulations of faith, and the standard teaching that expounds them, is a serious matter. It requires a solid consensus of the faithful. This is always hard to achieve for various reasons: some are not convinced by the arguments; for others the doctrines under attack are the well-spring of their spiritual life; others close ranks against anything which seems to threaten their Christian identity, and so on. This resistance to change is fortunate. It means that the critiques are subjected to full and thorough examination. (This cannot be done in a hurry in such complex matters; it is striking that the objections raised against some theological innovation in the first flurry are hardly ever the ones that later prove to be decisive.) In the case of the debates we have so sketchily outlined, moreover, many different disciplines are involved, and this adds to the difficulty of proper appraisal. Nevertheless, it is already becoming apparent that the arguments for jettisoning so much of traditional doctrine are not as sound as they may at first have appeared. In time the new knowledge and the new understandings of reality will further affect the way we define and express our doctrine, and will thereby leave it stronger and of more value to human living. But for the moment the debate continues.

The constraints of the past

These are of crucial importance in all great religions, but in doctrinal development today they seem to operate very unevenly and in many different ways.

At a popular level there is great confusion. Old landmarks, familiar forms are valued. Anything which seems like an attack on the creeds is widely condemned, yet it is doubtful how far even some of those who voice such condemnations are entirely happy with the creeds as an account of their personal faith. Old forms of service are defended not just for their language but also for the doctrines they enshrine; but it is hard to say whether the defenders of these doctrines fully understand their original import or would identify with it if they did. To say this is not to disparage such attitudes. They are rightly concerned with continuous identity. The words which meant much to our forebears, and which have been hallowed by long use at all the most mysterious and sacred junctures of human life, cannot lightly be jettisoned. There is a natural and proper, if seemingly illogical, attitude in which Christians will reserve the right to modify or interpret the faith for themselves, and yet prefer that the corporate formularies which they are modifying remain unchanged. There may be a parallel here with what has been said in earlier chapters about 'stories'. Do doctrines, for all their apparent verbal precision, operate in some ways like stories, so that there is actually a large degree of tolerance before the fit with reality becomes too loose to be serviceable?

Nevertheless, even among non-specialist Christians the gap between traditional loyalty and actual belief can widen to a point which threatens seriousness and integrity. In public worship we do a lot of interceding; but there is widespread doubt about its real value. This touches a fundamental matter of doctrine – the relationship between God and the world. The Church authorizes new lectionaries, and encourages the laity to take part in the public reading of the lections. But for many the use of the Bible is loaded with difficulties, and even those who turn to the Scriptures regularly and with conviction in their private devotion often do so in a monochrome way which denies them much of the light and leading they might actually receive. The kind of approaches to Scripture discussed in Chapter 2 and Chapter 4, for example, cannot be said to be yet in the bloodstream of congregations at large. How far is constructive help of that kind kept back from people because

280

the official voice of the Church has yet to give its authority to a truly developed statement of doctrines on such matters? That such a voice can be influential is suggested first by the inhibition of biblical studies in the Roman Church as a result of the anti-Modernist decrees, and then by the more recent stimulus given them by the Second Vatican Council.

But here a question of some significance presents itself. How can the Church commend a proper study of the Bible, when it often seems to make little use of the results of such study in arriving at its official teaching? The various pictures of God collected between the covers of Scripture – his character, his purposes, his modes of action – are not all mutually compatible. They cannot all be true as they stand. To appeal to the mysterious incomprehensibility of God to resolve the problem will not do. Talk need not, it is true, always be lucid, logical, propositional; it may be symbolic, allusive, suggestive. But the atmospheres, symbols, hints, evocations of the second sort of talk will also have their own kind of coherence, they will add up to something, indefinable perhaps, but felt to form a consistent world. Talk, whatever its nature, cannot be sheer contradiction or nonsense and still function, unless it is designed, as Job found, to reduce one to silence!

So the Bible cannot be taken in its entirety, as it stands, as God-talk all on the same level. It has to be presented, its parts given a certain relation to one another, if it is as a totality to be talk at all. This means, among other things, coming clean about viewing the Bible historically, taking account of sources, traditions, editors, recognizing cultural pressures, having a framework of thought within which to make use of such an immense aggregation of human experience and illumination. The Church, in the exercise of its teaching authority, must have a use of Scripture which it can justify and others understand. The Church has in the end to say, 'This insight of Scripture is to be preferred to that', or, 'If these insights are combined, the second has to be taken in a modified sense in order to marry with the first.'

Of all the constraints of the past, for Anglicans that of Scripture is unquestionably the most significant. For Romans or Orthodox this would not be so, but for Anglicans it is, because it is the one part of the tradition which all groups within Anglicanism acknowledge as authoritative. Hence there can be no serious development of doctrine at the corporate and official level until we arrive at a common mind on the proper limits and methods of its use. To say this is not to make a veiled plea for disowning or dethroning the Bible. Where there is no Bible, there is no Christianity. It is, however, to make the point that we cannot treat the Bible as unsystematically in doctrinal matters as in devotional. Doctrine is essentially the coherent, intellectual face of the faith, and is therefore bound to ask questions about the intellectual coherence of the material it is expected to use.

Where do we go from here?

'Doctrine' is a word that carries overtones of technical specialism. Some of the examples we have discussed may well seem to justify this. Nor should we indulge in the sentimental illusion that it is possible to define the beliefs of any faith that takes serious account of the complexity of life in our universe, and of the changes of history, without making considerable intellectual demands.

Nevertheless, it has always been a mark and boast of the Church that the essence of the faith can be voiced clearly and succinctly in words which transcend all barriers of culture and language and education, and which can be made their own by people of every race and nation. The 'canon' or 'rule of truth' may contain depths of meaning that libraries of books are not enough to expound, but in itself it is accessible to all. As Irenaeus put it in the second century:

> Neither do the churches established in Germany believe any differently . . . nor those established in Iberia, or among the Celts, or in the east, or in Egypt, or in Libya. . . . Nor will the man among the presidents of the churches who is a very capable speaker say anything other than these things . . . nor will the one who is a poor speaker reduce the tradition. For the faith being one and the same, neither does the man who is able to discourse at large upon it increase it, nor he who can say little diminish it (*Against the Heresies*, 1.10.1).

A later comment of his would find applause among many today: 'Of how much greater value is a pious simpleton than a blasphemous and shameless intellectual' (*ibid.*, 5.20.2)!

The point here is that the subtle and demanding corpus of doctrine and doctrinal teaching is the spelling out and justification of a faith that can be put clearly and simply. In that clear and simple form it may seem outrageous and incredible to the world, or something that would be nice if it were true but, alas, the evidence is against it. But the ideas in themselves are not opaque. It is because of this translucent, universal quality that the faith binds together the community in a fellowship of heart and mind, and becomes their marching song. It is also because the faith can be put in this concise and skeletal way that a phrase like 'development of doctrine' presents peculiar problems. Does this mean that the simpleton's 'canon of truth' is going to be revoked? Or expounded for the blasphemous and shameless intellectuals in ways that eat out its core from within? Or elaborated until it is far beyond the ordinary millions for whom Christ died?

Nor should we forget that it is the simple faith that is most commonly validated by life, for it is the world-shaking simplicities of the intellectually unselfconscious which usually motivate heroic sanctity. In our own day, indeed, there is just such a simplification going on before our eyes in the passionate determination of young Christians to unify belief and life in statements totally controlled by the ultimate affirmation, 'God is love.' For them this is the canon of truth. It has always been part of Christian belief. It has never been the thoroughgoing, exclusive, central principle. To make it so does in fact require a radical development of doctrine as we know it, but one which will certainly conform to a model of genuine organic growth, and will pass many of Newman's seven tests.

It cannot but strike one that such a development is more likely to unite Christians of different church backgrounds than some of the things we usually mean by doctrinal development. A developing doctrine of *episcope,* for example, has sucked in vast resources of theological expertise in order to move closely related denominations a few millimetres nearer to some sort of organizational co-operation. But the unity of the heart which demands expression in shared worship and service springs from loyalty to a common Master, whose person and work are understood in a few pregnant symbols.

The Niceno-Constantinopolitan Creed, of which we celebrate the 1,600th anniversary this year, and which has become the eucharistic confession of faith of the overwhelming majority of Christians, begins, 'We believe. . .' But that formula originally meant not, 'This is the official, complete faith of the corporate body to which members must try to get as near as they can,' but, 'This is what we, each one of us, personally believe.' A major transformation of life, a deep change in values and direction, calls for a profound new commitment in vision. We have to see life and the world differently, and to be in love with what we see. From that point we may go on to notice more and more things we failed to discern before, we may understand things that previously baffled us. Our doctrine, if you like, is enriched and elaborated. That is one kind of development.

The arguments we have surveyed in this chapter, however, seem to press upon us another kind of development, namely, the replacing of one vision by another, or at least the possibility that this may be demanded of us by loyalty to truth. If truth does not command our ultimate allegiance, we are doomed. Not only will our beliefs sooner or later corrupt and perish, but it is truth alone which ensures that a belief can be corporate, not just individual. For it is the very nature of truth that it presupposes a reality in essence the same for all. No two people will see it alike, but they will be aware that the inner mystery of what they see is one and not many. So truth is great and prevails, and the community of believers has to face the possibility that one day truth may ask them to admit they were mistaken.

Yet this is no argument against commitment. It is the badge of the pilgrim soul that it is passionately committed to affirmations it knows to be provisional. Supremely is this true of affirmations about God, for on that subject all words will always be provisional. In committing ourselves to such words, to the vision they try to convey, we declare simply that they are more right than wrong, that they set our feet away from the lie and towards the truth which is that 'other country' we seek. And in that pilgrimage we do not travel alone.

What, then, can the institutional Church do to help its members on their pilgrim way? At the risk of diverging a little from one or two views expressed in other chapters of this report, I suggest three answers to that question.

First, that theologians have a duty to show how the subordinate details of doctrine which they explore spring from the simplicities of a central vision, and how any developments they feel obliged to commend might change that vision.

Second, that the Church should call on its theologians to work with pastors and teachers to ensure that doctrine in its popular expression – as taught, for example, in Sunday

School, or confirmation class, or from the pulpit, or in adult education schemes – is always consonant with the demands of truth as a sober and balanced judgement will currently see them.

Third, that the Church should go beyond discussions of believing, individual or corporate, useful though these may be, and turn all its resources to stating what may properly be believed to our souls' health. The job can be done, as *A Declaration of Faith,* quoted earlier, splendidly shows. What *Doctrine in the Church of England* (1938) did for the last generation needs to be done again – and can be done, once we rid ourselves of the pride that will not commit itself to anything except eternal, and therefore inaccessible, verities.

Markers and Signposts

Anthony Harvey.

Our report has been concerned with what we have come among ourselves to refer to as 'corporate believing'. It represents an approach which differs from that of our predecessors, mainly in that we have looked at the believer, not so much as an individual who is set over against the tradition and the institutions of the Church, but as a person caught up in a complex system of church life and affiliation, which both influences him and in the long run is influenced, however slightly, by him. We have argued that to say what it is that we believe is not to attempt to make a judgement about the beliefs of individual church members, nor (at least in the Church of England) is it primarily to refer to formulations of doctrine officially promulgated by the Church, but to describe an intricate and continuing process in which every believer, to a greater or lesser extent, is involved.

To look at the matter in this way, as opposed to the more individualistic approach which is customary, has the effect of lessening that sense of threat and insecurity which has so often been felt when traditional Christian beliefs are subjected to radical questioning. When a bishop, or a Regius Professor of Divinity, or a group of distinguished theologians, publish interpretations of the Christian faith which seem to call into question doctrines whose truth is taken for granted by most church members, dismay is caused not only by the novelty of such thinking but by the apparent failure of the church authorities to make any clear response. *Honest to God, The Remaking of Christian Doctrine,* and *The Myth of God Incarnate* seemed to challenge the Church for a reply. But no official or authoritative reply was made. Or again, church members who adopt a fairly liberal approach to Scripture often feel dismayed by the (as they think) excessive literalism displayed by some with regard to such matters as hellfire, or the Second Coming;

but no generally accepted formulation of these doctrines seems to be available. Can it be that the Church does not know what it believes? Have the foundations been shaken beyond repair? Must every doctrine commission (like this one) disappoint the faithful by discussing only *how* we believe, and drawing back before the (as it seems) far more urgent question of *what* we believe?

These questions, and the dismay and insecurity they cause, are inevitable so long as the model with which we work is that of the individual believer having his faith supplied and monitored by the institutional organs of the Church. But they lose much of their menace if, as we have argued, the faith of both the Church and the individual is more accurately described as a kind of 'corporate believing', in which the individual, directly or indirectly, contributes to the formation of church doctrine at the same time as the Church, through its worship, its ethos and its historic formularies, moulds the belief of the individual. The novel thinking of a radical theologian, or the explorations of small groups in the Church into new ways of formulating and expressing their Christian faith, can then be seen, not as a challenge to traditional doctrine which must at all costs be answered, but as a necessary stimulus to the kind of thinking which must go on at all levels if the Church is to maintain a vigorous life. We have found again and again that we were anxious to sustain and encourage those who have in recent years been venturing to the very frontiers of Christian speculation, and who have thereby drawn a great deal of fire upon themselves. Their activity is as essential to the health of the Church as that of more conservative theologians; but it will be productive only if it is conducted within a Church which knows how to receive it. If church members simply wait to see whether some ecclesiastical authority will either authorize or disown the results of such thinking, then they are failing in their responsibility. In the long run it is only the common sense of the believer, trained by the Church's traditional teaching, nourished by its forms of worship old and new, and subject to the leading of the Holy Spirit within the worshipping and praying community of Christians, which can identify and make use of the real contribution which is made by those who accept the challenge and the risks of radical exploration.

So much is easy to say in general terms. To spell it out in detail and to illustrate its practical working is a complex task;

indeed the sheer complexity of it may be offered as a reason for
the somewhat impressionistic character of our report. Within
the total phenomenon of corporate believing there is a number
of factors which may appear at first to work against each other,
but which are, or should be, held together within the fellowship
of the Church. There is the necessary tension between the
freedom of individual judgement and the decisions and policies
painfully arrived at by the institution – of which the story of
the archbishop's hat provides a tantalizing illustration. There
is the subtle and often seemingly mysterious way in which the
Church of England is on the one hand bound to historic
formularies such as the Thirty-nine Articles, but on the other
permits itself a latitude in their interpretation, and a degree of
flexibility in the manner of assent to them demanded of the
clergy, which is unexampled in any confessional church. Most
of all, there is (or at least, as Anglicans, we sense there should
be) both the possibility to hold and express deep theological
convictions and at the same time a forbearance of (or perhaps
we should say, less patronizingly, a real respect for) those who,
though they belong to the same church, may instinctively
express their faith very differently. We sensed that to attempt
to subject so many factors to systematic treatment would not
only exceed our powers, it would inevitably misrepresent the
phenomenon we were trying to describe. We have accordingly
tried instead to approach it from different angles, in the belief
that the resulting diversity would give a more faithful picture.
Nevertheless, we have discovered among ourselves, and hope
we have succeeded in conveying to our readers, so many points
of agreement that we are confident that what we have been
describing are all different aspects of one and the same thing.

There is one further limitation of our enterprise to be
mentioned. Doctrine is not something we initiate ourselves,
whether individually or corporately. The Christian revelation
is of God; all we can offer is a response made with integrity and
faith. Our corporate believing stands under God's judgement.
We can never be certain we have done it correctly. The
explorers who shock us and challenge us may be raised up by
God for that purpose, or they may be wolves to scatter the
flock. The freedom of inquiry we cherish may turn out to have
been a mere pretext for permissiveness. We have to be
vigilant, humble and faithful. Our report, we hope, may have
things to say which may help the Church in its endless search
for a true response to the Christian revelation; but it cannot

pretend to offer a definitive account of the Church's believing, which must always be open to the innovating activity of the Holy Spirit.

Boundary markers

Continued attention to Scripture and tradition, making full use of the results of modern scholarship; critical and informed participation in worship; prayer which shows sensitivity to the real needs of the contemporary world; dialogue with men and women who hold a different world-view or profess a different religion – all this and more must be engaged in by church members according to their gifts and aptitudes, and constitutes that corporate believing which in turn acts as a principle of verification and control over the believer's individual quest for truth. That this manifold process should be maintained and extended is essential to the health of the Church; but it has the consequence that at any given moment it may be impossible to formulate an authoritative statement of 'doctrine'. One can take a sample of the beliefs of church members, or appoint a committee of theologians to work on a particular doctrinal topic. But in neither case will the result be more than a provisional approximation to what the Church may be said to believe. No final and authoritative statement is possible; at most one can describe the flavour of contemporary theological discussion, or establish the broad lines within which inquiry may be conducted.

At first sight, some may be dismayed by this apparent lack of clarity and accessibility with regard to the faith of the Church; and here there is a notable difference between the Anglican Communion and many other churches. The Roman Catholic Church, for example, has periodically attempted a definitive restatement of fundamental Christian doctrines, and is currently working on their crystallization in the form of ecclesiastical law; continental Reformed churches can normally refer to their confessional documents as a direct indication of their beliefs in a way that few Anglicans would be able to appeal to the Thirty-nine Articles. But the consequence of any such rigid formulations is that they immediately draw a boundary round the church. Those who cannot in conscience assent to them have to ask themselves whether they can continue to regard themselves as members, however much they may be in sympathy with the general ethos and activity of the denomination concerned. It is because of the danger of 'un-churching' good Christian people who happen to have difficulties with certain aspects of the faith that we endorse John McManners's insistence that (at least in the Church of England) doctrine should be authoritatively defined as little and as seldom as possible.

This does not mean that members of the Church of England do not hold beliefs of great strength and definiteness, nor that they cannot say exactly what those beliefs are (though the difficulties of doing so are well brought out in Basil Mitchell's introductory chapter, and should not be minimized). So long as they understand the nature and functioning of the Church to which they belong, and are aware of the sources and constraints of the corporate believing in which they participate, they need not fear any lack of clarity or vigour in their own convictions simply because the church as a whole does not publish authoritative statements of doctrine. Rather, they can rejoice to belong to a church which, though it displays a serious attention to the historical foundations of the Christian faith and to the formative documents of its own tradition, nevertheless permits a substantial variety of emphasis and understanding among its members. In faith (though in practice things may sometimes seem sadly different) they can believe that the subtle interaction between their own convictions and those of other Christians, and between contemporary attempts at formulation and the historic tradition and worship of the Church, may result in a response to God's self-revelation which approximates to the truth as nearly as is possible for sinful human beings like ourselves.

Statements of doctrine, then, must be provisional, tentative and infrequent. Corporate believing cannot flourish when subjected to a mass of authoritative definitions. But this is not to say that there are no limits to permissible formulations, no frontiers beyond which the explorer cannot be authorized to go. Like any other institution, the Church must have 'boundary markers' to regulate its life and public character. But these are set up, not only to mark out a theoretical framework to guide our thinking, and to serve as warnings to those whom a sense of intellectual and spiritual adventure might lead too far afield, but for strictly practical purposes. There are specific issues which arise in the life of the Church which demand authoritative decision. The remarriage of divorced persons, the ordination of women, the use of church buildings by adherents of other faiths, are matters which have to be settled here and now. It is widely and properly felt that these decisions must be taken in the light of doctrinal considerations; but it is never simply a matter, in this or any church, of bringing in a group of theologians to settle the question. Decisions of this kind may be made by a number of different authorities: a bishop (or the House of Bishops), the General Synod, even a Court of Arches. Each will attend as faithfully as possible to traditional Christian teaching, to theological opinion, to consensus and common sense – in short, to the good of the Church. The decisions reached are necessary if the Church is to continue as an ordered and disciplined institution. They are the inevitable boundary markers, provisional but definite, within which we enjoy our Christian liberty. They are the constraints which make creative action possible.

The subjects to which such decision-making is directed are severely practical: as we have said, we define doctrine only when necessary, and the necessity is produced only by the need for immediate practical decisions. To some, indeed, they will seem depressingly banal, as if the entire doctrinal apparatus of the Church is brought to bear only on matters which are marginal to the practice of our religion. But this (we have argued) is not necessarily to be deplored: the further the process of doctrinal formulation ventures into the central areas of Christian belief, the greater the risk that sincere believers will find themselves excluded by authoritative statements which they cannot in conscience assent to. On the other hand, it is possible that the new situation created by the presence in our midst of so many people of other faiths will require authoritative decisions on more fundamental matters. Fruitful contact and coexistence with other religious bodies may be found to depend on Christians knowing precisely where they stand in relation to specific beliefs held in other 'households of faith', and for this purpose members of the Church may need authoritative guidance. As the Bishop of Ripon has said (in Chapter 9), this is a matter which requires urgent study, but for which the present doctrine commission, even if it were the right body to attempt it, has neither the time nor the competence.

The agents of corporate believing
It is clear from all that has been said that corporate believing cannot be something static. It does not result in a definitive

formulation which can be repeated, parrot-wise, for generations to come. It is a process, an activity, which is essential to the health of the Church, and which will continue to throw up new forms and new idioms of Christian life and thought. It is true, of course, that in a sense Christian belief must always be the same. As Christians we are bound to the past, and we wish to be assured that our faith is continuous with that of the primitive Church. But we also live in the present and hope for the future, and we are engaged in the constant struggle to relate the traditional teaching of Christianity to the intellectual and social presuppositions of today, and to proclaim a vision for the future which will be meaningful to our contemporaries. This involves, at the very least, some change in the way we articulate our beliefs. Some would say (but here there is an area of controversy) that there is actual development of doctrine, and would point to some unspoken assumptions which underlie, for instance, contemporary forms of worship, and which can be shown to be different from (though not necessarily incompatible with) the assumptions of a previous generation. But in any case, whether it be in form or content, the corporate believing of the Church is perceptibly different (if one has learnt how and where to perceive it) from what it was before, say, the publication of *Honest to God.* As can be seen from the argument of several of our chapters, we believe this constant movement of thought within the Church to be a sign of health and vitality. It involves both the preservation and cherishing of traditional truth, and also the continual discovery of new forms and new implications. Indeed, to be interested in doctrine at all is to stand ultimately before the mystery of God. However much we may value what has already been revealed, it would be blasphemous to suggest that there is nothing new for us to know. Corporate believing, if it is to be (as it must be) directed towards God, for all the achievements of systematic theology, is a quest. It remains to suggest in more detail how, and by whom, this quest is conducted.

If we take first the more corporate and official aspects of believing and move towards those which are more informal and individual, at least six categories of agents suggest themselves. They are discussed in the following sections.

Authoritative decisions

We have seen that the Church will be required from time to

292

time to make a formal decision on a matter which has immediate practical implications; indeed, the comparison made with other systems and institutions in John Bowker's chapter (Chapter 6) suggests that it must be able to do this if it is to survive as a distinct and active organization. The bishops, synods or courts which make such decisions, if they are to retain their authority and respect, will need to rely on a general consensus in the Church; they are in effect the organs by which, when necessity arises, this consensus is articulated. We should be neither complacent nor overcritical about these decisions. If they seem to lack charity or Christian commitment, this will not necessarily be the fault of the authorities; it may just as well be that of local congregations which are unwilling to pay the price of a decision which might be costly in terms of patient tolerance and prolonged pastoral care. On the other hand, these decisions are unlikely to be seriously unfaithful to basic Christian principles: if they were, they would be repudiated by the Church as a whole. They are not (at least in the Church of England) irrevocable; they may be modified or reversed with the passage of time. The marriage discipline of tomorrow (to take only one example) may be different from that of today, and the individual decisions of bishops which will flow from it may effectively reverse those which have been taken in recent years. In short, such decisions, for all their authoritative appearance, are an expression of the corporate believing of the Church. On the one hand they are securely attached to traditional teaching; on the other hand they are no more than a provisional interpretation of that teaching appropriate to the needs and circumstances of the present day. In their turn, these decisions will enter the consciousness of the individual believer, so that he infers from them the character of that corporate believing with which he associates himself by becoming or remaining a member of the Church.

Authorized teachers

A large number of people in the Church – whether they be parish priests, dons, school teachers, Sunday School teachers or simply parents – have the privilege and the responsibility of instructing others in the Christian faith. As they do it, they can hardly fail to be aware of the seriousness of their charge. This is not the moment for trying out idiosyncratic ideas or airing highly personal opinions. The task in hand is that of passing on the Christian faith in terms which make it seem intelligible and relevant to the child, the inquirer or the confirmation candidate. In the past in the Church of England, as in many other Churches in more recent times, this task has been assisted and controlled by a written catechism. Today, Anglican teachers have to rely for the most part on their personal understanding of the faith and on such written material as they or their superiors find most helpful and authoritative. Their teaching, that is to say, is expected to be a faithful reflection of the corporate believing of the Church. But in so far as it is often also creative – for all effective teaching demands an effort of the imagination on the part of the teacher – it can exercise an influence the other way. The more successful the teacher in giving freshness and immediacy to the traditional content of his teaching, the greater the influence which is exerted on future corporate believing through those who learn from him.

This activity is carried on in various ways and on countless occasions in the life of the Church; indeed one can hardly be a Christian at all without at some time being called upon to communicate the essentials of the faith. But it also has a public side, and is regulated by a system of authorization which extends right down from senior clergymen to youthful Sunday School teachers. If the Church is to function as a system for the transmission of religious information (to use John Bowker's analysis once again), it is essential that all teaching done in the Church's name should be officially authorized. But this by no means separates this activity from the continuous process of corporate believing. The decision to grant or withhold a licence is made by the bishop or his deputy in the light of the standards of faithfulness to tradition in practice and belief which the Church expects of its teachers. And those expectations are formed in turn by the teaching which church members actually receive. These standards may of course be open to revision in view of changing educational methods or of shifts of emphasis in the presentation of Christian truth – a bishop might hesitate to license a reader, for example, whose teaching was known to show a medieval preoccupation with hell and damnation, even though what he taught could hardly be shown to be incompatible with the tradition of the Church. But the ultimate control is exercised once again by the corporate believing of the Church, which both influences and is influenced by the work of teaching in the Church.

Doctrine commissions

The Church of England has not always had a doctrine commission; indeed we are only the third, the first having been that which, after many years' work, published its famous report, *Doctrine in the Church of England,* in 1938 – a report which may still be referred to as a valuable guide to the style of doctrinal thinking characteristic of our church. We believe (though it is hardly for us to say so) that some body of this kind has an important part to play in the process of corporate believing. This is not to suggest that there is not normally enough theological thinking in the Church, and that it is necessary to set up a doctrine commission to provide some more. It is rather that, given the highly complex nature of corporate believing, it can be helpful if a group of qualified persons seeks to articulate both the process itself and the beliefs which are emerging from it. Such a group will not have an authority greater than that conferred by its official appointment and by the expertise of its members; but if it can help the Church to understand what the present state of its believing actually is, it may have an important part to play in the continuing process. But we should add that a future doctrine commission might look very unlike the present one. The most formative areas for Christian thinking are now those which bring us into contact, either with other religious traditions, or with more or less scientific worldviews. Consequently, future doctrine commissions may need to contain experts on other subjects in addition to Christian theology.

Explorers

An important part in the process is played by those who, starting from Christian convictions, are nevertheless prepared to call even the most cherished beliefs into question. If the Christian faith is to continue to speak to the world of today, it cannot just be reiterated in traditional language. Its meaning must also be conveyed by means of new concepts and new imagery, and this inevitably results in a critical reappraisal of the old forms and idioms. Those who are willing to follow the spirit of inquiry wherever it leads them deserve the sympathetic support of their fellow Christians. They risk, not only the dismay and distrust of their Christian friends, but also periods of doubt and disorientation in their personal faith. They are unlikely to be guilty of the charge so often laid against them, that of irresponsibly attacking some of the most cherished of Christian beliefs. It is often at great cost to themselves that they make the explorations which may ultimately enable less adventurous Christians to find their bearings in an increasingly unfamiliar world.

But here again, the corporate believing of the Church does not renounce all control and discrimination. Individual theologians have the right, if not the duty, to experiment with radically new formulations of doctrine. But equally, church members have the right to be shocked by what they hear. To authorize an inquiry is not the same as to endorse its findings. The Church may support its explorers, but it does not have to accept their conclusions. It may indeed have to disown them, if the path which has led to them appears to be one which the majority of Christians could not in conscience follow. There is played out in the Church a conflict which is familiar in other organizations also (witness the issue of the closed shop in the trade union movement): on the one hand the solidarity of the institution must be preserved, on the other the freedom of the individual conscience must be protected. A clergyman or a theologian who is genuinely led to doubt the existence of anything that would normally be meant by the word God, or who cannot see in Jesus anything more out of the ordinary than a gifted Galilean rabbi, presents such a problem. The Church cannot publicly accept his position and still remain a Christian body; on the other hand it does not wish to disown one of its members whose research and speculation have honestly led him to this conclusion. All it can do – and perhaps this is all it need do – is make a distinction between membership and responsibility. The explorer may remain a member of the Church so long as he can in conscience participate in its forms of worship and service; but there may come a point at which it is necessary to consider whether he can any longer be authorized to teach and minister in the Church's name. And this decision, too, will be one that can be taken only in the light of the corporate believing of the Church.

Neither out nor in

Here we encounter a factor in the formulation of Christian doctrine which is peculiar to the Church of England. This is the part which is played by those whom we would not normally think of as members, but who may turn out to care deeply about certain aspects of church life. The Bishop of Winchester has drawn attention to the influence exercised by a leaderwriter of *The Times* in the nineteenth-century controversy over baptismal regeneration. A similar part is played today by persons of distinction who write letters to the press or make comments in television interviews which bear on matters actually being debated within the Church. For it is one of the most distinctive features of the Church of England that it conducts its internal arguments in public, and anyone may join in. Often these participants appear to be snipers from outside: they might not wish to be regarded as church members. Yet their contribution to the debate often springs from a deep concern for the preservation of some Christian value or ecclesiastical tradition. As such it represents a current of opinion which must be taken account of in corporate believing. Those who recently protested so eloquently against new forms of worship were not all regular worshippers themselves; but no one can doubt that the protest represented the feelings of many who care deeply about the Church, and that this is a constituency which, in the Church of England, has its part to play in the formulation of doctrine.

A parallel phenomenon can be seen at a more popular level. Every parish priest is under considerable pressure from residents in his parish who may rarely, if ever, go to church, but who insist that their babies should be baptized. This pressure creates a dilemma. If it is yielded to, the Church's insistence on the connection between baptism and participation in the life of the Church is made to sound hollow; if it is resisted, the priest loses a pastoral opportunity and the Church is made to appear rigorous and exclusive. This dilemma, in its turn, affects the thinking of church people about baptism, and ultimately influences the choice of the words that are written into the baptism service. Indeed, this is only one of the ways in which what W. H. Vanstone has called 'popular religion' exercises an influence on the corporate believing of the Church. Subjective and impressionistic though it necessarily is, the section entitled 'Doctrine Diffused' is one in which every reader who knows the Church of England – or here one should perhaps just say 'England' – will recognize something familiar. No formulation of the belief of our Church can afford to ignore the pressure exerted by this multitude of sincere, if inarticulate, sympathizers.

The man in the pew

Perhaps in the end the most important agents of all are those who week by week come to church and seek to fashion their lives in conformity to what they learn and love there. These people have great power over corporate believing. On the negative side, if they frequently hear in church what they sense to be inconsistent with the doctrine they have learnt, or to be unworthy of Christian ideals, they will vote with their feet, and can be coaxed back only by a return to more traditional teaching or by the patient explanation of a priest who in the process will have come to subject his own interpretations of doctrine to careful scrutiny. On the positive side, the holiness of life and the sacrificial service displayed (or more often carefully concealed) by countless church members is a precious validation of that which is taught and believed. In the end the Church believes what it does because its belief bears fruit in the lives of its members: the priorities expressed in the prayer and the living of devout worshippers are what give content and authenticity to all our corporate believing.

These categories are not meant to exclude each other. All of us hope to belong to the last, but many, at one time or another, will have experience of at least one of the others. The intention is rather (as throughout this report) to indicate the variety of ways – and there may well be more – in which individuals actually contribute to the doctrine of the Church. And this leads us to our last section.

Signposts

Early on in this report it was pointed out how difficult it is to fill in the rest of a sentence beginning, 'The Church believes . . .' It should now be clear why this is so. One cannot give an account of the belief of the Church without attending to that complex process which we have summarily described in the last few paragraphs and which has been illustrated in one way or another in every chapter of this book. What the Church believes is certainly not something which can be formulated by a doctrine commission; the most that could be achieved would be a systematic statement by a group of theologians of what they sensed were the main theological priorities in the life and worship of the Church today. The time may come when such a statement may seem desirable, and a commission may be asked to attempt it. But even if they are successful, their presentation will be partial and provisional. The corporate believing of the Church continues incessantly and takes a bewildering variety of forms. It is not something which could ever be completely caught in a still shot and presented as a definitive statement. The only way of knowing what, at any given time, the Church believes is by attending to the manifold process as it is going on.

If it is asked, therefore, whether there is any useful outcome of the inquiry in which we have been engaged, our first answer must be that it has at least helped us – and we hope our readers also – to understand better the situation in which we stand. It may be true – as it is true, for example, of sociology – that our approach has not enabled us to discover anything that was not known before; but (as is also the case with sociology) by seeing familiar facts in a new light one can often see relationships between them which were not apparent before. We have learnt, for example, to appreciate better the function of theology in the Church – not to be wheeled in when more practical considerations are exhausted, nor to be seen deferred to as a final arbiter, but as something which arises out of every authentic Christian activity and then needs to be articulated in order that the true significance of different options may be perceived. We have been able to assure ourselves (and we hope others) that the challenges occasionally presented by *avant-garde* Christian thinkers are a sign of health, not of weakness, and that the lack of an official response by the church authorities need cause no dismay: the real response is to be found diffused in all levels of the Church. Above all, we have come to see that doctrine in the Church can never be the creation of a team of experts, but is the product of the engagement of every church member in the complex process which we have called 'corporate believing'; from which follows the important corollary that the Church will best perform its stewardship of doctrine when its members faithfully make their contribution to it in thought, prayer and sanctity of life.

This advance in self-understanding would be enough in itself to satisfy us. In any case it would hardly be expected that a report on such a general topic as this would conclude with specific recommendations. But perhaps, in our final paragraphs, we may be allowed to draw out of our study four consequences which, if they are not programmes for future action, may be taken as signposts to renewed effort and awareness.

The first will sound utterly banal: it is simply to encourage

299

every member of the Church to play his part to the full. But in the context of our argument, the exhortation may take on a fresher meaning. If it is the case that the corporate believing of the Church is a product of the prayer, worship and Christian living of its members, of their attention to the received tradition and of their creative individual response, then it follows that a Church which has sound doctrine is a Church in which Christians are playing an active part in its corporate believing. Every member of the Church of England (and other people outside it) can be encouraged by the realization of the responsible part they have to play in the formation of the Church's belief.

But the process is a subtle and complex one, and for much of the time may pass unnoticed. It is essential that there should be regular procedures for taking soundings. Christians need to know where they are. They have a right to expect from their Church a means by which attention may be directed to those areas of church life which at any given time are doctrinally significant.

Several chapters in our report have placed emphasis on the importance of 'story' in the corporate believing of the Church. The fundamental story proclaimed by Christianity, and the many subsidiary stories contained in the Bible, have been until recently a part of our national culture, and have greatly assisted the transmission of the faith. A generation is now growing up which is largely ignorant of these stories; yet the success of these same stories in such productions as *Jesus Christ Superstar* and *Godspell* show that they have by no means lost their attractive power. The Church must not neglect this part of its heritage on the grounds that these are 'merely stories' and that what really matters is Christian doctrine. The stories themselves, and above all the master story of our redemption, carry a great load of doctrinal significance, and are still our most powerful means of conveying the essentials of our faith. It is an urgent responsibility laid upon all Christians to ensure that these stories are constantly attended to and imaginatively retold in each successive generation. Indeed, this should be a conscious objective in training for any form of ministry today.

An entirely new feature of life in England is the proximity of devout and practising members of all the other world faiths. This causes us to ask difficult and pressing questions about our own beliefs, and it is an urgent matter to find ways of speaking which both respect the integrity of our Muslim or Hindu neighbour and at the same time do justice to the unique significance we find in our own faith. This is an exploration which is only just beginning in the churches. We urge that it be given the highest possible priority, and that it be conducted in the light of any insight which may have emerged from our own study of believing in the Church.

Index of Names

Index of Subjects